MW00396054

PRAISE FOR *AMERICAN RECKONING*

"I have been deeply indebted to Jonathan Alter for his political wisdom and journalistic experience these last 20 years, and I'm grateful for this gripping guidebook through a bizarre chapter in the life of our strangest president."

—Stephen Colbert

"No cameras in the courtroom but Jonathan Alter's brilliant book is the next best thing or better when he zooms in on Trump's hair and finds the shiny dome underneath, when he catches every 'dirty look' Trump throws at his enemies, when he sees the resemblance between the porn star witness and a certain senator, and when he describes Trump's 'pained face' after the verdict. Alter was the best writer filing reports from the courtroom and the only one who knew Trump's favorite lawyer, Roy Cohn. He brought his whole life as a journalist into that courtroom and delivers the historic drama as no one else could. And, oh yeah, there's a happy ending."

—Lawrence O'Donnell

"Jonathan Alter's *American Reckoning* is a wonderful hybrid—a memoir of an extraordinary career in journalism, a political history of our recent past, and above all an insightful account of Donald Trump's criminal trial in New York. It's also a cry for decency and democracy at a critical moment."

—Jeffrey Toobin, author of *Homegrown: Timothy McVeigh and the Rise of Rightwing Extremism*

"A must-read for anyone who truly cares about the majesty of the rule of law during these perilous times."

—Retired New York Judge George Grasso

"I loved reading about Jonathan's formative years and the powerhouse women who influenced him. Now I know why he's such an original thinker! This is a great read."

—Susie Essman, actress on *Curb Your Enthusiasm*

ALSO BY JONATHAN ALTER

The Defining Moment:
FDR's Hundred Days and the Triumph of Hope

Between the Lines:
A View Inside American Politics, People and Culture

The Promise:
President Obama, Year One

The Center Holds:
Obama and His Enemies

His Very Best:
Jimmy Carter, A Life

For Dwight Garner:
Remember the June monthly dinner at the Century?
This was hatched at our table.
Warmest regards,

American Reckoning

INSIDE TRUMP'S TRIAL—AND MY OWN

JONATHAN ALTER

BenBella Books, Inc.
Dallas, TX

This book is based on the author's notes from interviews with participants, recollections of conversations, trial transcripts, and public statements. Quoted dialogue has been lightly edited for readability, including the removal of stuttered speech, vocal tics, and repeated words. While every effort has been made to ensure accuracy, some conversations and events may be paraphrased or reconstructed from memory.

BenBella Books, Inc.
10440 N. Central Expressway
Suite 800
Dallas, TX 75231
benbellabooks.com
Send feedback to feedback@benbellabooks.com

BenBella is a federally registered trademark.

Printed in the United States of America
10 9 8 7 6 5 4 3 2 1

Library of Congress Control Number: 2024943480
ISBN 9781637746660 (hardcover)
ISBN 9781637746677 (electronic)

Copyediting by Scott Calamar
Proofreading by Lisa Story
Indexing by WordCo Indexing Services
Text design and composition by Aaron Edmiston
Cover design by Sarah Avinger
Cover image © Getty Images News, Michael M. Santiago
Image on page 85: DOONESBURY © G. B. Trudeau. Reprinted with permission of ANDREWS MCMEEL SYNDICATION. All rights reserved.
Image on page 229: Lorie Shaull/Flickr
Printed by Lake Book Manufacturing

For Emily

PREFACE

This is the story of two reckonings—Donald Trump's and my own.

Trump's reckoning came on May 30, 2024, when he was convicted of multiple felonies in one of the most significant criminal trials in American history.

My own reckoning—with my image of America and its commitment to democracy—is still underway. I have lost my claim to be, as John F. Kennedy described himself, "an idealist without illusions." I'm still idealistic but it turns out I had more illusions about this country than I thought I did.

Watching Trump desecrate the presidency and other democratic institutions over the last several years has been an ordeal—a trial—for me and for millions of others. Now American voters face their own reckoning as they render a verdict at the polls.

Historians who overwhelmingly rate Trump as the worst president since the founding of the republic will have a hard time explaining how a convicted felon, serial liar, and malignant narcissist mounted a political comeback. I'm not going to try here, and details of Trump's unAmerican election denialism and contempt for the rule of law are beyond the scope of this book. So is the full story of the 2024 campaign, though I do provide some fresh reporting on the fateful political events of July, especially Nancy Pelosi's historic efforts to convince her reluctant friend Joe Biden to withdraw from the race. Overnight,

Kamala Harris's thrilling candidacy eased the dread of Democrats and put Trump's criminal conviction front-and-center in the most pivotal election since the Civil War. Harris's signature line is "I know Donald Trump's type." Beyond articulating a "We are not going back!" vision of the future, she and her running mate, Tim Walz, are prosecuting much of the broader case against Trump that I lay out in this book.

My aim here is to show how a tawdry trial about hush money payments to a porn star became an inspiring if provisional locus of democratic accountability—a place where, for the first time since his father died twenty-five years ago, Donald Trump was forced to sit down, shut up, and face the consequences of his actions.

Amid my contextualizing of presidents and my journal of the trial, I try to tap into the anxiety that so many Americans feel about Trump and his enablers—the fear of what they are doing to our sense of ourselves.

My focus here is partly personal. Trump's disrespect for the Constitution and for the presidency is an assault on many of the assumptions that have underpinned my life. In the nation that I thought I knew, an obvious con man would not have been elected president; in that nation—receding into the past—the Republican leaders who support Trump despite knowing better would not have failed the character test of their generation.

All of this has caused me to question my faith—not in God or democracy, but in the common sense and good judgment of roughly half of the American people.

The portentous question at hand is whether the two "Black Swan" events of 2024—the criminal conviction of an American president and the last-minute replacement of the Democratic nominee for president—would together put America, and the world, on a better path.

If Trump wins the election, this book will be in the tradition of William L. Shirer's *Berlin Diary*, which chronicles what it felt like to watch Adolf Hitler consolidate his power after he overcame a criminal conviction to become the dictator of Germany.

If Kamala Harris wins, my story will be more in the spirit of Jimmy Breslin's post-Watergate book *How the Good Guys Finally Won*, with the felonies I write about looming large in Trump's defeat at the hands of a former prosecutor.

Whatever happens, the criminal trial—the first ever of an American president—will remain a subject of compelling historical interest.

The case was highly publicized, but little understood. Without television or even audio, the millions of people who said they were closely following news from the courthouse had to settle for brief reports that often felt like messages in a bottle from a distant shore.

As one of a handful of journalists with a pass that let me in the courtroom every day, I had essentially a front-row seat for this twenty-three-day drama. I kept a journal that recorded everything I saw, from the judge threatening Trump with jail time, to jurors stifling giggles, to the defendant's bald scalp.

I've been a reporter and historian of sorts since I was a little boy. I've interviewed nine of the last ten American presidents (all except Ronald Reagan)—either before, during, or after their presidencies—and written books about three. And I've covered politics over the last forty years for the old *Newsweek* and other publications.

While I have always approached candidates and presidents with a critical eye, I revere the office the founders created and mourn the way Trump's Supreme Court has now endowed it with monarchical powers. In assaulting the Constitution and the rule of law, Trump has inadvertently given me greater appreciation for the other men, flawed but decent, who have assumed "the glorious burden" of the presidency.

I don't like to admit it, but I'm a figure from another age—a straight, white, sixty-six-year-old legacy journalism holdover. The late Texas Governor Ann Richards famously said that George W. Bush was born on third base and thought he hit a triple. (In Trump's case, it's a homer.) By contrast, I want to be upfront about my life of privilege and the additional obligations that incurs. Like soldiers or jurors, I feel a tugging duty to serve—to be the eyes and ears of anyone who appreciates journalism and history and still loves this infuriating country.

I start with the premise that democracy is a muscle that needs exercise and that our democratic institutions must be protected from criminals, whatever the political fallout may be. The stories I tell—and the accountability I witness—flow from there.

My tale of Trump's encounter with the criminal justice system moves from frustration to satisfaction and at least some measure of hope.

The frustration came when it looked as if Trump's strategy of delay, delay, delay would let him skate until after the election.

The satisfaction and hope came when he finally faced the music—an Irish-born jury foreperson chanting "Guilty" thirty-four times.

That was one of the most dramatic public moments of the twenty-first century and the genesis of this book and *cri de coeur,* which I deliver as a series of discrete epistles to myself and to you.

Part One is a mini-memoir of growing up in a political family in Chicago, where, as a child, meeting Martin Luther King Jr. and experiencing the turmoil at the 1968 Democratic National Convention helped set me on my path. I tell a few stories about my encounters with flawed but decent presidents and would-be presidents to illuminate how much of a departure and shock to my system—and our system—Trump has turned out to be. And I explain how my enduring civic faith helped power my desire to see him held accountable.

Part Two is my barbed journal of the winter and spring of 2024. In it, I undertake a frenzied mission to capture the dispiriting run-up to this Trumpiest of Trump trials; review how the judge, the lawyers, and the witnesses performed; and (with a hat tip to the late Dominick Dunne's coverage of celebrity trials) collect color aboard the dizzying Tilt-a-Wheel ride inside the Manhattan Criminal Court Building—from Stormy Daniels' stiletto heels clacking on the grimy floor, to the legal arguments proffered in the line to the bathroom, to the chaotic scene when a furious Judge Merchan cleared his courtroom.

As the trial moved forward, I found myself alternating between confidence in a conviction and concern that the prosecutors had blown it. Everyone knows how the story ends, but not the strange ups and downs en route.

Part Three chronicles the aftermath of the trial and the astonishing Black Swan Summer that followed, an historic period when the political world turned on its axis in just a few short weeks. I try to synthesize some of what I've learned about presidents into an assessment of the broader meaning of this national moment, then end on a hopeful note.

American Reckoning is my chance to give readers of today and the future a tactile sense of what it felt like to be a troubled but hopeful American looking for justice in a dangerous and dispiriting time.

Jonathan Alter
Montclair, New Jersey
August 2024

PART ONE

JIM AND GEORGE DEFEND DEMOCRACY

One night in October of 2023, I had a strange dream. All I knew was that it involved vodka and cigarettes and my dad with a gun.

When I woke up, I pieced the shards of the dream together into a memory of a real story that my late father, Jim Alter, liked to tell. During World War II, Dad flew thirty-one harrowing missions over Nazi-occupied Europe in a B-24 Liberator. As a navigator/bombardier, he handled a device called the Norden bombsight, a primitive computer that was supposed to help bombardiers lock on to targets. Dad told me that it didn't work well when an airplane was in the clouds. Slight detail.

Dad had orders to destroy the classified Norden bombsight if he and his crew were captured. On one of his last missions, the B-24 came under heavy German fire and made an emergency landing in Hungary. Dad emptied his Colt .45 into the bombsight and crawled out of the plane with his hands up. Fortunately, he and the crew were greeted by friendly Soviet troops. After a night of drinking, Dad ripped a page from a log and scrawled out a contract: the Russians could keep the unflyable airplane in exchange for vodka, cigarettes, and safe passage back to the American base in Italy.

First Lieutenant James Alter, Army Air Corps

Three years earlier, Dad was a sophomore at Purdue when the Japanese attacked Pearl Harbor. He liked college, was in love (not with Mom yet), and had what he then would have called a "swell" new convertible. Leaving all that was hard. There is no right time in anyone's life to do what you can to help defend democracy. But he did. He enlisted.

When he got home to Chicago in 1945, Dad learned from my great-grandmother that he had bombed the town in Hungary where she said "our people" were from, though by that time almost any Jewish relatives in the area who hadn't emigrated to America had been carted away to the camps.

Dad had no regrets. He was part of what Tom Brokaw dubbed "the Greatest Generation." The men and women who survived the Great Depression and World War II and built a powerful postwar economy shared a set of beliefs: appeasing enemies never works; alliances matter; and America is great, as Alexis de Tocqueville said, because America is good.

George H. W. Bush was the last American president from that storied generation. In 1942, Secretary of War Henry Stimson gave the commencement address at Bush's graduation from Andover. The speech was about fighting for freedom and democracy. Stimson told the graduates to go to college before they went to war, but Bush didn't listen to that. Days later, on his eighteenth birthday, he enlisted and soon became the youngest pilot in the navy.

When I covered his 1988 presidential campaign for *Newsweek*, I learned that Bush bailed out of his TBM Avenger near the island of Chichijima in the South Pacific, where cannibalistic Japanese soldiers were said to be eating the livers of downed American aviators. With his two crewmates dead, he gave himself first aid and sat for four hours in his inflatable life raft before being rescued by a submarine.

Bush said he spent his time in the ocean thinking about his next meal; his fiancée, Barbara; and . . . the separation of church and state embedded in the Constitution. Lots of jaundiced reporters—including me—snickered at this, assuming that Bush was just trying to show moderate voters that he hadn't sold out entirely to the Christian Right.

Perhaps so, but shame on us. The young pilot was also expressing a genuine motivation for his service. George Bush, Jim Alter, and thousands of other brave volunteers were risking their lives for an idea. When I recall the Greatest

Generation nowadays, I think about Trump calling veterans and dead soldiers "losers" and "suckers." A personal, political, and occupational question reverberates in my head. It's a question, to be honest, that keeps me up at night:

What am I doing to help defend democracy and save the Constitution? At any other time in my adult life, this would be a grandiose, laughable question. Not now.

Unlike Dad and Bush and the combat reporters I've known who have died abroad doing their jobs, I don't have to risk my life. I just have to inconvenience myself a little to bear witness—do *my* job—and urge others to get into the fight in whatever way they can.

It's a fight alright. From the start, Trump called the press "the enemy of the people," the exact words of Stalin, Hitler, and Mao.

When I heard this, my first reaction was: No, *we* represent the people (as the founders intended when they singled out the press for protection in the Constitution) and *you* are the enemy—of decency and democracy. But then I thought that descending to Trump's level by describing even the most odious character (e.g., Trump) as the "enemy" takes us down a path toward violence. We have to fight hard and sometimes get personal, but stay decent.

Democracy is supposed to be America's civic religion. It's certainly mine. Trump doesn't believe in this creed. He and J. D. Vance are classic nationalists, who believe not in the power of ideas but in the idea of power.* They're blood and soil, divide and conquer, might makes right. This is how demagogues and despots have scarred human history.

I'm glad that Dad's gone and can't see all this.

---

* Vance stressed "home" and "homeland" over our founding ideas in his nationalistic acceptance speech at the Republican National Convention. His "Great Replacement Theory" lies about Democrats importing immigrants so they can vote for them, his denigration of single women, and his repellent policy proposals giving parents an extra vote for each child are all familiar fascist tropes.

HONEST ABE

I can trace my fascination with politics back to a single afternoon of dorm room small talk.

In 1948, my mother, then Joanne Hammerman, had an experience that would change her life and, by extension, mine.

As a senior at Mount Holyoke College, she was assigned to give Eleanor Roosevelt a tour of campus. After the tour was over, Eleanor asked her, "Now where do you live, Joanne? I want to see your dormitory." When they arrived, the most famous woman in the world—the author that year of the Universal Declaration of Human Rights—plopped down on Mom's bed and said to this Jewish girl from a non-political family in the Chicago suburbs, "Now tell me all about yourself. Do you want to help make a better world?"

Mom was dumbfounded. Eleanor Roosevelt was asking about *her*! From then on she was intensely interested in public affairs and intensely curious about other people, the foundation of both good politics and good journalism. She could be blunt and unfiltered, but her belief in working within the American political system to change lives never wavered, and she infected first her husband and then her children with it.

After the war, Dad began working in his father's wholesaling business. In the 1920s, the Harry Alter Co. distributed Majestic Radios, the Apple Computer of its day (until it collapsed in the Crash). Someone in the family saved a 1928 invoice for a $167.50 radio sold by Harry Alter to "Benito Mussolini, Rome, Italy." Il Duce ("The Leader")—who must have liked Majestic's motto, "the Mighty Monarchs of the Air"—was popular then in both Italy and the United States.

My parents were married in 1952 at Chicago's Blackstone Hotel, where the phrase "smoke-filled room" was coined to describe how the Republicans nominated Warren Harding there in 1920. Mom was already a pioneer for women in politics, serving alongside a young county official named Richard J. Daley as an officer of the Young Democrats of Illinois. Daley would soon become the most powerful mayor and party boss in the country—a local Trump, only a thousand times smarter and more competent.

At the 1952 Democratic National Convention in Chicago, my parents worked to nominate Illinois governor Adlai Stevenson for president. Adlai was derided as an "egghead," which meant an intellectual. A woman told him that he had the votes of every thinking American. "That's nice, ma'am," Adlai replied. "But I need a majority." He didn't get one. Retired General Dwight D. Eisenhower—with grievance-nursing Richard Nixon as his running mate—crushed Stevenson in November and again in a rematch in 1956. The lesson I later drew was that elite opinion has little to do with winning elections.

I was born the year after that second defeat, and by the time I was three, I was smitten with my fellow Illinoisan, Abraham Lincoln. At dinner parties, my parents hauled me out in my pajamas to discuss Honest Abe and recite all the presidents in order in a made-up song that I later taught my siblings and eventually my children.

My earliest memory in life is of Mom and Dad leaving us with a babysitter in 1960 when they flew to Los Angeles to see John F. Kennedy nominated. ("Whistle while you work! Nixon is a jerk!" was the song my older sister Jennifer taught me that summer.) My uncle, Bill Rivkin, was a Kennedy man and got an ambassadorship out of it.* The photograph of Uncle Bill and Aunt Enid in the Oval Office with JFK hung in our hall and fueled my youthful dreams.

The author with his hero

My first campaign was in 1968. As a ten-year-old, I accompanied my parents as they rang doorbells on the South Side for Abner Mikva, an

* His son, my first cousin, Charlie Rivkin, who was four years old when his father died, grew up to become Barack Obama's ambassador to France.

inspiring candidate for Congress. Mikva was running against incumbent Barratt O'Hara, a veteran of the Spanish-American War. I had a connection to Teddy Roosevelt charging up San Juan Hill!

That was around the time I learned of my father's three-handshake history of the American republic. A drummer boy in the American Revolution could have shaken hands with a future Civil War veteran who, in fact, did shake hands with my father at a Chicago 4th of July parade in the late 1920s, who shook hands with (or kissed) grandchildren who may live into the twenty-second century.

After learning that American history is so short, I thought in second grade that I could write a short history of the country. I made it about two or three pages in.* Dad called me the only American historian who didn't know how to read. When I finally learned, I inhaled Landmark Books about presidents and Mike Royko's funny and pointed columns in the *Chicago Daily News*.

My little friends played with Legos and dinosaurs. I preferred Lincoln Logs, of course, and on the wall of my room I hung a copy of the Gettysburg Address (which I memorized) and a Styrofoam eagle, above the seal of the president of the United States, with an olive branch in one talon and arrows in the other. I also hung a 1964 *Sports Illustrated* poster of Cassius Clay (soon to be Muhammad Ali) decking Sonny Liston.

MLK

In 1966, when I was eight, Dr. Martin Luther King Jr. was living in a slum on the West Side of Chicago. He was there to draw attention to the plight of the urban poor and to pressure Mayor Daley for concessions on housing. A local politician had planned to host a party for King to raise money for a big civil rights rally at Soldier Field, but he feared Daley's wrath. So he asked my parents to do it, and one spring night, King and his Chicago associate, Al Raby, came to

* Franklin Roosevelt had a similar problem. In 2005, while researching my book *The Defining Moment* at the FDR Library in Hyde Park, I noticed that in the 1920s, while recovering from polio, he set out to write a history of the United States but only managed to scribble a few pages.

our North Side house. The haul was disappointing—just a few hundred dollars, my father recalled. Many of my parents' white friends didn't show up because they, too, feared alienating Daley, whose iron grip on Illinois Democrats was as strong as Trump's hold on Republicans would later become.

I got King's autograph on the lined paper of my school notebook. The next day I stood exactly where he did in front of our fireplace and tried to recreate the mini "I Have a Dream" speech he had softly delivered. Could I stand up for justice like him? It wouldn't be easy. That summer, I read in the *Chicago Sun-Times* how King was pelted with rocks when he marched through Marquette Park.

I wish I could report that I began my journalistic career by covering King in my handwritten newspaper that Dad xeroxed at his office so I could deliver it to the neighbors. Instead, I covered the Cubs (Wrigley Field, where bleacher seats cost a dollar, was only six blocks away) and wrote a banner headline that read: JON LOSES FOUR HARD BALLS IN THE BUSHES IN ONE SUMMER.*

For years, I took my unusual childhood experiences for granted, from attending campaign rallies in a stroller to skipping school every Election Day to work a precinct. Mom brought us to see the Beatles at Chicago's Comiskey Park when I was seven and to see *Hair* (with full frontal nudity) when I was eleven. This was life as an "under-deprived Alter," as my wife, Emily, later put it. We weren't rich or spoiled, just exposed—to everything.†

Mom was, by all accounts, a force of nature. In third grade, my interest in history took a back seat to sports—Cubs, White Sox, Bears, Blackhawks, and a brand-new lousy basketball team called the Bulls. She marched into the Francis W. Parker School and confronted the teacher, Mrs. Horst. "My son could have been the next Henry Steele Commager," she scolded, referring to the renowned historian. "And now you've made him into just another little boy!" I had no idea who this Commager was, but I was relieved that Mom didn't tell Mrs. Horst

* The legendary columnist Jimmy Breslin did better. When he was eight, he used his handwritten newspaper to cover his mother's attempted suicide. I interviewed him for an HBO documentary, *Breslin and Hamill: Deadline Artists*, and asked why he did that. He was offended by the question. "I had to write an ahticle!" he honked from Queens.

† Emily and I tried to do something similar. My interview with Mikhail Gorbachev in New York happened to take place on Take Your Children to Work Day, 2001. I took them to it.

her real career ambition for me—to be the first Jewish president of the United States.

I considered that occupation but also weighed being a TV anchor. On stage at school, my friend Casey and I re-created *The Huntley-Brinkley Report*, which, like the *CBS Evening News with Walter Cronkite*, was seen every weeknight by about twenty-five million people, more than five times today's evening news ratings and ten times today's top cable ratings, even though the country was only two-thirds the size that it is now. I played David Brinkley. "Goodnight, Chet," I said to Casey, who played Chet Huntley. "Goodnight, David," Casey said, completing the storied sign-off.

CHICAGO '68

The summer I was ten, I was footloose at the infamous 1968 Democratic National Convention. Having seen war, Dad hated it and was working for the peace candidate, Gene McCarthy; Mom had a job on the staff of Hubert Humphrey, who won the nomination that year without entering a single primary. A McCarthy aide saw my parents eating together in the Haymarket restaurant, soon to be the site of violence, and reported back to headquarters that Mr. Alter was conspiring with a female Humphrey operative. "That's my wife!" Dad said.

Even as a kid, I could feel tension between anti-war protesters and police mounting on Michigan Avenue. We fled by car through Grant Park, and soon after, images of police clubbing demonstrators there would be flashed around the world. I have no idea why my parents let me go back the next day. But I can still see the glint of the National Guardsmen's bayonets and smell the stink bomb that a protester threw into the lobby of the Conrad Hilton hotel.*

In 1969, federal prosecutors were determined to send hippies and Black radicals to jail for disrupting the previous summer's convention. The result was

* Some analysts have made facile comparisons between the 1968 and 2024 campaigns. It's true that President Lyndon Johnson stood down, just as President Joe Biden did, and that in both years the Democrats held their convention in Chicago. In 1968, the Democratic Party was deeply divided over the Vietnam War; in 2024, the Democrats are remarkably united.

the Chicago Eight Trial, with Judge Julius Hoffman—one of the worst federal judges in the country—presiding. Bobby Seale, co-founder of the Black Panther Party, had been in Chicago only briefly during the convention and was completely innocent of any conspiracy to disrupt it. With his lawyer hospitalized, he protested to the judge that he lacked legal representation.

Judge Hoffman didn't like his tone. He ordered him bound and gagged in the courtroom, then severed him from the other seven defendants and sentenced him to four years in prison for contempt of court, an absurd sentence he never served.

I remember poring over the *Sun-Times* courtroom sketches of Seale shackled to a chair with a rag in his mouth—and feeling my conscience stirred.* But as bad as the racial politics of Chicago were in those days, I don't recall any white politicians claiming, as Trump did with Kamala Harris, that a Black rival wasn't really Black.

In high school, defining myself as an outsider, I chose journalism over politics. My mother seemed OK with it, perhaps because she was otherwise occupied. She was a tireless "professional volunteer," as she called herself, spearheading civic organizations, as many women of her generation did. But her big focus was getting women to run for public office. Our dining room table was given over to women's causes, from races for state representative to unsuccessful efforts to ratify the Equal Rights Amendment.

THE JACKIE ROBINSON OF CHICAGO GENDER POLITICS

In 1972, Mom went to see Mayor Daley on behalf of a women's group she organized and bluntly told him that "women are people, too" and he should slate them for public office. This was a polite but bold request (not a "demand") three years before wives were even allowed to have their own credit cards. She gave the mayor a list of accomplished women who, unlike her, were loyal to

* Thirty years later, I interviewed Seale and was struck by his lack of bitterness.

his "Machine." Daley thought Mom was a pushy critic, but he was a clever politician. So he offered her a place on the Democratic ticket (primaries being a mere formality in Illinois in those days) for commissioner of the Metropolitan Sanitary District. Mom told "Hizzoner Da Mare" that she knew nothing about sewage. He reproached her in his flat, harsh-consonant Chicago accent, "Joan [her real name was Joanne], I thaaat you sa'd you wanted women in politicks." She said yes.

It was just after the first Earth Day, and Joanne Alter—with the help of a field organization made up mostly of housewives—ran one of the first environmental campaigns in the country. That and the novelty of her sex propelled her from the bottom of the ticket to being the top vote getter in Cook County. Over the years, I came to think of her as the Jackie Robinson of gender politics in Chicago, with Dad as her Denis Thatcher or Doug Emhoff. Friends had a joke campaign poster made: "When You Flush, Think of Me. I Won't Stand for No Shit."

Once in office, Mom didn't. She made a lot of enemies but saved taxpayers millions and spearheaded the removal of industrial slag heaps in favor of beautiful walkways on the banks of the Chicago River, now a gem of the city. One day

Joanne Alter, civic pioneer

in the mid-1980s, her office phone rang. The caller was a community organizer from the South Side who was surprised to be put through to a commissioner. Mom always refused to have her calls screened; she believed she worked for the people and they deserved to be heard just as much as any big shot. The young man had a problem with a nearby sewage treatment plant that he discussed years later in a book called *Dreams from My Father.* That was the first time Mom ever spoke to Barack Obama.

Mom owed her political career to Daley, but unlike Trumpsters, she wouldn't take orders from the "Boss," as the columnist Mike Royko called him. "Joanne, you're one of those brainless braless broads who is ruining America," another commissioner told her. That was mild compared with what he and other hacks said behind her back. "They couldn't deal with a 'girl from the kitchen' making big budget decisions," she told me years later, noting that path-breaking women engineers and lawyers she knew faced similar derision.

Remembering these men makes me think of Ted Cruz, Lindsey Graham, Kevin McCarthy, and other Republicans. They sound tough but are putty in the hands of their Dear Leader. After Mom opposed Daley's reelection to a sixth term, he slated another candidate for lieutenant governor. She ran anyway, and lost with no regrets.

THINKING IN TIME

My work as a journalist began at sixteen when I wrote press criticism for the *Chicago Journalism Review*, a prelude to my job a decade later as *Newsweek*'s media critic. At Andover, which I attended for two years, I got the chance to interview Teamsters boss Jimmy Hoffa for the school paper. I asked him a tough question about the Teamsters muscling Cesar Chavez's farm workers off the roads in California. "Where'd they get this kid?" Hoffa asked a thuggish aide, gesturing to me with a look that could kill. My interview turned out to be one of the last with Hoffa before he mysteriously disappeared.

At Harvard, I majored in history, with David Herbert Donald's class on the Civil War my favorite. Things are bad now, but not nearly as bad as they were in the 1850s. I took a course at the Kennedy School taught by Richard Neustadt and Ernest May called "Thinking in Time: The Uses and Misuses of History." Neustadt and I stayed in touch, and he helped me to embrace historical analogies in my *Newsweek* column but also to stay careful in how I deployed them.*

History doesn't repeat itself, and when it rhymes, the meter is sometimes off. Columnists, historians, and the guy at the gym with a bone to pick should reject "presentism"—analyzing history through the prism of the present. That doesn't mean rationalizing slaveholders or the callous treatment of women, but it does require avoiding facile historical analogies.

Beyond history and English classes and my senior thesis on Vietnam, I didn't study much. I remember one class taught by a guy named Roger Revelle that had something to do with boring meteorological patterns. I ditched it often and only learned later that Revelle (like Neustadt) was a mentor to Al Gore and one of the founders of climate science.† My loss.

In the summer of 1978, I was an intern in the speechwriting office of Jimmy Carter's White House. The emotion I remember is awe. This was what I had dreamed of when peering up at night at the styrofoam eagle and Gettysburg Address on the wall of my childhood bedroom. After a few weeks, I scored a hard pass for the West Wing, which allowed me to take my friends to see the Oval Office. If the president wasn't there, the door was open and we could stand in front of the velvet rope and stare inside for as long as we wanted.

My boss was twenty-eight-year-old Jim Fallows, who later wrote that "Being Jimmy Carter's chief speechwriter was like being FDR's tap dance instructor." Carter was a good president but a so-so speaker, especially compared to his

* As a reporter for the *Harvard Crimson* I got my first experience covering sex stories. I learned that two MIT women had slept with thirty-six men they identified by name and rated them one-to-four stars on their sexual prowess. The story was picked up by the pre–David Pecker *National Enquirer*.

† Gore deserves more credit than he gets. While he didn't "invent" the internet, he secured much of the government funding that made it possible, which is all he ever claimed. Unfortunately, politics got in the way of his vision. When I interviewed him just before the 2000 election, he downplayed his climate-change agenda, which his campaign worried (with good reason) would hurt him in fossil fuel states such as West Virginia and Ohio that were already trending red. But without passion on climate, his campaign had a stolid uninspiring quality. That hurt him in a breathtakingly close election.

successor, "the Great Communicator," Ronald Reagan. One week, none of the grown-up speechwriters wanted to write Carter's remarks at a North Carolina tobacco warehouse. I happily obliged. The only line of mine the president used was a joke saying he would bring back some tobacco for staffers caught smoking pot "so they smoke something regular for a change."

In 1980, my former teacher, Alan Brinkley, got me a job as a research assistant to his famous and dry-witted father, David, my grade school role model, who was writing a history of Washington during World War II. David had been put out to pasture at NBC News and was still a year away from being hired by Roone Arledge at ABC News to launch his Sunday show, *This Week with David Brinkley*. That year, I loved interviewing old people who had known FDR personally. I vowed to become a journalist of some sort. My mother had planned for me to go to law school, but it slipped my mind.

NIXON HAD MY NUMBER

I came of age when Richard Nixon was president and I hate-watched him on TV every chance I got. Like many of my friends, I was inspired to go into journalism in part by the dogged work of Bob Woodward and Carl Bernstein, whose articles in the *Washington Post* broke the Watergate scandal wide open.

Not long ago, I moderated a discussion with Woodward and Bernstein, both in their early eighties, on the fiftieth anniversary of the publication of their classic book, *All the President's Men.* Bernstein, comparing Trump's conduct to the treason of Jefferson Davis, explained how George Washington warned against a party very similar to the GOP in his Farewell Address, in which he described a dangerous faction that "kindles the animosity of one part against another, foments occasional riot and insurrection." Woodward, who has spent more time with Trump than any other reporter, thought the similarities between Nixon and Trump were "stunning." During the Watergate hearings, Sam Ervin, chairman of the Senate Watergate Committee, asked the larger question: "Why did this happen?" Woodward said the answer fits both Nixon and Trump: "A lust for political power. It's a disease."

I remember being influenced in the 1970s by a Watergate book called *Breach of Faith*, by Theodore H. White, whose best work I later tried to emulate. White argued that Nixon shattered a national myth that the presidency "would make noble any man who held its responsibility."

Just before the 1988 election, I arranged to bring Nixon to *Newsweek*. I wanted to meet the man before he croaked. Toward the end of a long session between Nixon and the magazine's editors, I asked him how history would view outgoing President Reagan.* He gave a perceptive answer: "Well, you have to distinguish between history and the historians," he said. "The historians are like you, they're liberal. If you're a conservative, you go into business. If you're a liberal, you write history and journalism."

Nixon—this man I despised—had my number. He had, as they say, *seen* me. These days, as I weigh how to respond to Trump, I have to see myself and my responsibilities more clearly. Historian and journalist. Bearing witness. That's all I got.

Is it enough? In Woodward and Bernstein's day, aggressive journalism brought down a president. Nowadays, reporters still break big stories, but the fragmentation of the news business has dramatically curbed the influence of people like me. That's fine, but I worry that readers now seek and receive (through algorithms) "news" that mostly validates their worldview. There's a big difference between a fact-checked 1988 *Newsweek* cover story and "I read it somewhere online—can't remember where—but it must be true and it really pissed me off!"

THE NIXON PARDON

I've done a 180-degree turn on the Nixon pardon—actually a flip-flop on a flip-flop. When Gerald Ford granted it in 1974, I was in high school and

* When I was at *Newsweek*, I was too young to be assigned to interview Reagan in the White House, and after he left office, he was too old to sit down with reporters. So Reagan was the only president going back to Nixon whom I didn't get a chance to question.

strongly opposed the decision. Later, Caroline Kennedy gave Ford the Profile in Courage Award for a decision that helped cost Ford his presidency.*

Over time, I and a lot of other people also decided that in retrospect he deserved the award—that the pardon was necessary to help heal the country. I wanted to talk to Ford about it and had my chance in the summer of 2000 when our family was on vacation in Colorado. I took Emily and our children with me to Ford's ski chalet in Beaver Creek. As gracious Betty humored the kids while packing for a trip, I asked the former president about the pardon, and he offered a vigorous defense of it.

For years, the pardon seemed prudent because we thought Nixon was an aberration and that basic democratic accountability had been achieved. But by short-circuiting a trial of Nixon for his Watergate crimes, the pardon set a harmful precedent and should not have been issued. It left open the question of whether the president is above the law. "When the president does it, that means that it is not illegal," Nixon told British television host David Frost. Fifty years after Nixon's resignation, the Supreme Court—in *Donald J. Trump v. United States*—essentially agreed.

CHARLIE PETERS

On Thanksgiving Day 2023, I saw a *New York Times* bulletin on my phone that Charles Peters, the founder and editor of the *Washington Monthly*, had died. I left the living room and wept in the hall.

Charlie was ninety-five, so the news was hardly unexpected. But for me, Jim Fallows, and many of the other magazine writers and editors in our informal *Washington Monthly* alumni association, it was like losing a second father.

* My present for my college friend Caroline Kennedy on her twenty-first birthday was "soap on a rope" shaped like a microphone for singing in the shower. In an especially classy college boy move, I brought it over to her apartment at 1040 Fifth Avenue in a paper bag. "That's the most phallic thing I've ever seen," Jacqueline Kennedy Onassis said before turning on her heel to leave the room.

Charlie hired me in 1981 for a princely $8,700 a year. He expected that I and his other young editors would work eighteen-hour days doing everything from taking out the garbage to writing cover stories for two years before graduating to something bigger in journalism. I was twenty-three and intimidated by his patented "rain dances," where this squat, raccoon-eyed, West Virginia iconoclast would jump up and down and explain at a high-decibel level what was wrong with your article, the government, the country—and you.

The abuse was worth it, because eccentric Charlie was one of the few genuinely original thinkers I've ever met. He believed in the compassionate ends of liberalism but was often critical of the mindless means of achieving them—and of the smug pieties of many on the left. As we learned to meld idealism and skepticism, he urged us to fasten an anthropological lens on our reporting, as if Washington politicians and bureaucrats were some exotic tribe in the South Sea islands. Charlie taught us to appreciate human complexity by writing "something bad about the good guys and good about the bad guys."

Charlie and I last spoke in the spring of 2023 as he sat propped up in his basement, surviving thanks to an oxygen machine and the glow of an artificial Christmas tree that—his own person to the end—he kept lit all year long. We talked about his road trips with JFK during the critical 1960 West Virginia primary, and agreed that Trump was the exception who proved the rule—the only bad guy about whom there was nothing good to say.

ROY COHN

Charlie was the one who got me a job at *Newsweek*, where I spent twenty-eight years as a New York–based writer, senior editor, and columnist. Early on at *Newsweek*, I covered the media, and that brought me into contact with a figure who years later would cast a shadow over Trump's criminal defense team. In 1985, S.I. Newhouse, heir to a newspaper fortune, bought the *New Yorker*. The week of the sale, I learned that one of Newhouse's friends was Roy Cohn, the infamous New York lawyer. As a young man, Cohn helped prosecute Julius and Ethel Rosenberg for espionage. He went on to be the top aide to

Senator Joseph McCarthy, the most dangerous postwar American demagogue until Trump.

I called Cohn, who told me that he and the new owner of the *New Yorker* were not just friends, but best friends from Horace Mann School in the Bronx.

Cohn informed me that every morning at 6 AM, he, Newhouse, and their other best friend from high school, Generoso "Gene" Pope Jr., who founded the *National Enquirer* with a loan from New York crime boss Frank Costello, talked on the phone. That was the lede of my story, which I was later told almost blew the roof off the old *New Yorker* building on 44th Street: "Our new owner's best friends are *Roy Cohn* and the founder of the *National Enquirer*? We're toast!" It turned out that Cohn and Pope did nothing to harm their best friend's new purchase, which Newhouse kept prosperous and strong editorially until the day he died.

Roy Cohn did a lot for Trump. He represented him in the 1970s after Trump and his father were sued by the Nixon administration's justice department for blocking Black people from renting apartments in their buildings. Fred Trump had been arrested at a Ku Klux Klan rally in New York in 1927, and the poisoned apple didn't fall far from the tree. Fred Trump III later reported that he heard his uncle use the N-word.*

Cohn also represented big-time mobsters, including Anthony "Fat Tony" Salerno, Carmine Galante, and Paul Castellano, the latter of whom was whacked by John Gotti, the original "Teflon Don" before the New York tabloids bestowed that title on Trump. These gentlemen were part of what federal authorities called "the largest and most vicious criminal business in the history of the United States." Starting in 1979, "Fat Tony" struck a deal through intermediaries with the brash young developer: Trump would pay a mobbed-up construction company a premium for ready-mix concrete in exchange for labor peace with the mobbed-up unions he needed to build Trump Tower. Later, when erecting his casino in Atlantic City, Trump's contractors dealt with a *Sopranos*-style New Jersey mob called "the Young Executioners."

* Fred Trump III has a disabled son. In a 2024 book, he charged that Trump got tired of contributing to a medical fund for him and told his nephew, "Maybe you should just let him die and move down to Florida."

I didn't know it, but at the time I talked to Cohn, he was dying of AIDS. The next year, Trump and Barbara Walters were among those testifying as character witnesses before the bar association after Cohn was credibly accused of ripping off a clueless elderly client. Just weeks after Cohn was disbarred, as Cohn's secretary reported, Trump dropped his terminally ill mentor "like a hot potato."

When he was president, Trump often asked, "Where's my Roy Cohn?" He meant, Where's my brilliant and surpassingly unscrupulous lawyer who would do anything to win? Too bad they couldn't locate one for the New York trial. It would be fun to watch a reincarnated Cohn in the courtroom. I don't think the jury would like him.

PEZ-DISPENSER PRESIDENTS

Since 1994, my family has lived in a Queen Anne Victorian house that was built in Montclair, New Jersey, during the administration of Rutherford B. Hayes.

President Hayes has a place in our home, along with almost all of the other men who have held the highest office. We've got silver spoons of presidents, supermarket figurines of presidents, bobbleheads of presidents, paintings of presidents (including one by our daughter Charlotte of Martin Van Buren), bookends of presidents, and Pez dispensers of presidents. Did I mention the busts? We have bronzes of Washington, Lincoln, FDR, and JFK, and a wax Nixon, plus a foot-high peanut with Jimmy Carter's grin and a classic print of Obama by Shepard Fairey.

There is one president whose likeness does not appear anywhere in our home. I think you can guess who he is.

TRUMP'S SHOPWORN HAIR SALON

In 1991, I was interviewed for a documentary about Trump's business career and said two things: Trump was not the richest real estate developer in New York, much less the United States, as he insisted. And Trump was lying when he claimed Mikhail Gorbachev planned to visit him at Trump Tower. Both the Soviet embassy and the State Department told me this was complete bullshit—never any such plans.

The film, a critical look at his bankruptcies called *Trump: What's the Deal?*, was underwritten by the billionaire Leonard Stern, who owned the Hartz Mountain pet food company. Trump paid Stern to squelch the film—a kind of early catch and kill—and I received a harsh letter from one of Trump's lawyers threatening to sue me for defamation. I was young and a little intimidated. But when I showed the letter to *Newsweek*'s attorney, she laughed and said, "Join the club." Nothing ever came of the lawsuit, of course.

Six years later, Trump had completely forgotten the flap over the film. I needed a sound bite for a TV piece and—like a lot of New York reporters—knew where to get one. Calling Trump a publicity hound in those days was unfair to hounds. We sat down in his Trump Tower office, which looked like a shopworn hair salon where the owner insists on hanging photos of himself between the mirrors.

This was for a *TODAY* show story about how everything in America is now super-sized, from McMansions to coffee cups at Starbucks. He tried to be thoughtful about the trend but did not succeed. We included him in the story anyway.

In the years that followed, I tried to think about Trump as little as possible. He was just an obnoxious celebrity who embarrassed New York in the eyes of the world.

Unfortunately, by 2009 he was impossible to ignore. Trump believed in Joseph Goebbels's "Big Lie" technique, which means not just lying with relish but pushing outlandish lies so incessantly that they worm their way into public consciousness. He began with the absurd claim that Barack Obama was not born in the United States. After Obama, as president, released his birth certificate, Trump just moved on to the next of more than thirty thousand other documented lies. Trump's lies were picked up by the Tea Party, a huge and now forgotten movement that hassled Obama for years before morphing into MAGA, which in turn spawned QAnon and its insane conspiracy theories.

I made a point of listening to some of Trump's lies at one of his 2016 rallies in New Hampshire. Standing in the crowd, I sensed an air of menace, especially when the crowd turned on reporters gathered near the camera stand, booing them on Trump's cue. But the crowd seemed happy and entertained, and there was power in that.

The weekend before the 2016 election I was with Vice President Biden when he campaigned for Hillary Clinton at a lackluster rally in Pennsylvania. Afterwards, a student at Bucks County Community College told me that as many as half of his classmates were for Trump. I asked why. He said it was because Trump was funny. That's when I knew Hillary Clinton was in deep trouble. Many Americans ignore or indulge Trump's norm-breaking because they view him as they would an eccentric uncle telling gay jokes at the other end of the dinner table.

I've rarely tried to report on Trump World and here's why: At the 2016 Republican National Convention in Cleveland, I ambushed Paul Manafort, Trump's campaign chair (and later a jailbird), and asked him why Melania Trump plagiarized Michelle Obama in her speech the night before, and why support for Ukraine had been mysteriously deleted from the Republican platform. He was pleasant enough but didn't even bother with the usual spin. He simply denied everything, which was preposterous.

Since then, I have steered clear of these guys even though I know they are prodigious leakers. That's because I've long subscribed to the maxim that a fish rots from the head—Trump's bottom-feeders are serial liars, too, so why waste time trying to figure out if they're lying 50, 75, or 100 percent of the time?

The feeling, of course, is mutual, not just from Trump World but from the broader MAGA universe. Despising the press is hardly new. Sixty years ago, Barry Goldwater's delegates at the 1964 Republican National Convention loudly booed reporters at the Cow Palace in San Francisco. But it's worse now. After the 2016 election, I asked a friend from South Carolina why so many people voted for Trump. "Because they hate you," he said—not me personally, but everything that I, as a "lamestream" journalist, represent.

INSIDE THE BEAST

Bret Stephens, a conservative columnist for the *New York Times*, asked me recently: What's worse, covering up hush money payments to Stormy Daniels or lying under oath about Monica Lewinsky?

For me, it's not a close call. Both involved law-breaking, but the stakes were higher with Trump. In 2016, Trump did more than lie about sex; he took part in a conspiracy aimed at securing his election. In 1998, Bill Clinton lied like any cheating husband—to avoid embarrassment. One thing is for sure: the reaction of Republicans was worse. After they denounced Clinton, they didn't just back Trump, they anointed him. By contrast, Democrats all chastised Clinton and breathed a sigh of relief that he wasn't eligible for a third term.

Thinking about all of this took me back to the 1990s. That was the pre-9/11, pre–Iraq War, pre–Great Recession decade of peace and prosperity—the era when we had the leisure to obsess over Clinton's sex life and the O. J. Simpson trial.

I'm not ashamed of my coverage of sex and politics but not proud of it, either. Much of what I wrote about Gary Hart, Bill Clinton, and, later, John Edwards, was prompted by tawdry articles in supermarket tabloids that we in the mainstream press thought could not, alas, be ignored.

My guidance in matters of sex and presidents came from Charlie Peters, who in 1979, at the time Ted Kennedy was challenging incumbent Jimmy Carter, published a widely read article by Suzannah Lessard in the *Washington Monthly* entitled "Kennedy's Women Problem—Women's Kennedy Problem," that argued persuasively that Ted Kennedy's philandering and cavalier treatment of women should be openly discussed. Charlie wrote that the sex lives of presidents and presidential candidates—but not senators or governors—were newsworthy because "We should not have to wonder from whose bed the commander-in-chief will be summoned at the moment of nuclear decision." He wrote this in the context of saying that he knew and revered JFK and didn't think his womanizing was disqualifying, but that friendly reporters should not have covered for him.

So aside from the legalities, is it necessary for the public to know that Trump had sex with a porn star when his wife was pregnant? I vote aye—and still believe that when vetting candidates for president, everything is fair game.

After a rocky start, Clinton led the country through eight years of relative peace and prosperity. According to a book by Howard Kurtz, Clinton said of me: "Alter bites me in the ass sometimes but at least he knows what we're trying to do." Sounds about right.

In 1997, a senior White House aide asked if I wanted to come down to Washington and interview for the job of chief speechwriter. I was tempted but decided that a job interview would compromise my column if it didn't work out, so I immediately declined. Thank God, because the next year I would not have enjoyed cranking out the party line on the allegations against Clinton in the Monica Lewinsky case.

Lewinsky was a twenty-two-year-old White House intern when Clinton first kissed her, before they moved on to phone sex, an unlit cigar in her vagina, and tell-tale stains on a blue dress. I opposed his impeachment but supported censure, which I still think is the right punishment for lies about sex that do not rise to the level of the "High Crimes and Misdemeanors" required by the Constitution for removal from office (like, say, extorting the government of Ukraine or attempting a coup). But in retrospect, it's remarkable how many Democrats defended him, including prominent feminists who would later champion the #MeToo movement. Imagine if he'd done all of that now—he'd be forced to resign before lunch.

Of course the rules are different for Trump, whose base didn't care at all when he was found in a civil trial to have sexually assaulted E. Jean Carroll in a changing room at Bergdorf Goodman. Same for his involvement in Jeffrey Epstein's harem or with Stormy Daniels. Swing voters—especially women—may not be as forgiving.

Like Kennedy's many dalliances, Clinton's sins did not discredit his presidency. But his handling of the matter did make it easier for men like Gary Hart, John Edwards, and Donald Trump to play the victim.

All told, I interviewed Clinton seven times when he was president, and all but one involved foreign affairs or domestic affairs, not the affairs and other sexual encounters that were causing him such problems. The exception proved memorable.

After he was impeached in part on the basis of reporting by my *Newsweek* colleague Mike Isikoff, he cut me off for a year or so. Then I spent time with Clinton touring impoverished areas of the country, and he agreed to let me interview him again. This was more than a year after he admitted the affair with Lewinsky, and no reporter had yet been able to question him about it. So in the fall of 1999, I rode with him in "the Beast" (the presidential limo) to Hartford, Connecticut, and posed what may be the most impertinent question I've ever asked anyone, though one I don't regret:

"Are you seeking any psychiatric counseling for your self-destructive behavior, Mr. President?"

Clinton blew up. "I can't believe you're asking me that question, Jon!" I mumbled something about Tipper Gore working to end the stigma around mental health, then reframed the question to refer to his publicized *pastoral* counseling. He said that counseling was going well, calmed down, and finished the interview before he and an aide bolted the Beast without saying goodbye.

At the end of his term, I sought another interview with Clinton and was rebuffed. "After that 'Are-you-crazy-Mr.-President'? question, no way," his press secretary, Jake Siewert, told me. But here's the thing about Clinton: Because *he* needs forgiveness, he forgives others. A year later, I got the first interview with him after he left office. "I can't believe I'm giving my first interview to the house organ of Paula Jones," he complained to me when I was shadowing him for a week at his Harlem office, referring to the fact that *Newsweek* had twice put his Arkansas accuser on the cover. But he cooperated and allowed me to question him for the first time about his pardon of fugitive financier Marc Rich, a decision that received a hundred times more negative coverage than all of Trump's more egregious pardons combined.

Back in New York after the presidency, the Clintons let Trump ingratiate himself with them. He gave $100,000 to the Clinton Foundation and supported Hillary's Senate campaigns; they attended his 2005 wedding to Melania at Mar-a-Lago. Just another celebrity transaction.

Then came 2016. Trump—reeling after the release of the *Access Hollywood* tape—brought three women who had accused Bill Clinton of sexual harassment or assault as his guests for his second debate with Hillary Clinton.

We all saw the resurrection of this tabloid drama. But another tabloid story—a story about Trump and a porn star—was hidden from view that fall, known only to Trump, Michael Cohen, and a couple of others. It would surface much later in the dusty files of the Manhattan DA.

UNCLE FUN

Getting to know John McCain did as much as anything to nourish my nonpartisan civic faith. I fell for him harder than a journalist should for a politician. We met in 1995 when he and his fellow war hero and Senate colleague, John Kerry, were providing cover for President Clinton (like Trump, a draft dodger) to normalize relations with Vietnam. I told McCain I was headed for Vietnam, and he set me up with Communist officials who offered me strong evidence that—contrary to feverish conspiracy theorists—no POW/MIAs were held or buried there.

McCain was a bad boy with a good heart and we called him "Uncle Fun." He spent two of his five and a half years of captivity in North Vietnam in solitary confinement and now craved company. "I'm Luke Skywalker getting out of the Death Star!" he'd exclaim.

I was a frequent passenger on "the Straight Talk Express," his 2000 campaign bus where day after day about ten reporters got to talk to the candidate for five or six hours straight about everything from being viciously beaten by his captors at the "Hanoi Hilton" to why he felt Mitch McConnell and many of his Republican colleagues were jerks.

McCain's positions on most issues were too conservative for my tastes but that didn't matter in primaries. He was essentially running to be another John F. Kennedy—"to inspire a generation of young Americans to commit themselves to a cause larger than their own self-interest," he'd say. Just mentioning the need for inspiration was inspiring to me, and the contrast with Trump—who has no ideals of any kind—could not have been more stark. In 2015, Trump said of

Aboard the "Straight Talk Express" with (left to right): John McCain, strategist Mike Murphy, journalist Jonathan Karl, and the author

McCain, "I like people who weren't captured." I was surprised and disappointed that this comment did not end Trump's campaign. That was an early sign that, politically, we were no longer in Kansas.

Before the South Carolina primary, Jeff Zucker, the executive producer of the *TODAY* show, arranged a wildly expensive live shot aboard McCain's Straight Talk Express, which in those days required two hovering helicopters and a fleet of satellite trucks. After Katie Couric tossed to me to open the broadcast, I said, "Good morning, Senator McCain," and he replied, "Good morning, Jonathan, you communist."

When Trump says something vile (i.e., almost every day), he often claims afterwards that he was just joking. It's a clever way of revving up his base while simultaneously slagging his critics for lacking a sense of humor and denying responsibility for the inflammatory remark. But the "jokes" are more than just part of his lounge act. Most of them also reflect his actual views. Even sick humor contains truth.

In McCain's case, the "communist" jab really was a joke, and a funny one. He was amusing in private, too, and proved more even-keeled than his reputation suggested. While he tongue-lashed Senate colleagues for selling out to special interests, he treated his loyal staff with great respect.

I was in his Columbia, SC, hotel room when his aides told him that exit polls showed he had not only lost to Bush in South Carolina, but had lost among veterans. Racists in Bush's campaign had—without Bush's knowledge—spread the word that McCain fathered a Black daughter. This was an unconscionable attack on eight-year-old Bridget McCain, whom the McCains had adopted from a Bangladeshi orphanage in 1991. Cindy McCain, sitting next to me on a small couch, burst into tears. John, who had seen a lot worse in Vietnam, calmly said, "It's just politics, honey."

I put my columnist's thumb heavily on the scale for McCain, who began losing a string of primaries to Bush. On a day off from the 2000 campaign, he had me and John Dickerson of *Time* to his ranch near Sedona, Arizona, where he kept four "Turbo" grills. His war injuries prevented him from raising his arms above his shoulders, so hiking and moving from grill to grill were his only forms of recreation. His specialty was spicy chicken, which he patiently grilled on low heat "to cook everything bad out of it—a purification thing."

For me, McCain embodied a purification ritual in American public life. Instead of bitterness, great suffering can bring grace—if survivors tap their curiosity, idealism, and sense of humor. Even so, the rest of 2000 tested my faith in democracy. After defeating McCain, Bush beat Al Gore in the disputed 2000 general election, despite losing to him in the popular vote (the first time a president was elected with a minority of the popular vote since Benjamin Harrison in 1888).*

In 2008, McCain won the GOP nomination after Rudy Giuliani blew up on the launchpad. By then we had drifted apart, mostly because he had the poor judgment to name Sarah Palin to the ticket. I angered his staff by writing that he didn't know how to use a computer—a relevant detail for a possible future president—and he knew I was partial to Obama.

---

* I was at a county building in Tallahassee, Florida, watching the counting of ballots when the conservative Supreme Court—hypocritically violating its own long-standing deference to states on election issues—ordered the counting stopped and handed the election to Bush. Gore's graceful concession stood in sharp contrast to Trump's shameful and criminal behavior after the 2020 election.

Five years after that, we reconnected when he agreed to do a cameo on a comedy I was working on.* John loved show business. During his captivity, he entertained the other American POWs by acting out all the parts in movies. One day on the campaign trail, I watched a conspiracy monger confront him. "And Angela Lansbury turned over the queen of diamonds," he deadpanned, a reference to nutjobs calling him "the Manchurian Candidate."

McCain had limited patience in life and art. If he hadn't succumbed to brain cancer in 2018, Trump's "January 6th Choir" would have killed him.

FEARLESS

On Super Tuesday 2004, I was in a Starbucks in Penn Station when a doctor called to say that a CT scan of my abdomen showed a large tumor, with extensive lymph node involvement.

I endured a chatty lunch with anchors and political reporters at the Palm restaurant, where we bet on the outcome in Super Tuesday states. My head was throbbing as I absorbed what I knew to be true: I had cancer. Our group hosted a guest that day—Roger Ailes. I remember wondering: Why do I have cancer and Roger looks fine?

The diagnosis was worse than I expected: stage four mantle cell lymphoma. Two-year survival rate of 50 percent. The five-year survival rate was so bad they didn't want to tell me.

Dr. Andy Zelenetz and the Sloan Kettering team saved my life. I was there for twenty-nine days in all, including the bone marrow transplant. Our children—Charlotte, Tommy, and Molly—handled it remarkably well, in part because we didn't overshare the details.

In the hospital, I set my doubting nature aside—the crap I read online that understandably irritated Dr. Zelenetz—and listened scrupulously to doctors' orders, which I later recounted in a long *Newsweek* article about my ordeal.

* In 2013–2014, I co-produced *Alpha House*, a two-season Amazon show starring John Goodman. The show, written by Garry Trudeau, was about four Republican senators who live in a man-cave on Capitol Hill. McCain played himself.

Before I grew too weak, I even managed to write a column about New Jersey governor Jim McGreevey resigning after a gay sex scandal. Yep, I was still covering politics from my near-death bed.

I have a memory about Trump from this period. Because of my severely compromised immune system, I refused to shake hands, cheerfully telling friends that I was just following the example of germaphobe Donald Trump, who did the same without having cancer.

I never learned what caused my lymphoma, though I have my suspicions. After I recovered, I received a call from Joe Lhota, the former deputy mayor of New York. In the days and weeks following 9/11, I had accompanied Joe and his boss, Mayor Giuliani, on several shattering visits to Ground Zero, which struck me as the closest I will ever get to *Dante's Inferno.* I thought Giuliani had been a bad mayor overall but respected his leadership after 9/11, a period that strengthened my patriotism. At lunch, Joe told me that he, too, had been diagnosed with lymphoma, and he thought we both might have gotten it from all that unmasked exposure to chemicals in the steaming pile of rubble.

In the last twenty years, the sword of Damocles hasn't dropped. Not yet, anyway. The fear of recurrence never evaporates, but I don't think about it much anymore. It'll probably be something else that gets me—a heart attack or a Mack truck.

I love getting older, because I wasn't sure I would. It's a miracle I'm still here and have more time.

One of the things I don't take for granted: the future of this country. We're on a knife's edge. I've never been a Voltaire guy, so I don't understand retreating to cultivate one's garden without any connection to the wider world. I don't understand why ostriches put their heads in the sand. And I don't understand how any person can be so happy-go-lucky or self-absorbed that their private life is not shadowed—at least part of the time—by the alarming condition of public life.

When I was sick, a friend of mine joked, "Oh, God, now you're gonna get deep." I told him he didn't have to worry about that. But I did get more fearless, a quality in depressingly short supply in politics.

I'm not sure where Liz Cheney, Adam Kinzinger, Mitt Romney, Brad Raffensperger, Rusty Bowers, and a few other lonely patriots got their guts, or why so few of their colleagues in the Republican Party have any. One explanation is fear of violence; Romney said several of his Senate colleagues didn't vote to convict Trump in his impeachment trial out of concern for their personal safety. But the larger reason is moral cowardice. When faced with a choice between power and conscience, only the bravest will listen to the latter.

ROGER AILES

To understand what Trump is doing to this country, you have to understand what Roger Ailes did to us first. A bad guy long before he was caught sexually harassing women, Ailes, like Trump, could dish it out but he couldn't take it, as I learned when I wrote a satirical column about him in *Newsweek* in 2006. Ailes went crazy, writing me a charming letter that began: "Jon, I'm afraid your cancer has affected your judgment." Later, he denounced me publicly and threatened to sue me after I described his paranoia in a book. I knew that just like Trump, Ailes would never follow through, so I didn't care.

I did care that the new indoor records Ailes set for nastiness were, with the help of the internet, being matched and broken all over the place. It was as if the gossamer layer of basic human decency that we assumed protected us was a spider's web after all. Ailes was a huge spider—the biggest and most influential of the era—and his poison spread through much of the national bloodstream.

Ailes and Trump had their ups and downs but were good friends in Manhattan for forty years. When Trump began toying with the idea of running for president, Ailes sent him strategy memos from Fox News headquarters, just as he had done for George H. W. Bush and his son. He died four months after Trump's inauguration.

Whatever happened later between Trump and Fox after Ailes's death, the work of the master was done. He had bolted the Republican Party to a powerful propaganda machine (and its imitators) and changed American politics forever.

OBAMA AND GRANT PARK

It's often said that Barack Obama made Donald Trump possible; the backlash against him sent things spinning in the wrong direction. Maybe so, but Obama also made genuine, unbridled idealism possible. For a whole generation, he did what John F. Kennedy had done in 1960 and Kamala Harris would do in 2024. In that sense, the success of Obama's presidency made the dread and disillusionment of the Trump Era feel even worse.

I met Obama in early 2002 when we were sitting shiva in Chicago for my Aunt Enid, the aunt whose photo with her husband and JFK in the Oval Office had helped fire my boyhood imagination. Enid's son, Bob Rivkin, and his wife, Cindy Moelis (a work colleague of Michelle Obama), had been urging me to meet him, and here he was, this cocky Illinois state senator who had just lost to a former Black Panther for the House. Now he was heedless enough to be launching a long shot campaign for the U.S. Senate with a name that a year after 9/11 sounded suspiciously like Osama bin Laden. But he was impressive that day and grew more so over time.

Mom agreed. By 2008, she had Lewy body dementia, but she was clear enough for me to write a *Newsweek* column that detailed her "excruciatingly painful" choice between two candidates she knew personally and admired. She resented the sexist comments directed at Hillary Clinton ("Iron my shirts!" chanted imbecilic future Trumpsters in New Hampshire), but she finally chose Obama because she saw that her grandchildren were inspired by him. The next president was for them, she reasoned.*

Even so, Mom felt bad for Hillary and conflicted: A woman president was what she had been working toward for more than half a century. In more lucid moments, she never let me forget that a year earlier, *Newsweek* and *Time* both

* One of Obama's most powerful themes in 2008 was that it was time to "turn the page" generationally from the Clintons. Kamala Harris is making a similar argument against Trump. Ironically, the Clintons, Obama, Trump and Harris are all technically baby boomers, born between 1946 and 1964. But the early boomers have little in common culturally with contemporaries Obama and Harris, who were born in 1961 and 1964, respectively. The latter—shaped more by the 1970s than the 1960s— are more properly known as Generation Jones, which is named for all the lyrics of the era containing the name Jones.

neglected to put Nancy Pelosi on their covers after she was elected the first woman Speaker of the House in US history. "That's outrageous!" Mom said. And she was right.*

Obama's decade-long run of political success is almost unprecedented in recent American political history and it's a big reason why Trump resents him. He seems easygoing in public but can be tough and contemptuous in private. When the staff gets sloppy, he grows angry, as Jimmy Carter did.

Midmorning on Election Day 2008, I put Mom in her wheelchair and took her downstairs to the polling place in the Chicago nursing home where she lived with Dad. She was weak and disoriented but determined to vote one last time. I went into the polling booth with her, guided her hand to Obama's name, and—like a machine precinct captain of old—helped her pull the lever for him.

On election night, I was in Grant Park, marveling that the children of police officers and of anti-war protesters were on the same sides of the park's barricades now, celebrating together, forty years after that horrific Democratic National Convention broke the party and the country apart.

It felt good to be an American, with a brilliant Black president bending Dr. King's arc of the universe toward justice. He was the face of a changing America—a new, more equal country, but one that proved threatening to millions of its people, including a buffoonish real estate developer from New York.

My mother died a week after the election, and the president-elect found time to leave a voicemail message for me and my sister Jamie and to send me this email: "I loved your mom, and will miss her. I hope, despite the loss, that her remarkable life will be a source of celebration. Barack." It was.

* In 2012, I compensated a bit by inviting Pelosi to appear as part of the Joanne H. Alter Women in Politics and Government Lecture series at the Chicago Humanities Festival, which we established in memory of Mom.

UN-TRUMP

Toward the end of the Obama presidency, I began work on a full-scale biography of Jimmy Carter. Like Obama, he was an UnTrump.

On the day in June of 2015 when Trump came down the Trump Tower escalator and announced his candidacy, I was in the Jimmy Carter Presidential Library in Atlanta and had to hustle over to a local studio to analyze it on MSNBC. On the air, I was right and wrong that day. Right in calling him a dangerous demagogue for attacking Mexican immigrants as "drug dealers, criminals, rapists" and wrong in discounting his chances of being the Republican nominee.

What I remember most is returning to the library, where for the next three years of research I could take vacations from Trump and find refuge in Carter's integrity and decency. Turning the pages of Carter's papers brushed away the Trumpist toxins.

Trump never got to live in my brain rent-free because Carter already occupied the premises. He was a much more complicated and thus intriguing person than a simpleton like Donald Trump could ever hope to be.

Over time, my eyes grew wide at the scope of Carter's unheralded achievements. His presidency was a political failure—Ronald Reagan crushed him in 1980—but a substantive and often visionary success. Carter signed more major bills in one term than Clinton and Obama did in two—and more than ten times as many as Trump. In the six decades since Lyndon Johnson's presidency, Carter's legislative successes are rivaled only by Joe Biden's.

And yet amid my many interviews with him about his epic American life, I grew annoyed with Carter when talk turned to Trump. Carter seemed to take more shots at Reagan and Clinton than he did at the new president. He'd gruffly acknowledge that Trump was divisive, then change the subject, usually to the Middle East.

I hoped Carter would use his moral authority to discredit Trump, but he was playing a longer game. Even in his nineties, he considered himself a player who needed to keep his options open in case Trump would let him get back in the action, as Secretary of State John Kerry had done when he welcomed Carter's reports on his meetings with Putin and other world leaders. In early 2019,

Carter wrote President Trump a long, smart letter about China, which Trump called "beautiful." After they spoke on the phone, a pleased Carter seemed to me to be falling a bit for Trump's flattery.

But within months, Trump started to trash Carter again, and it was clear he wouldn't give him any assignment. By that summer, Carter was calling Trump an "illegitimate" president who had been put into office by the Russians.

ROSALYNN

When Rosalynn Carter died in 2023, I realized it is not just presidents who are capable of renewing my faith in our civic religion. It's first ladies, too. In researching my book, I found a lot of people who had critical things to say about Jimmy, but no one had a single bad thing to say about Rosalynn, a tough-minded woman of many unsung accomplishments.

One example: Rosalynn convinced scores of states, most of them conservative, to require that children be vaccinated before entering school—a huge public health victory that Trump wants to reverse.

Rosalynn blamed Reagan, indirectly, for the Confederate flag flying on a porch across the street from their modest home in Plains, Georgia. She told me that he made Americans comfortable with their prejudices. "Just like Trump," she said.

At her funeral, their daughter Amy read one of the passionate love letters Jimmy wrote Rosalynn when he was at sea as a naval officer. Amy told me a few years ago that her mother kept the letters in a drawer close by for seven decades.

I'm sure Melania would do no less.

EAVESDROPPING ON BIDEN

I'd learned over the years that Joe Biden knows the issues well and is no lightweight. Familiarity has bred respect. One day in 2009, I was sitting in his vice-presidential office when his secretary said Iraqi president Jalal Talabani was on the line. I got up to leave and he motioned me to sit down. For the next half hour, I eavesdropped on a master class in how a good politician massages another to get his way. Biden did that for Obama and for himself and has the legislative record to show for it.

As I pondered why Biden didn't keep his pledge to be a "bridge"—a transitional president—and instead fought so hard to stay atop the 2024 ticket, my mind turned to 2016, when he was the outgoing vice president. For three months that year, I traveled on and off with him as I prepared a profile for *The New York Times Magazine*. He was a haunted man, bent by grief over the loss of his son, Beau, in 2015, but determined to stay in the arena in 2020. "I'll run," he told me on Air Force Two. "If I can walk."

One night, en route home from South America, I looked at the vice president's shoulder and thought I could see the chip. He was talking about how Obama aides referred to him dismissively as "Middle-Class Joe"—a moniker he was proud of, but not from the mouths of Ivy Leaguers whom he thought (often wrongly) looked down on him. There was nothing bitter and Nixonian here, but the class resentments weren't far from the surface.

Obama and Biden had a close, complex relationship in the White House that I chronicled in my Obama books. They didn't play golf together or socialize much, but their partnership was inventive, as I learned just before they left office. Both men—and former Defense Secretary Leon Panetta—confirmed for me that they had a secret code in meetings so that Obama could get the honest views of subordinates too inclined to agree with him. To keep the discussion flowing, Obama would not disclose his position. When the president leaned back in his chair, it was a signal for the vice president to chime in with the pre-arranged Obama-Biden view, which could then contribute to the debate without tilting it.

But in 2016, Biden was a little sore at Obama for backing Hillary Clinton over him for president. He was genuinely grateful to Obama for his emotional support after Beau's death; the president, who had amassed some wealth from book royalties, even offered to pay the college tuition of Beau's children. Biden didn't take him up on it, but appreciated the gesture. And when Obama advised him that he was still too distraught to run, Biden agreed. But I could tell in 2016 that he felt conflicted about it.

That's because Biden believed he would have beaten Clinton in the primaries and Trump in the general election.* This was unlikely. He finished fifth in the 2008 Iowa Caucuses, fourth in the 2020 Caucuses, and fifth in the 2020 New Hampshire primary. The brutal political truth is that Biden had been a rambling and unimpressive presidential candidate as early as 1988, when I first watched him bore the pants off audiences.

THE TRUMP COUP TRIAL

In 2022, I followed the January 6 Committee hearings like a frenzied fan. Bennie Thompson, Liz Cheney, Adam Schiff, Jamie Raskin, and all the other members of the committee became my demigods of democracy. They forced a tardy Merrick Garland to get with the program and start investigating the coup plot.

Jack Smith, the top-notch special prosecutor finally appointed by Garland, tried to make up for lost time with a streamlined indictment of only four counts and just one defendant: Trump. The question was whether he made up *enough* lost time to convict Trump before the election.

For a while, it looked as if he had. In mid-2022, we had real hope that both of Jack Smith's federal cases could bear fruit—the big one in Washington and a winnable but less constitutionally significant one in Florida, where Trump was indicted for hoarding classified documents at Mar-a-Lago and, worse, not returning them when asked to do so. FBI agents raided Trump's mansion and came away with a ton of incriminating evidence. Smith, fresh from trying Kosovo war crimes in The Hague, seemed to be on a roll.

The Florida case was viewed in legal circles as a slam dunk until it was assigned to Judge Aileen Cannon, a dim-witted Trump appointee and apparatchik. At every turn, she ruled for delay and more delay, even after being reversed by the appellate court. After the odds of a Florida trial before the

* When Hillary wrote her book, *What Happened*, about the 2016 election, she came to Montclair on book tour. We assembled a few girls and young women to greet her in our home. I had been critical of Trump in my coverage but apologized to her for not doing more to illuminate the historic stakes.

election plummeted to somewhere between zero and none, I stopped reading stories about that case. Why bother? The lucky bastard had slithered free again.*

Meanwhile, the Trump coup trial, supervised by the formidable Judge Tanya Chutkan, was delayed by Trump's immunity appeals, which he eventually won in the Supreme Court. But Smith's case will likely survive in some form in a Democratic administration. If it does go to trial, it will be the most monumental test for the rule of law and the US Constitution since, well, ever.

VETERANS DAY

Dad always liked Veterans Day. He taught me as a kid that it was originally called Armistice Day in honor of World War I ending at the eleventh hour of the eleventh day of the eleventh month, 1918. It's not a day to be taken for granted.

I can't bear to imagine how he would react to Trump's 2023 Veterans Day speech in New Hampshire, especially the part where he said: "We will root out the communists, Marxists, fascists, and the radical left thugs that live like vermin within the confines of our country, that lie and steal and cheat our elections." Trump posted almost identical messages on the 4th of July and Thanksgiving. How patriotic.

It's easy to make fun of this—the redundancy of "communists, Marxists"; the fact that communists are on the left and fascists on the right; the irony and gall of the party of Trump, Bannon, Giuliani, and their legions of goons-in-waiting calling Biden, Harris, Schumer, Jeffries, and millions of moderate Democrats like me "radical left thugs." Calling my dad that!

Demagoguery is dangerous. A dictator's first move is to dehumanize.

This is not a drill.

---

* This was confirmed in July 2024 when Cannon dismissed the case, citing Clarence Thomas's concurring opinion in *Donald J. Trump v. United States*, the landmark immunity case. There's still a chance the stolen documents case will be revived in a different judge's courtroom.

SMASHING THE GYROSCOPE

Over the years, I've tended to agree with Barack Obama's observation that things are never quite as bright or as dark as they appear at the time. We muddle through. Events loom large for a while, then become just more flotsam floating down the river of history. To mix metaphors, it's as if there's an invisible gyroscope responsible for stabilizing our politics. If Harris wins, the 2024 election may well be remembered as the time when stabilization kicked in.

But unlike parliamentary systems where poorly performing prime ministers can be turned out of office any time, our system invests great power in one person for at least four uninterrupted years. That places a premium on the character of the president and of the other political actors who are charged with keeping him (or her) in check. What's terrifying about Trump is that beginning in 2016 he hijacked not just the Republican Party but public life itself. The raised fist after he survived an assassination attempt is not just a powerful iconic moment of defiance; it's a reminder that Trump plans to use that fist to smash this gyroscope, perhaps as soon as the aftermath of the 2024 election, which he will of course refuse to concede if he loses.

That's what makes moments of accountability and the rule of law so critical. And that's why it's important to invest a sordid trial with the constitutional grandeur it now deserves.

PART TWO

JANUARY

1/1/24
NEW YEAR'S RESOLUTIONS

I'm starting a journal today. Let's hope I'm disciplined enough this time to keep it up for a while. As Trump likes to say: We'll see.

One of my New Year's resolutions is to listen more when Emily tells me to get off my high horse once in a while and let the poor beast drink.

But while I'm still up there: I spent a lot of last year arguing in print that Joe Biden should not run for reelection. Now it's too late for him to get out.

Or is it?

1/15/24
GRANT'S SPEEDING TICKET

I amused myself today looking for precedents for when a president or former president faced a criminal trial. There are none.

In 1803, Aaron Burr was tried and acquitted of treason, and in 1973, Spiro Agnew took a plea deal for accepting bags of cash in the White House. But they were *vice* presidents. In 1872, President Ulysses S. Grant was ticketed for driving his horse and buggy too fast on 13th Street in Washington, and in 1953, Harry Truman, after he left office, was stopped for driving his car too slow on the Pennsylvania Turnpike. In 1974, Richard Nixon was pardoned before trial, and in 2001, Bill Clinton agreed to give up his Arkansas law license and pay a fine in exchange for prosecutors dropping perjury charges.

That's it.

1/26/24
E. JEAN CARROLL

Tasting a little justice. A jury in a civil case is forcing Trump to pay E. Jean Carroll *$83.3 million* in damages. That's a ton, but he had this coming because he kept slandering her after she won the first time. The only way to shut him up is to ram tens of millions of shredded dollars down his throat.

Lisa Birnbach, best known as the author of *The Official Preppy Handbook*, was the key corroborating witness in the case. Carroll—"breathless, hyperventilating, emotional"—called her right after Trump assaulted her. E. Jean told Birnbach, "'He pulled down my tights, he pulled down my tights,' almost like she couldn't believe it had just happened to her." Last summer, Lisa told me about the hard-ass Trump attorneys who tried to intimidate her during her deposition.

The judge concluded that the jury had found that because Trump "penetrated her vagina," his offense went beyond "sexual abuse" to what is commonly, though not legally, considered to be "rape."

FEBRUARY

2/5/24
BAIT AND SWITCH

The Trump coup trial is going nowhere—slowly.

It's clear the Supreme Court wants to slow things down so Trump cannot be tried in federal court before the election.

I thought back to Mitch McConnell on the Senate floor in February of 2021 when he made sure Trump wasn't convicted by the Senate after his second impeachment, this one for January 6. After he sabotaged the fastest and easiest way to prevent this man he knows is dangerous from further harming the country, McConnell tried to cover himself. He fashioned a sound bite noting that Trump had been guilty of a "dereliction of duty" and was "practically and morally responsible for provoking the events of that day."

"We have a criminal justice system in this country," McConnell said. "And former presidents are not immune from being held accountable." Trump's attorneys went further in the Senate trial. They insisted that a former president "is like any other citizen and can be tried in a court of law."

Then, a couple of years later, Republicans argue that Trump has absolute immunity from prosecution. Sounds like a bait and switch to me.

RUNT OF THE LITTER

With the trials in Georgia, Florida, and now the big one in Washington almost certainly delayed until after the election, that leaves only the runt of the litter before November—District Attorney Alvin Bragg's hush-money trial in Manhattan.

The feds passed on it, as did Bragg's predecessor, Cy Vance, but apparently there is now much more evidence. Bragg had originally asked for a trial date in March but moved the date so Jack Smith's Washington case could go first. Now Bragg will go first. It's not ideal, of course, but as Donald Rumsfeld said during the Iraq War, you fight with the army you have.

This is the time and place to hold Trump to account. That's why I'm focused now on a sassy porn star, a lying fixer, and a once-minor prosecution that is the trashiest of all the cases against him—and just might be a turning point in the most crucial election since the Civil War.

Or not.

2/6/24
UNTELEVISED

What's the matter with New York? It used to lead on everything from worker safety rules to quality public education. Now New York is one of only two states that still ban cameras in the courtroom. The other is Louisiana.

I get why they don't want another Lindbergh kidnapping case, where early camera operators stood on witness tables for a better angle, and bulbs popped throughout the sensational 1935 trial.

But this makes no sense in 2024. A year ago, as Trump was arraigned, New York State Supreme Court Judge Juan M. Merchan ruled that he would not make an exception and allow cameras, as a consortium of news organizations had rightly sought. He sided with Trump's attorneys, who claimed that televising the trial would create a "circus-like" atmosphere.

Trump apparently weighed a lifetime of winning publicity for his own circus act against other, more immediate concerns. I guess he didn't think Stormy Daniels talking about bad sex with him would play well on TV. Imagine the memes and TikTok videos if the trial had been televised.

2/14/24
FANI WILLIS

The "Find me 11,780 votes" call that Trump made to [Georgia secretary of state Brad] Raffensperger is so incriminating—such an obvious violation of Georgia state law—that I could almost smell a conviction in Fani Willis's case. But with so many defendants, it always felt like a 2025 trial.

So even before Willis was revealed to have had her stupid affair with the prosecutor she hired, the odds of a trial in Georgia before the election weren't great. I'm done with that case, too. Call me after the election.

In the meantime, I'm going to try to get a credential for the hush money trial, which is closer to home, anyway.

2/16/24
I HAVE TO

Do I want to bring my life to a standstill for weeks or even months to cover this trial?

In a funny way, it's not really up to me. I'm gonna cover it because I have to—I'm compelled to.

I have to, after Trump didn't lift a finger to save the lives of Capitol police officers, the House Speaker, and his own vice president;

I have to, after Kevin McCarthy visited a disgraced Trump at Mar-a-Lago and threw him a lifeline that makes this comeback possible;

I have to, after the "Find me 11,780 votes" tape from Georgia and Trump ruining the lives of election workers with his lies;

I have to, after Trump refused to return the nuclear secrets he had stolen, then sold out Ukraine and promised to bring "retribution" and "suspend the Constitution";

I know he's on trial in New York for different crimes, but he is a career criminal and must be stopped where there is the evidence to do so.

His crimes against decency and democracy are now so numerous that they blur together and numb us into complacency. Which is one more reason I have to slap myself in the face and report for duty.

2/28/24
SUPREME INDIFFERENCE

After a new ruling, it's clear that the US Supreme Court is on Team Trump. There won't be time for a coup trial before the election. If Trump wins, he will kill the case. Six justices are apparently fine with that.

So this looks like a serious constitutional injury coming our way. Even granting the president partial immunity—the expected outcome in the high court—would, as Judge Chutkan put it in an interim decision, "confer a lifelong 'get out of jail free' pass" to every president.

Yes, the United States now resembles a game of Monopoly. If you control the SCOTUS board, which Trump does, you get that card where prison-striped Mr. Monopoly flies out of the birdcage. For a guy who built hotels on Boardwalk (though not Park Place) in Atlantic City, it all makes sense.

2/29/24
TRUMP IS LAST

Went to a historians' dinner organized by Princeton professor Julian Zelizer. The topic: A new survey of historians that ranks Biden fourteenth out of forty-six presidents, just ahead of Wilson, Reagan, and Grant.

Historians credit Biden with many achievements, but most of all, they cite his 2020 defeat of Trump, who ranked dead last behind Richard Nixon, James Buchanan, and Andrew Johnson.

All six of us (including the great Robert Caro) saw this as unexceptional news. *Of course* Trump was last. But we didn't do enough to acknowledge how peculiar it is in historical terms that he's making a comeback. It's as if the despised Buchanan won a second term; or Johnson, after being impeached, was nominated by the Republican Party for president in 1868; or Nixon, after Watergate, became a cult leader.

MARCH

3/11/24
MY GOLDEN TICKET

I learned from Al Baker, who runs communications at the Manhattan Criminal Courthouse, that there are still courtroom press seats available for the hush money felony trial. Baker recognized my name and said he would get me credentialed to cover it for the *Washington Monthly*. So I'll get to return to my log cabin forty years after I worked there. I realized Al wasn't giving me special preference. I just did something I almost never do: advance planning.

3/18/24
TRUMP'S PRE-TRIAL LOSSES

Big win for Manhattan DA Alvin Bragg and a big loss for Trump. Judge Juan Merchan—showing again that he is a careful, by-the-book judge but will take no legal hooey from the Former Guy's lawyers—granted, in writing, almost all of the DA's pre-trial motions and denied almost all of the Trump team's motions.

Most significant: the DA now has permission to argue in court for elevating the case from a squalid tabloid dispute into a monumental historical case about whether Trump sought to illegally influence the outcome of the 2016 election, which turned out to be one of the most pivotal in American history.

So this is not really akin to getting Al Capone for income tax evasion. It's about 2016 joining 2020 as American elections that were poisoned by Donald Trump.

3/25/24
JUDGE MERCHAN

Some reporters were here last year for the arraignment, but this is my first day in the courtroom. It feels like the first day of school. The trial was scheduled to start today, but Trump successfully delayed it for three weeks. Now, we're scheduled to begin for real on April 15.

Today is devoted to pre-trial motions. Even for those, the defendant is required to be in the courtroom, as he—and we—will be throughout the trial.

By good luck, I'm on the aisle (with one seat roped off), which means Trump walks in and out about four feet away from me. It's the first time I've seen him in the flesh since the 2016 Republican convention in Cleveland, where I swore off covering him.

Trump is taller in person than one might imagine on TV and a little lighter. In an earlier trial, he told a courtroom artist that she was sketching him too fat, and he seemed self-conscious about it. His face is more haggard than I expected, and it lacks the sprayed-on orange pancake makeup that normally makes him look like a ghoul.

I am very sorry to report that at six foot two and 215 pounds (down from 240 as president), he possesses an alpha male presence that goes beyond him being one of the most famous men in the world. He is still perfectly groomed, and the standard red tie still extends over his crotch, which we may hear more about when Stormy Daniels testifies.

The Honorable Juan Merchan presiding (REUTERS/Jane Rosenberg)

This is my first look at New York State Supreme Court Justice Juan Merchan, who sits beneath huge brass letters reading: "In God We Trust." The "Supreme Court Justice" title is misleading so, like many reporters, I will call him "Judge."

With Peter Graves–gray hair and attractive utilitarian glasses, Merchan looks impressive on the bench. His soft, soothing voice has just a touch of Queens and some wisdom in it.

Merchan's father was a military officer in Bogotá who emigrated to New York with his family in 1968 when Juan was six. I'm surprised that the irony of

Trump facing trial under an immigrant judge has occasioned so little comment, but it's hard to imagine Trump holding his tongue on this for long.

The judge was the first in his family to go to college—Baruch and then Hofstra Law School—and he started as an assistant Manhattan DA, prosecuting financial frauds that included falsification of business records, a common charge. Mike Bloomberg—a Republican—appointed him to family court in the Bronx, and he soon ascended to the state supreme court, where he has presided over criminal trials for fifteen years.

I was glad to hear that Judge Merchan has experience reining in Trumpsters, having handled cases involving the Trump Organization, Steve Bannon, and Allen Weisselberg, whose attorney praised Merchan as firm, practical, and a good listener.

And I'm impressed by how Merchan spends his Wednesdays, when this court will not be in session. He presides over a special mental health court he founded, and he's respected there for his compassion in adjusting punishment.

After Merchan was assigned the case a year ago, Trump immediately attacked him as a "Trump hater" for donating thirty-five dollars to Biden and the Democrats in 2020. (Rumor has it that it was for a T-shirt for his daughter.) The contribution wasn't smart, though according to New York State rules, the minuscule amount doesn't require recusal.

Trump thinks he's scoring points by attacking Bragg for a political prosecution, and maybe he is. But what is Trump suggesting—that Republicans can only be prosecuted by Republican DAs and Democrats by Democratic DAs?

In the meantime, he's spreading a lie that Bragg said during his 2021 campaign that he would "get" Trump. This is part of Trump's intentional effort to confuse Bragg with NY attorney general Letitia James, who takes a much harder personal line. All Bragg said on the campaign trail was that he knew "how to follow the facts and hold people in power accountable." Completely kosher.

Trump's defense lawyers are shameless. Now they're accusing the DA of "widespread prosecutorial misconduct" and "unethical actions" in connection with the discovery process. They sought another ninety-day delay, which was the point of the gambit in the first place.

Merchan said no way and patiently explained how defense lawyers were unfairly characterizing the document collection process.

As Todd Blanche, Trump's lead attorney in this case, persisted with his weak argument, Merchan, after a pregnant pause, asked Blanche how long he had been an assistant US attorney. When an unnerved Blanche said thirteen years, the judge eviscerated him.

Given that background, the judge scolded, "You know the defense has the same ability as the prosecution to obtain these documents . . . [but] for whatever reason, you waited until two months before trial [to raise this matter]."

The judge wasn't done. "This is very disconcerting. Incredibly serious," Merchan said, referring to the defense's lack of any precedent. You are literally accusing them [the DA] of prosecutorial misconduct and making me complicit in it. And you don't have a single cite!"

I could see Trump on the monitor shaking his head in anger. Another bid to put off his criminal trial until after November was in tatters.

3/26/24
LUCKY BASTARD

I'm in a ranting mood today. This is not an attractive side of me. When I occasionally look back at old *Newsweek* columns, I'm struck by my calm, thoughtful tone. Now, I'm more vituperative—not mean like Trump, but harder edged. That's part of what he's done to us.

So here we go:

Judge Aileen Cannon slow-walks the Mar-a-Lago documents case.

Lucky bastard.

The US Supreme Court slow-walks the immunity claims.

Lucky bastard.

Fani Willis got romantically involved with one of the prosecutors she hired, effectively delaying the case until after the election.

Lucky bastard.

Truth Social, which last year had $3.39 million in revenues—less than your dumb cousin's failing Chipotle franchise—is going public today. Trump boarded the last SPAC scam train out of town, and this pathetic company is now worth billions on paper. Trump controls the board, which can help him out financially this fall if needed. In the meantime, MAGA World is buying an option on his election.

Lucky bastard.

And finally:

"Katie Johnson"—also known as "Jane Doe"—was an underage girl in Jeffrey Epstein's harem who claimed in an unconfirmed story to have had sex with Trump. After death threats, "Katie" canceled her press conference and withdrew her lawsuit.

Lucky bastard.

Will Trump get lucky in this felony trial, too? That's why I'm here.

3/27/24
GAG ORDER

This trial could be wild. Citing Trump's history of making "threatening, inflammatory, denigrating" statements against people at all levels of the justice system, including jurors, Merchan yesterday issued a sweeping gag order. It bars Trump from trashing witnesses like Michael Cohen and Stormy Daniels, plus jurors, attorneys, court staff, and their families. Trump is free to continue attacking the judge and the DA—and you can bet he will.

After MAGA World spread a phony story about Merchan's daughter lampooning Trump that almost certainly endangers her, the prosecution moved that the gag order be extended. Trump's lawyers said no; they would do nothing to protect the safety of the young woman.

What's scary is that Trump's attacks work. He's a master at driving a message through repetition, flooding the zone with "witch hunt" and "crooked trial" until large numbers of Americans believe this especially pernicious lie—a lie that threatens a criminal justice system that, for all its faults, is the bulwark of American freedom.

Trump is getting his day in court. He is being afforded all of the protections of our system: grand jury, jury of peers, strict standard of evidence, reasonable doubt, right of appeal. Then he turns around and pretends we're Salem in 1692 or Moscow in 1938, as if this is some kind of show trial that ends with him being sent to the gulag; as if any public integrity case must be fundamentally illegitimate if it happens to involve him or his toadies.

Lock Hillary up. Lock Hunter up. But for Michael Flynn or Steve Bannon or Roger Stone or Paul Manafort or Bernard Kerik or Joe Arpaio or Scooter Libby or Dinesh D'Souza, it's pardon time. Trump has even promised to pardon the January 6th insurrectionists who wounded 146 Capitol police officers. He backs the blue—unless it's a coup.

He'll seek "retribution" against his political enemies if he's reelected, which likely means efforts to prosecute Merchan and Bragg. And Biden, too. He'll be in the dock for something if Trump wins.

But for now, anyway, the wheel has turned. Whether it has turned enough will be up to the Big Jury–the voters–in November. In the meantime, Trump will have to listen to an honorable judge and, eventually, twelve honorable Manhattan neighbors. These are his peers, and it is the glory of our system that he must submit to them.

3/30/24
DIRTY ROCK

I've had a hand in covering eleven presidential campaigns—back to 1980—but never in my most fevered, ersatz gonzo imagination did I think that I'd have a reserved seat in the criminal trial of the front-runner. It's the new ramshackle press bus.

Trump will face the music (preferably "Doin' Time" by Lana Del Rey) in a dreary courtroom in a decrepit courthouse featuring the cheapest worn-out wood paneling that bureaucratic money could buy, a venue several cuts below not just federal courts but a hall of justice in Albania.

The courthouse opened in 1941 on the site of "the Tombs," the infamous prison. It was designed by one of the same architects who gave us the gorgeous Rockefeller Center. But this is Dirty Rock, not 30 Rock, and it seems nothing has been done to fix the place since at least the Ford administration. You have to search for the Art Deco details in the elevator doors and stair railings, and they don't show well in the old-style fluorescent lighting. It's all reminiscent of the Bronx Criminal Courthouse that Tom Wolfe describes in *Bonfire of the Vanities*.

I have great respect for public servants and sympathy for the time they spend in dispiriting surroundings. So I'm glad to see signs of repairs and new construction.

What it lacks in grandeur, *The People of the State of New York v. Donald J. Trump* makes up for in historical significance, whatever the verdict's effect on women swing voters in the suburbs may turn out to be.

Trump seemed to know before the press did that his jig—delay, delay, delay—may finally be up, if not in the other criminal cases, then at least in this one.

APRIL

4/10/24
"HIS EYES WERE COALS OF HATRED"

Dan Barry and Michael Daly—two talented chroniclers of New York—spoke at Roosevelt House in celebration of Jimmy Breslin's classic work being collected by Dan for the Library of America.

My lens on the trial will be influenced by Breslin's work, as well as that of Pete Hamill and Murray Kempton, the gaunt, pipe-smoking, midcentury columnist and essayist who rode around New York on his ancient three-speed bicycle decades before that was fashionable.

In 1984, when I was a pup at *Newsweek,* I covered two famous libel suits going on simultaneously in the same courthouse in Foley Square: Ariel Sharon vs. *TIME* magazine and William Westmoreland vs. *CBS News.* That's where I met septuagenarian Murray, then with *Newsday,* who would hold court in the hallway, rehearsing his next column aloud while offering a brilliant journalistic amicus brief on the trials, the city, the nation, and the world.

"His eyes were coals of hatred," Kempton wrote of J. W. Milam, who was wrongly acquitted in 1958 of the murder of Emmett Till.

What could I make of Trump's blue eyes?

4/11/24
O. J. AND TRUMP

O. J. Simpson is dead. Ah, the nineties. I spent a good chunk of 1994 and 1995 writing thumb-sucking *Newsweek* columns about O. J.

Murder trials, no matter how juicy or socially resonant, are not as significant as a trial like this, which is about accountability for the most famous man in the world—a demagogue bent on destroying democracy.

But the O. J. trial sure was fun. One afternoon, Emily and I scored press passes to Judge Lance Ito's LA courtroom. I thought Simpson looked shrunken and gray. Emily, by contrast, felt his powerful magnetism from the moment he walked in. She could sense his connection to the jury—a connection Trump will not likely experience.

At least O. J.'s story of race, class, and celebrity was quintessentially American. Is Trump's? That's what scares me. Con men have always been in the American grain. But they aren't supposed to be the wood itself.

04/15/24
DAD ON MY BOOTS

O. J. had his Bruno Magli shoes. I have my brown Ecco low-laced boots with some of my father's remains on them. When we spread his ashes in 2014, I spilled a little.

A decade later, as I dressed in the dark for the first day of the trial, I pondered those old dusty boots in my closet. They were held together by masking tape and thus would violate the decorum of the court, not to mention make me look like a bum.

So Dad would not be coming with me to see Trump, which was just as well since he couldn't stand the man. I chose another pair of shoes and a suit coat with purple lining that I plan to wear with black jeans as my easy-to-remember uniform each day.

And I go beltless for quicker passage through the metal detectors, even at the risk of resembling a couple of the shackled defendants I've seen in the halls, berating their beleaguered public defenders. The six weeks Trump will spend here are probably the closest he'll ever get to the feel of a real (rather than country club) jail.

I arrived at the courthouse pumped, as if some atom inside me has split and released levels of energy far beyond what I should have at my age. If Trump skates or gets a hung jury, this won't be a big deal. But if I witness him being convicted, it'll be a good and important day for democracy. Setting aside the MAGA screeching, we'll have won some justice, even if it doesn't swing the election.

I'm sick of being asked what's gonna happen in November. Predicting who will win the election six months ahead of time is like predicting where the stock market will go. I learned long ago to avoid prognosticating more than a week or two ahead, and we're usually wrong about those predictions, too.

So I'm excited about this trial in part because it gives me a chance to focus on what *did* happen, not on what *might* happen. That's what journalism is supposed to be about: the past and present, not the future. A pen or keyboard, not a crystal ball.

BROADCASTING FROM THE BATHROOM

At 7:30 AM Al Baker greets me near one of the front entrances. I'm #31 out of fifty-four on Al's Golden List, including six from the foreign press. Being on the list entitles me every day to a paper "hall pass" to the courtroom.

Other reporters have to hire "line sitters" to queue up at dawn for a chance to get into "the overflow room"—another courtroom down the hall, where they will see closed-circuit video on overhead screens but have no views of the jury.

The rest of the world will see nothing. I guess people can imagine it by reading thousands of pages of transcripts, though of course those dry pages can't convey the feel of the event itself. More often the public will have to settle for "Top Takeaways" written from inside the courthouse that will, by necessity, be short and incomplete. I know, because I will be writing some of them for the *New York Times* Opinion section.

In the nineteenth and twentieth centuries, this was common; in the twenty-first, it's strange to cut off 99.999999999 percent of the globe from the historic trial of an American president. Critics pooh-poohing the level of interest in the trial report polls showing "only" 16 percent of 160 million voters plan to follow it closely. That's about 25 million people.

The ban on cell phones in the courtroom is rigorously enforced, with eagle-eyed court police immediately on top of you if you forget and habitually start to pull it out of your pocket.

Because silenced laptops are allowed, several reporters are live blogging or live tweeting, two or three sentences at a time. This is seen in some quarters as an impressive media innovation. It's fine for junkies who need a short quick fix in real time but strikes me as a throwback to the 1930s, when Ronald Reagan would receive brief telegraph messages about Chicago Cubs at bats and "announce" the games for WHO Des Moines.

Every day I'll get a different seat inside Room 1530 of the Manhattan Criminal Courthouse. It depends on the serendipitous flow of the lines through the metal detectors on the first and fifteenth floors. I could be in the first row in the morning and the last in the afternoon, or vice versa. Arriving early helps, but the seating is also a matter of which of the two aisles—left or right—the jumpy court police guards arbitrarily lead you down and make you fill the rows. No switching seats allowed.

The only press with specially assigned seats are the four women courtroom artists sitting in the first row behind the prosecution lawyers on the right. My new friend, retired judge George Grasso, a former deputy commissioner of the NYPD, is attending as a spectator. He knows everyone and scored a regular seat in the rear.

Per usual courthouse rules, there's no eating or drinking in the courtroom. Trump will have to fight his addiction to Diet Coke; it's only water inside. The police guards allow you to quickly scarf down snacks in the hallway but only if you're in line for the restrooms. No loitering allowed. Sometimes you have to finish eating in the bathroom or you lose your place in line. If you happen to be in the bathroom when Trump and the Secret Service are on the move nearby, you're locked in, and have to put your ear to the inside of the bathroom door to strain to make out a little of the bullshit Trump is spouting to the press pool in the hall.

I'm told that in the women's room, two of the courtroom artists prop up their canvases against a radiator and a garbage bin so they can photograph their sketches on their phones and send them to editors. The bathroom mirrors are scratched.

The men's room has no mirrors at all because perps might smash them and use the shards to shank a guard or snitch. The garbage bin is sprayed with graffiti. Above the two sinks, there's an urgent sign saying "Wash Your Hands!" But the separate water taps for hot and cold only flow when you push one on and hold it, which means you can only wash one hand at a time.

Some reporters risk talking on their cell phones in the bathroom, with at least one even filing a live radio report from a stall. When he was on the air, he neglected to acknowledge his location.

"COOL, CALM, COLLECTED"

Day One did not disappoint, as Merchan set the tone for the trial, which can basically be summed up as: this court is not going to take any shit from Donald Trump.

The judge reminds me of the old deodorant ad for Ice Blue Secret—"cool, calm, and collected."

Todd Blanche started the day trying to relitigate issues that the judge settled last month in his written responses to pre-trial motions. I hear from a couple of Trump's former lawyers that this maximalist strategy will be pursued throughout the trial at the defendant's insistence and to the annoyance of the judge, who is determined not to let his courtroom resemble *Groundhog Day.*

Blanche went to American University and worked as a paralegal for the Southern District of New York to help pay for Brooklyn Law School at night. He was at WilmerHale before becoming a partner in 2017 at Cadwalader, Wickersham & Taft, New York's oldest law firm. He quit last year when his partners didn't want him representing Trump; it didn't impress them that he's a former president and, more important, they knew his long record of not fully paying his lawyers.

Blanche, on the cusp of fifty, saw a chance to be a part of history and—who knows?—maybe become attorney general next year. After commitments of up-front money from Trump, he moved to Palm Beach, set up a new firm with offices near Mar-a-Lago, and hired an experienced defense attorney, Emil Bove, who will serve as his second chair in this trial. If Blanche and Bove don't realize Trump will eventually stiff them as he has his other attorneys, they're fools.

Square-jawed, blue-suited Blanche has a full head of black hair and a record of completing two Ironman Triathlons. Trump likes everyone who works for him to be good-looking and Blanche fills the bill. He's plenty smart but woefully inexperienced for this criminal trial. Almost all of his courtroom experience is in civil cases or as a federal prosecutor. He has handled only two criminal cases as a defense attorney—a plea deal for Igor Fruman, the Russian goon hired by Rudy Giuliani to dig up dirt on Biden in Ukraine, and motions and appeals for Paul Manafort, the former Trump 2016 campaign chair convicted of witness tampering and fraud. That is astonishingly little preparation for a defense counsel, a job that requires different skills than those of a good prosecutor.

Trump's decision to put Blanche in charge of keeping him out of prison is like scheduling a journeyman hurler with two short stints of middle-inning relief to pitch game seven of the World Series. Blanche may have a good fastball

Trump with attorneys Todd Blanche and Emil Bove (REUTERS/Jane Rosenberg)

and slider, but no one has seen it yet. And his delivery in the pre-trial bullpen had no snap. His plaintive voice might work for the plaintiff in a civil case but not in the show. Its contrived tenor urgency is somewhere between a legal plea and a desperate personal one.

From the start, Blanche tried to bean the judge, arguing that in 2019 Merchan was quoted as saying, "I hate that politicians use Twitter. It's unprofessional. That's not how politicians should behave." I guess he's hoping that some appellate judge views Donald Trump and social media as indistinguishable and reverses Merchan on those grounds.

The judge responded that five years later, his dim view of Twitter reflected no bias in this case. Nor did the fact that a "family member" (his daughter) worked in politics. He noted for the third or fourth time that a state ethics panel had said he had no obligation to recuse himself over what his adult daughter did for a living, and the charge that she stood to benefit financially from a conviction was the product of "inference, innuendo, and unsupported speculation."

"To say these claims are attenuated is an understatement," he noted drily.

When the defense complained about the juror questionnaire, Merchan replied evenly that this is the "most exhaustive questionnaire this court has ever used."

Merchan did end up ruling a couple of times in favor the defense. He refused to allow any references during the trial to the three women who, in October of 2016, alleged that Trump had sexually assaulted them, which he described as "hearsay" and "just a rumor, gossip." Merchan knows that the decision of the judge in the Harvey Weinstein case to let that kind of thing in may get Weinstein freed on appeal.

Merchan reiterated his decision to not allow the *Access Hollywood* tape to be played. And in a new ruling, he refused to let the prosecution refer to the fact that Melania was pregnant and gave birth to Barron while Trump was what you could call a double cheater, having sex with Stormy Daniels while still undertaking a months-long affair with Karen McDougal, a former Playboy Playmate of the Year, who will figure heavily in the case though is not expected to testify for the prosecution.

Let's just unpack this for a second. Evangelical Christians—the same people who despised Bill Clinton as a degenerate—love a president who is so selfish and so determined to satisfy his sexual appetites at any cost that he feels entitled to look elsewhere when his wife cannot have sex with him because she's very pregnant or postpartum. And when a Playboy model—who thinks they are having a love affair, by the way—is not enough, he cheats on her with a porn star.

In suburban and rural churches, Trump wins overwhelming majorities. If you dissent from the party line backing Trump, as conservative *New York Times* columnist David French did in the Presbyterian Church he once loved, they shun you.

They apparently believe their cult leader, who told Chuck Todd in the third person on *Meet the Press* in 2016: "Nobody respects women more than Donald Trump."

SLEEPY DON

We learned that jurors will likely see an exhibit of Trump's all-caps Truth Social post: "IF YOU GO AFTER ME, I'M COMING AFTER YOU."

He directed that at witnesses in this case, but it's his philosophy of life, courtesy of his mentor, Roy Cohn. Unfortunately, the exhibit, despite the all caps, downplays Trump's real MO. He has said on many occasions that he likes to hit back *ten times as hard.*

Trump almost certainly didn't hear today about the all-caps post. As *Times* reporter Maggie Haberman first noticed on the monitor, he fell asleep in court. The good news is that this means he can no longer call Biden "Sleepy Joe."

Trump dozed through much of his trial (Barry Blitt)

4/16/24
JURY SELECTION

Jury selection is often the most important part of any trial, and Trump has a hard row to hoe. In New York State, convictions and acquittals must be unanimous among the twelve jurors. After seeing how many potential jurors checked NPR on the questionnaire as a major source of news, unanimous acquittal seems well nigh (I was always hoping to find a chance to use that phrase) impossible. There's just too much evidence against Trump for members of the reality-based community—i.e., most of the jury—to ignore.

Conviction is more likely, but a hung jury is also a distinct possibility. It takes only a single stubborn juror to scotch the whole thing, which would be a big win for Trump.

It isn't easy being orange in Manhattan. The judge dismissed two jurors for cause—a guy with Lands' End on his resume for ending a 2017 Facebook post with "Lock him up" and a bookseller at Shakespeare & Co. on the Upper West Side for posting an AI-generated parody with Trump saying of himself: "I'm dumb as fuck." I loved watching Trump have to sit and listen to that one without betraying any emotion.

In the first round of jury selection, fifty out of ninety-six potential jurors were dismissed after answering yes to Question #34 on the jury questionnaire:

"Do you have any strong opinions or firmly held beliefs about former President Donald Trump, or the fact that he is a current candidate for president, that would interfere with your ability to be a fair and impartial juror?"

Of course, had I been in the jury pool, I would have answered yes, too. There's no chance I could be fair and impartial. But in analyzing the trial, I plan to be tough minded about what the evidence shows. If the prosecution isn't proving its case, I'll say it.

Manhattan has one of the most liberal jury pools in the country, which is bad news for a defendant who lost the borough by seventy points in 2020. If the Mar-a-Lago documents case ever goes to trial, he'll have better luck with the jury pool in Florida.

Trump's best bet so far for a holdout was a bearded native Texan and golfer who watches Fox News and is a partner in an accounting firm. He said that in the accounting world, "a lot of people tend to slant Republican intellectually . . . so there could be some unconscious bias," and added that his background from Texas could make him have bias, but he was "not sure."

Merchan told him, "We need an unequivocal assurance." After the man acknowledged that "It's probably going to be tough for me to be impartial," the lawyers had a private sidebar with the judge, and, to Trump's chagrin, he was excused.

The ones who stayed said they could put any personal and political feelings aside in the interest of fulfilling their duties as jurors. I believed them. They reminded me of why, despite the hours of waiting around, I have enjoyed my own experiences with jury duty. It's inspiring. People generally do their best to be fair and stick to the evidence presented and to the judge's instructions.

It was impossible to track which prospective jurors were dismissed by a peremptory challenge (each side has ten). But it's a safe bet that the defense removed a woman who mentioned that she heard Trump "targeted some females," and the prosecution didn't want a man who said, "I have a lot of friends in law enforcement who are pro-Trump."

There's a strong chance the six additional jurors and five or six alternates will be selected by the end of the week. That's much faster than anyone anticipated.

STEINGLASS'S HIT MAN

In his informal remarks to prospective jurors, Josh Steinglass for the prosecution said he wasn't looking for jurors "who have been living under a rock for the last eight years or the last thirty years." This process, he stressed, "has nothing to do with your personal politics" or "what you think of Donald Trump." He said it's about not just whether jurors could be fair but whether "you can give assurance that you won't speculate why it [the prosecution] hasn't happened sooner."

Steinglass is a portly but pleasant-looking prosecutor whose $155,000 salary is less than what some twenty-five-year-old first-year associates make at white-shoe New York firms. He could have left years ago and made twenty times as much money in private practice. But he stayed because he believes in public service, a commitment that inspires me every time I see it.

This is not Steinglass's first Trump rodeo. Two years ago, in a civil case that was quickly forgotten, he and Susan Hoffinger, a former defense attorney who came on as Alvin Bragg's chief investigator, dismembered the Trump Organization with a meticulous case that exposed a web of fraud.

Steinglass asked prospective jurors to consider the case of a husband who hires a hit man to kill his wife. Would they consider that "the husband may be as guilty as the person who pulled the trigger, even though he wasn't there?" Trump glared at the prosecutor. "Can you hold him [Trump] responsible for acts he didn't do personally?" Steinglass said. "You're gonna have to assess Mr. Trump's intent."

Blanche for the defense told the panel of prospective jurors that if selected, they were obliged to avoid drawing any conclusions about the defendant until they began their deliberations. He used almost all of his time to suss out potential jurors who might be not just Biden voters (nobody can be asked who they voted for) but unable to give Trump a fair shot or follow the judge's instruction that they should draw no conclusions if Trump doesn't take the stand.

4/18/24
JESSE WATTERS, PUBLIC MENACE

Jury selection is usually tedious, but not in this trial. Today felt like voir dire on steroids, as the first jury ever to possess the power to convict an American president ended up being selected in about a third of the time most people expected.

The day began with Judge Merchan perturbed that Juror #2, the cancer nurse, was hearing from her friends that she had been targeted. It turned out that Jesse Watters, a menacing Fox News host, had said the nurse's claim of impartiality was "concerning" because she said during jury selection that "no one is above the law."

I was shocked but not surprised that a Fox host—with more viewers than Rachel Maddow—would go there. Think about this for a second. The house organ of one of our two major political parties—a cable network with millions of viewers—has a big star who believes that the idea of "Equal Justice Under Law" emblazoned on courthouses across the country is just another libtard talking point.

With the prospective jurors out of the room, the judge told us he had invited the oncology nurse into his chambers where she asked to be excused.

Then came a moment of unease for the journalists in the courthouse and their editors. Merchan said, "I am directing" the press to "use common sense" and not be specific about the jurors. Referring obliquely to Juror #1's brogue, he said there was no need to report that any jurors spoke with a foreign accent.

After the judge addressed the media, it emerged that Juror #4—a Puerto Rican IT consultant—was revealed by the prosecution as having been arrested for ripping down right-wing posters in Westchester County.

Late in the day, I found out this guy had a beef with the DA over an investigation of him. If the prosecution hadn't learned this overnight and moved to dismiss him, the original Juror #4 could have been Trump's best hope for a hung jury.

By now, everyone in the courthouse was thinking the same thing: brrrrrrr!

I was wearing my overcoat but more importantly I was also, like Trump, a little "disgusted" by the bathrooms, especially those on other floors, which later in the day some of us had to use because of lockdowns in the hallway when Trump or jurors were passing through.

When jury selection resumed in the afternoon, there were six alternate seats to fill. Voir dire now went smoothly, with well-educated Manhattan professionals (who didn't post insults on social media) sailing through.

More than half of the people in the second jury panel (about one hundred reluctant jurors in all) also decided before being questioned that they could not be impartial and were excused.

The DA team's peremptory challenges were used to dismiss those they suspected might be in the 15 percent of Manhattan voters who voted for Trump in 2020, including a self-described "wannabe hockey player" who was impressed by Trump's ability to rebuild Central Park's Wollman Rink in the 1980s when the city could not, and a banker confessing that her uncle was an accountant for disgraced casino owner Steve Wynn, who gave his friend Donald $1.5 million for his 2020 presidential campaign.

After lunch, the pace quickened. Prospective juror B430 ran afoul of Trump's jury consultants, who hit pay dirt when they researched her social media posts.

"I wouldn't believe Donald Trump if his tongue was notarized," she wrote in 2016 in a line that was often used about Trump in New York in the 1980s.

Later that year, Juror B430 posted: "He is anathema to everything I was taught about love and Jesus. He could not be more fundamentally unChristian." Trump listened impassively to this abuse. She claimed to be impartial now and told the former president, sitting twelve feet away, "I'm sorry."

The defense asked the judge to dismiss her, saving them a peremptory challenge, which they had to use on potential jurors like the woman whose son worked for Hakeem Jeffries. Merchan, who dismissed a juror on Tuesday for posting "Lock him up," agreed and excused B430 for cause, too.

Trump didn't do as well with Juror B500, a woman employed by an apparel company, who told the court that she didn't have strong opinions about Trump and was sure she could be impartial but added, "I don't like his persona—how he presents himself in public . . . He is selfish, self-serving, and I don't like him . . . He's not my cup of tea." She qualified that with, "I don't like some of my coworkers, but I don't try to sabotage their work," which got some laughs and also indicated that she thought she could be fair.

Susan Necheles, one of Trump's attorneys, said B500 should be dismissed by the judge for cause. This kicked off a fascinating debate over whether jurors can separate their personal feelings about the defendant from their commitment to be impartial and fair, which the judge said was more important.

Prosecutor Steinglass said jurors had preconceived notions about, say skinheads, but that didn't prevent them from being fair.

Necheles made a good point that with most criminal defendants, including sex offenders, it's the crime, not the individual, that potential jurors are reacting to, and preconceived notions about the crime are perfectly fine. But in this case, it's the person, Trump, not the crime, and B500's views of Trump are current, not from the past.

The judge, stressing that B500 was convincing in saying that she could be impartial, said preconceived notions about people were impossible to avoid: "If we eliminated everybody with a preconceived idea, we would never have juries." He denied the motion to dismiss the juror for cause. B500 was seated as Juror 11.

"We have our jury," said the judge at 4:35 PM, and afterwards I felt as if I saw a puff of white Vatican smoke waft out of the chimney of the courthouse.

4/19/24
"THE DEVIL"

I cannot report hearing or smelling Trump cut the cheese—the big question on social media today—though he did look tired and unhappy. For the first time in his life, he has to sit down and shut up while listening to ordinary people savage him.

The day began with Trump's typical nonsensical blather. With uncharacteristically messy hair thanks to the wind outside, he had reporters hanging on his every word, "They've taken away my constitutional rights to speak, and that includes speaking to you." This was delivered with no sense of irony because he has none.

As we saw on Monday, Trump intermittently snoozed, with his head drooping a couple of times. But he seemed awake enough when prospective jurors unloaded on him, either directly or through old social media posts read aloud by his own attorneys when arguing for the judge to dismiss them.

All morning, Trump had to sit still and listen to the insults:

"I never read any of your books."

"[He gives people] permission to act on their negative impulse."

"Egomaniac, sociopathic incompetence."

"I do believe that he was the devil."

The prospective jurors who said these things at some point in their lives didn't make it onto the jury. But Trump had to sit there and take it. He was trapped, unable to use his remote to change the channel to Fox or Newsmax.

SELF-IMMOLATION

The jury seems to be made up of impartial New Yorkers who will listen to the evidence with an open mind. There's one who is African American; one who is Asian American; one teacher; one salesman; one in tech; two lawyers; two people in finance; three in small business. Each will have an individual screen attached to the seat for the viewing of exhibits. With all the alternates selected, the court recessed. I went down from the fifteenth floor and left the building to eat my brown bag lunch.

Four minutes earlier, a mentally ill Florida man had self-immolated in the small park just across the street and about twenty-five yards beyond the long row of camera positions.

Eric Shawn, a veteran Fox News reporter, was on the air when it happened. I later watched a tape of him describing live, with great poise, what it was like to see the man burn.

I arrived after police had extinguished the fire and rushed the victim to the hospital, where he died. But I was there in time to see the smoldering pile and to interview distraught eyewitnesses. I glanced at cell phone video of the self-immolation but couldn't watch it. Another reporter told me that he could still smell the burning human flesh. I could not.

I mentioned to a young reporter that in 1963, monks protesting the South Vietnamese government set themselves ablaze in Saigon. "Did you cover that?" she asked. "No," I told her. "I was six years old."

I went back upstairs to take refuge in the courtroom. Court police guards sternly reminded us that we would be ejected—possibly for good—if we took out our cell phones. No photos are allowed there (or anywhere on the fifteenth floor) except those taken by a tiny pool of credentialed still photographers who are given a ninety-second photo "spray" of Trump each morning before the trial begins. When Olivia Nuzzi of *New York* magazine tried to take a cell phone shot of the overflow room, she was permanently ejected.

The good news is that spending seven hours a day in the courtroom for six weeks without being able to take my cell phone out of my pocket may be just what the doctor ordered to break my addiction to it.

In place of my phone, I am increasingly reaching for my binoculars. We're allowed to use binoculars in the courtroom as long as we don't focus them on the lawyers' open laptops, which could contain something confidential—or on exhibits that are shown on the big overhead monitors but have not yet been introduced into evidence. I plan to use my binoculars mostly to check the monitors to see if Trump is sleeping and to birdwatch jurors.

JUROR #2

MAGA World is already pinning its hopes on Juror #2—the one who replaced the cancer nurse. He's a gray-haired banker with a hard-assed look and a short-on-the-sides haircut that I associate with Trumpsters, though I realized that my Trump-loathing son also has one.

People keep saying #2 was on Truth Social, when what he actually said in voir dire was that he saw on X what Trump, Kellyanne Conway, and others were posting on Truth Social, but he also used X to track Michael Cohen's tweets. And the MAGA wishful thinkers didn't seem to notice that he mentioned *Mueller, She Wrote,* a podcast about the Mueller investigation into Russian collusion. Whichever way he comes down, Juror #2 will come under heavy scrutiny.

"SIR, WOULD YOU PLEASE HAVE A SEAT"

After lunch, defense attorney Emil Bove tried one final delaying tactic. He asked the judge to order the prosecution to redact "personal information" from tens of thousands of pages of documents before they were entered as exhibits.

Prosecutor Susan Hoffinger noted that this would be "extremely burdensome." For example, Michael Cohen had 39,000 contacts on his phone.

I have a few thousand in mine. I hope we'll hear testimony about how the hell Cohen acquired so many.

By the end of the day, Merchan was out of patience with Trump's team. "The defense is targeting my decisions one by one by one," he said. "That has to end . . . There comes a point where you have to accept my rulings. There's nothing else to clarify. Nothing else to argue. We are starting this trial Monday morning."

Trump thought that was his cue to leave. But when he stood up, the judge said: "Sir, would you please have a seat."

This was my favorite part of the trial so far. Trump's older sister, the late Judge Maryanne Trump Barry, described her brother as "a brat" who was sent to military school by his father to learn to follow orders. As an adult, Trump had to listen to domineering Fred Trump, but not since 1991, when Fred got Alzheimer's.

That means that for thirty-three years, Trump has not had to listen to anyone about anything. Until now. Merchan made the former president meekly sit down like the obedient little boy he never was.

This sent a strong signal. Trump will continue to trash everything when he goes to the press pen in the hallway. But inside his courtroom, Merchan has all the power, and Trump better get used to it.

4/22/24
OPENING STATEMENTS

With the jury selected, it was time for opening arguments. But first came a hearing about what would be admissible if Trump decided to testify in his own defense. The answer: almost everything, including a bunch of lies he told in other legal proceedings.

Only a foolish megalomaniac would take the stand under such circumstances—so perhaps Trump will.

The judge noted that "delays are inevitable" but explained that in his courtroom, time is a precious commodity:

"I never take it for granted, and I *never* want to waste it," Merchan said, with the first little edge I'd heard in his voice. I noticed from behind Trump's golden mane that he seemed fully awake for that one. His delaying games won't work.

Matthew Colangelo is handling the opening statement for the prosecution. He's a crisp former senior federal prosecutor who took a new job in New York to help with the case. Colangelo's background working in the Obama and Biden administrations has made him a MAGA target, though there's nothing unusual about federal prosecutors using their skills on local cases.

Colangelo began his opening statement with "the Trump Tower conspiracy," a reference to a key meeting in August of 2015 where Trump, Michael Cohen, and David Pecker "formed a conspiracy" to "conceal information" with "intent to defraud and intent to conceal another crime."

Under New York state law 175.10 on falsifying business records in the first degree—the subject of the thirty-four-count indictment—prosecutors are not obliged to identify (much less indict on) "another crime"; they are only required to show that the defendant intended to break other laws, in this case, on taxes, campaign finance, and falsification of other documents.

That might be a strange, poorly worded law, as right-wing legal scholars like to claim, but as these legal eagles know perfectly well: IT'S STILL THE LAW. What Trumpsters call "bookkeeping errors" are criminal acts, and laws against them have been used for generations to keep businesses from turning corrupt.

As Colangelo's story got juicier, the clicking sound of fifty-eight reporters tapping on their laptops sounded like the cicadas we're going to hear this summer in different parts of the country.

When Colangelo read the transcript of Trump using the expression "grab them by the pussy" on the *Access Hollywood* tape (the judge deemed the audio itself "too salacious" and thus prejudicial), there was no audible gasp or reaction of any kind I could discern in the jury box. It was as if jurors thought to themselves, *Oh, yeah, I remember that. It'll be interesting to see how it relates to this case.* Trump himself was hard to read as "pussy" reverberated in the courtroom.

The defense will refer to their client as "President Trump" out of "respect for the office," but Todd Blanche wanted jurors to know, "He's not just Donald Trump . . . he's a man, he's a husband, he's a father, he's a person like you and me."

Really? This sounded to me like a pathetic effort to prepare a Melania defense—that he wanted to kill what he claims are false stories about his sex life in order to protect his family. Thus, Trump's strategy: deny absolutely everything.

There are a couple of problems with this approach:

First, Melania isn't here and isn't expected to come any time in the next six weeks.

Second, we will hear testimony that Trump at first tried to avoid paying Stormy Daniels. According to Cohen and other witnesses, he figured that after the election, it wouldn't matter if the stories came out. So much for appreciating the tender feelings of his family.

Blanche also previewed an implausible argument that Trump "put up a wall" between himself and his business when he was elected. Please.

The defense will argue that "a man who pinches pennies" would never pay $420,000 to repay a $130,000 debt. It does sound uncharacteristic of Trump—if you haven't seen the paper trail those of us following the case have already begun inspecting.

Blanche closed by arguing: "Use your common sense. We're New Yorkers. That's why we're here . . . You said you would put aside" your views of Donald Trump. "If you do that, there will be a very swift verdict of not guilty."

In private, Trump's attorneys see that as a pipe dream. They're gunning for a hung jury, not an acquittal.

4/23/24
CONTEMPTIBLE

Trump is likely to be held in contempt of court, but somehow I doubt he'll be bound and gagged like Bobby Seale in Judge Julius Hoffman's courtroom in Chicago in 1969.

Prosecutor Chris Conroy outlined ten alleged violations of the gag order Judge Merchan imposed on Trump to compel him to stop insulting jurors and witnesses—eight posts on Truth Social and two on official campaign websites.

Conroy noted that Trump has "willingly and flagrantly" violated the protective order, a nicer way of describing a gag order.

Witnesses, jurors, family members—"nobody is off-limits to the defendant."

Under normal circumstances, violating a gag order would bring jail time. But the prosecution isn't asking for it, and not just because it would let Trump wear a jumpsuit the color of his hair, which would help him play the martyr. Jailing Trump for contempt would also interrupt the trial and open the door to time-consuming appeals.

So all that's left is for the defendant to be fined—a maximum of only $1,000 for each count, the amount specified by law because it is extremely rare for a disruptive, rule-breaking defendant to be a person of means. Trump would owe $10,000 if held in contempt on all counts. If, as expected, he remains in contempt, the judge will have to revisit the question of jail time.

Defense attorney Emil Bove argued that under the gag order, Trump is allowed to respond to attacks and speak out politically. And he does. Daily. Sometimes hourly. Because the judge specifically excluded himself and the prosecutor from his order, Trump attacks them practically every time he opens his mouth.

The question for Merchan is which of Trump's social media posts are largely political responses to those protected by the gag order and which cross the line into intimidating witnesses and jurors or the jury pool.

Most of the social media posts covered in the motion are attacks on Michael Cohen, the key witness in this case. The judge repeatedly pressed defense attorney Todd Blanche to explain which political attacks Trump was responding to:

"You've presented nothing. I've asked you eight or nine times: 'Show me the exact post he's responding to.' You haven't been able to do that even once."

En route to the men's room during a break, I asked my new friend and fellow trial spectator, retired New York judge George Grasso, the chances of a contempt citation. Because Trump attacked the jury, he said—"99.999 percent."

I remembered how a few days ago Jesse Watters went after Juror #2—who later left the jury, thanks to all the publicity—for saying during voir dire that "no one is above the law." Watters promoted his smear with the line: "Catching undercover liberal activists lying to the judge."

This line became important in the contempt hearing because Trump did not simply post it, which would have been bad enough. He added that these "liberal activists" were lying *"in order to get on the Trump jury."*

Trump was attacking the jury—a big no-no in any trial anywhere in the United States or other countries with trial by jury.

Merchan reprimanded Blanche for failing to cite any case law to back up his claims that it is permissible to re-post or otherwise disseminate content that violates the gag order.

"Case law!" the judge demanded. "Suppose someone's holding a placard that says terrible, terrible things about the jury, and your client picks it up. [Are you] saying that he's done nothing wrong?"

Blanche, sounding like a schoolboy pleading with the principal, said it was "just common sense" that re-posting dangerous attacks on jurors is permissible. He continued:

"This gag order—we're trying to comply with it . . . President Trump is being very careful to abide by your rules."

Then, Merchan delivered an unforgettable smackdown from the bench:

"Mr. Blanche, you're losing all credibility with this court."

DAVID PECKER, TRASH COLLECTOR

The first witness in this case is David Pecker, seventy-three, the former publisher of the *National Enquirer* and former chair of the parent company, AMI, where he still works as a consultant.

Pecker looks like a well-tailored hyena past his prime. His name, like Anthony Weiner's, is a bad joke.

This guy is an important witness for the prosecution but that doesn't mean I have to like him. From what I've heard about him over the years, he's a tyrant in the office and a jerk-about-town. I'd call him a disgrace to journalism, but that would imply that he is in journalism, which he is not. He's in the trash business.

Prosecutor Joshua Steinglass and key witness David Pecker
(REUTERS/Jane Rosenberg)

Supermarket tabloids can be funny, so why do I feel so strongly about this? Because like other real journalists, I've spent my career trying hard to be accurate. This is a time-consuming but vital part of our jobs.

Think of your occupation and your reaction to others who act in a shoddy and irresponsible way, making a mockery of your hard work even as they rake in (notice I didn't say "earn," which implies honest toil) a lot more money. Now you have some idea of how I view the David Peckers of the world.

We all know journalism is a business, but the press is the only business mentioned in the Constitution.

With First Amendment rights come responsibilities that deserve more than lip service. We have to at least try to be truthful.

Pecker would say he, too, tries to be truthful. But he doesn't usually try very hard.

Until today. Something important and unexpected is slowly unfolding in the courtroom. This tabloid carnival-barker has morphed into a sober and compelling witness. After helping wreck the country by doing as much as anyone to help Trump win the cataclysmic 2016 election, Pecker is now working to get him convicted. While he is testifying under subpoena, there's nothing in his plea agreement requiring him to remember every detail and spin every answer against Trump.

And yet, as his testimony moves forward, that's exactly what he's doing, from describing how Trump hatched "the Trump Tower conspiracy" shortly before he announced for president in 2015, to corroborating key parts of Cohen's story, to describing Trump as a "detail-oriented . . . micromanager," the opposite of what the defense hopes to show.

Pecker even explained why his number two, Dylan Howard, an Aussie who directly managed "catch and kill" and other parts of what Pecker calls the *Enquirer's* "checkbook journalism," could not be present to testify, a question that will no doubt occur to the jury.

Howard is supposedly back in Australia, suffering from a spinal condition that prevents travel. Or so we're told by Trump's old pal, David Pecker, who—like so many of Trump's transactional "friends"—eventually ceased to be one.

Pecker detailed the Trump Tower conspiracy that launched "catch and kill": catching negative stories about Trump and sex and killing them so they will never be published.

"They asked me what can I do and what my magazines could do to help the campaign," Pecker recounted. "I said I would publish positive stories about Mr. Trump and I would publish negative stories about his opponents. And I said I would be your eyes and ears because I knew the Trump Organization had a very small staff . . . I said that if I hear anything negative about yourself or if I hear anything about women selling stories, I would notify Michael Cohen and he would be able to kill negative stories."

This is much worse than what the Russians were doing in 2016, which was mostly sowing confusion, not directly sliming American politicians.

Soon after the conspiracy was launched, the *Enquirer* began savaging Trump's rivals for the nomination with headlines like these:

TED CRUZ SHAMED BY PORN STAR

TED CRUZ SEX SCANDAL—FIVE SECRET MISTRESSES

FAMILY MAN MARCO RUBIO'S LOVE CHILD STUNNER!

There were also phony stories about Dr. Ben Carson's so-called "medical malpractice" and—most infamously—Ted Cruz's father being connected to the JFK assassination. "We [took] the photos [of Cruz's father] and the different picture [of] Lee Harvey Oswald. And mashed the two together. And that's how that story was prepared—created I would say," Pecker said on the witness stand.

Pecker testified that after Republican primary debates, Cohen would tell the *Enquirer* which Trump rivals had done well and thus needed to be lied about next. Later, Steve Bannon collected all of the *Enquirer's* old lies about Hillary Clinton for use by the campaign in the general election.

These tabloid lies might be amusing, but they're also kinda sick. They're a departure from the norm in American politics for the last century or so, which is: you hit the other candidate very hard but you don't *directly* make shit up about them.

It's true that for decades, a few campaigns have benefited from "stink tanks" producing dirty tricks that crossed the line. Part of the Watergate scandal revolved around a thirty-year-old dirty trickster named Donald Segretti, who went to jail for what he called "ratfucking"—in his case, for forging letters on the letterhead of Senator Edmund Muskie, the Democratic frontrunner in 1972 and the candidate most feared by Nixon operatives. Roger Stone, who has a tattoo of Nixon's face on his back, still describes himself as a "dirty trickster" and was pardoned by Trump for what he did on his behalf in 2016.

Unlike Trump, Nixon did not personally authorize dirty tricks. But that didn't get him off. When the Supreme Court ordered the release of June 1972 tape recordings that showed Nixon personally approving hush money for the burglars who broke into Democratic Party headquarters at the Watergate complex, he was forced to resign.

The Watergate break-in and the Trump felony trial are both essentially about the same thing: covering up hush money.

Trumpsters trying to minimize catch and kill say it's no different than attack ads, which are ubiquitous. But the whole point of "oppo research" is to dig up negative stuff about your opponent that is based in truth, so that it's credible in attack ads. Using supermarket tabloids to make stuff up that screws rivals is—like so many other horrible things in American politics—a Trump innovation.

DINO THE DOORMAN

The first catch and kill that stemmed from the Trump Tower conspiracy involved Dino Sajudin, now known in the tabs as "Dino the Doorman." He gave the *Enquirer* a tip about Trump fathering a child with a Trump Tower maid.

Even after the *Enquirer* learned that the story was false, Dino the Doorman was paid $30,000—at least three times the *Enquirer's* highest tip rate. The point was to make sure that Dino didn't embarrass Trump before the election by selling the story elsewhere, even if it was untrue. If he did, under the terms of the non-disclosure agreement, he would owe AMI $1 million.

Pecker testified that from the start, Cohen was adamant that the love child story was untrue. Cohen said Trump would be happy to take a DNA test and he told Pecker: "He is German-Irish, and this woman is Hispanic, and that would be impossible."

Was Trump so racist that it was "impossible" he would have sex with a Latina? Enquiring minds want to know.

4/25/24
"ALL RISE"

In most trials, jurors stifle a laugh and finish a whisper as they enter the courtroom. They've often developed a little bond with each other during their long hours together, so they're still sharing something about lunch or sports or a funny movie. Anyone who has served on a jury—as I have three times—knows this to be the case.

Here, there's no chatting. The jurors march in and out like soldiers with a silent sense of duty, eyes straight ahead as they walk just three feet from the defendant.

"All rise," the bailiff says as they pass. On the monitor, where the camera is focused on Trump from the front, I detect an expression I've never seen before: compliance.

Several times a day, the former president of the United States must stand to honor these ordinary citizens. He doesn't think he's honoring them, of course. He detests them as biased liberals, even if they aren't. But he must bend to a system that is enshrined in both the Declaration of Independence and the Constitution. It's a beautiful thing to see.

When they begin their deliberations, these twelve men and women will be sovereign. Can you imagine Vladimir Putin being judged by twelve ordinary Russians? Xi Jinping being judged by twelve ordinary Chinese?

Whatever the verdict, the accountability has already begun.

But will it be sustained? We learned today that in a four-to-three decision, a New York appellate court overturned Harvey Weinstein's New York sex crimes conviction. The court ruled that the trial judge made a reversible error when he allowed prosecutors to call as witnesses several women who testified that Weinstein had assaulted them, even though none of their allegations had led to formal charges.

Some legal experts outside the courtroom think Merchan might have a problem on appeal with such "Molineux witnesses." But lawyers who have witnessed his rulings and read all of the judge's responses to pre-trial motions are confident he has taken steps to prevent reversal on these grounds.

PLAYBOY PLAYMATE OF THE YEAR

The man who published bullshit turned out to be a truth teller on the witness stand. David Pecker could have stuck to "yes" and "no" answers. Instead, with the memory of an elephant, he detailed example after example of Trump's criminal intent and contextualized the prosecution's theory of the case.

If Tuesday was about Dino the Doorman, Thursday (there's no court on Wednesdays) revolved around Karen McDougal, the model and former Playmate of the Year who told AMI that she didn't want to be "the next Monica Lewinsky."

In September of 2016, Dylan Howard, AMI's chief content officer and Pecker's deputy, learned of her ten-month affair with Trump in 2006–07 from one of his very best sources, Keith Davidson, a suave, well-connected Beverly Hills attorney who also happened to be the lawyer representing both Karen McDougal and Stormy Daniels.

Dylan Howard reported to Pecker that ABC was offering McDougal a spot on *Dancing with the Stars*, but Pecker concluded that this gig—like rumors about a Mexican group offering her $1 million for her story—were almost certainly false.

Pecker concluded that he would have to buy the story to protect Trump as he had promised. "I believed the [McDougal] story was true, and it would be very embarrassing to him and to his campaign," Pecker said. This was powerful testimony and a glance at the jury box suggested it had landed.

Pecker then testified that Trump placed an urgent call to him when he was attending an investor conference in New Jersey. What follows is important evidence because it shows direct contact between Pecker and Trump:

"Mr. Trump said to me, 'I spoke to Michael [Cohen]. Karen [McDougal] is a nice girl.'"

This pre-corroborates Cohen's testimony that he and Trump talked about how to deal with women Trump had sex with.

Trump told Pecker that he wanted AMI to buy McDougal's story and take it off the market.

Pecker testified that he was under the misimpression that he would be reimbursed for the $150,000 "lifetime rights" contract that Keith Davidson, McDougal's lawyer, negotiated, which stipulated that she could say nothing about "any relationship with a then-married man."

In exchange for keeping her mouth shut about the affair, McDougal would be allowed to put her name on ghostwritten articles for AMI publications and appear on a few covers.

Pecker thought all of that was worth $25,000 and that Trump would thus owe him $125,000. Pecker tried to explain to Cohen "why it was so important to be reimbursed . . . He [Cohen] basically said at the end of each conversation,

'Why are you worried? I'm your friend. And the boss [Trump] will take care of it.'"

Of course, the boss never did because that's the way he rolls. His deadbeat MO goes at least as far back as his repeated practice of stiffing Trump Tower contractors and vendors in the early 1980s, as Hillary Clinton pointed out in the first 2016 debate. But having shelled out $150,000, Pecker was determined to get most of the money back.

Pecker was right to be getting cold feet. After the scandal broke in 2018, he signed a non-prosecution agreement with prosecutors stipulating that he broke the law. Political contributions of $150,000 for unspecified purposes are not legal.

Around this time, I looked through binoculars at the monitor—the only way to see Trump from the front—and saw him cross his arms. One of the courtroom artists who has covered other Trump trials told me that this is usually a sign he is frustrated about some portion of testimony.

"I AM NOT A BANK"

Pecker's testimony helped the jury understand the case's chronology.

On October 8, 2016, one day after the release of the *Access Hollywood* tape that seemed to cripple the Trump campaign (before James Comey's resurrection of Hillary's emails bumped it out of the news), Pecker was having dinner in Greenwich, Connecticut, with his wife. He took an urgent call from his deputy, Dylan Howard, telling him that two of his biggest sources, Keith Davidson and Gina Rodriguez, were trying to sell a story about Trump having sex with a porn star named Stormy Daniels.

Pecker told his deputy, "We already paid $30,000 to the doorman and $150,000 to Karen McDougal. I am not a bank. We are not paying any more . . . If anyone were to buy it, it should be Michael Cohen and Donald Trump."

All day, Pecker sketched the pattern of the conspiracy by detailing the McDougal payoff—a prelude to the real show—and connecting Trump directly to Stormy Daniels.

One morning after the election, Pecker asked if he could walk the president-elect back to his Trump Tower office.

Trump asked after McDougal, the woman he now denies having known. "How's our girl doing?" he asked. Then he told Pecker, "I want to thank you for handling the McDougal situation" and "the doorman situation."

Just in case there was any misunderstanding about his critical testimony, Pecker added, "He was thanking me for buying them and not publishing any of the stories and helping the way I did . . . He said the stories could be very embarrassing."

Embarrassing for whom? "I thought it was for the campaign," Pecker told prosecutor Josh Steinglass in a moment that went straight at Trump's intent. Trump said, "It would be very damaging to his campaign and election."

Then, in a mild tone, Pecker went further. "His family was never mentioned," Pecker said, by either Cohen or Trump.

After Trump was inaugurated and Pecker visited the Oval Office, Trump asked if he wanted to walk with him to dinner. As they passed the Rose Garden, Trump asked again about McDougal. "I said she's doing well," Pecker said. "Everything is good."

In early 2018, Trump's mind was still on his old mistress. "Donald called, and he said to me, 'Did you see the Anderson Cooper interview with Karen McDougal . . . I thought we had an agreement with [her] that she can't give any interviews or be on any television shows.'"

Pecker replied, "I said yes, but I amended it to let her speak with the press. He got very aggravated and couldn't understand why."

Pecker may be a reptilian creature but he's delivering the goods for the prosecution.

4/26/24
TRUMP'S SCALP

We may look back at the second Friday of the Trump trial as one of the most significant days of the entire case. That's when Emil Bove—arguably Trump's best defense attorney—failed to break David Pecker on cross-examination. But I'm going to start today with the story of my great view of Donald Trump's scalp. Here's how it happened:

After wolfing down my brown bag lunch on another floor of the courthouse, I was early at the metal detectors, caught a lucky aisle break, and found myself with one of the best seats in the house—the third row on the left side. This was two rows in back of the Secret Service and one row behind where the defendant's family would sit if any of them showed up.

So far, none have. Before court, Trump was at "the pen"—the camera position in the hallway—and wished Melania a happy birthday. Then he spent the morning enduring hours of testimony about Karen McDougal, whose affair with Trump overlapped with his wife's 2005–06 pregnancy with Barron.

For the next three hours, I was sitting about twelve feet directly behind Trump, perfectly positioned for what may be the very first eyewitness tonsorial report:

On the upper left side of the back of his head, the meticulously coiffed soufflé and industrial-strength hairspray mostly did their comb-back job covering evidence of the truth. But by peeking through peachy strands, I could

The defendant prepares for court (Garry Trudeau)

clearly see the pink-as-a baby's-bottom scalp beneath. We're talking cue ball here and the baldness is almost certainly present higher, lower, and to the right, with not a sprout to be seen.

Like a few other reporters, I often use binoculars to determine Trump's sleeping patterns. I focus them on the overhead video monitor that offers a camera view of him from the front. Today I didn't see any of the telltale head bobs we witnessed in earlier days of the trial—slow nod down, quick jerk up, a snoozing ex-president in airplane mode.

By my rough calculations, Trump closes his eyes about a third of the time, but it's often not clear whether he is resting or sleeping. While he sometimes consults Todd Blanche on his right, or Emil Bove on his left, he rarely talks to the best attorney and only woman on his team, Susan Necheles.

BELA LUGOSI FOR THE DEFENSE

Emil Bove is a second-team All-American lacrosse player and Georgetown Law grad with a stint as a federal prosecutor in the Southern District of New York. As he sucks the blood of witnesses on cross examination, he looks like Bela Lugosi playing *Dracula*.

I'm sure some of his liberal New York friends have asked him how he can defend Donald Trump. And I imagine his answer is that if he can defend Venezuelan drug dealers and the notorious "Chelsea Bomber," the terrorist who detonated explosives in New York and New Jersey, then he could, with a clean conscience, represent a former president.

Bove joined Todd Blanche's new firm to help handle this case, and he and Susan Necheles are the only members of the defense team who really know their way around a courtroom.

Bove started strong. He scored points on certain shakier parts of Pecker's direct testimony, including the publisher's admission that tabloids had used source agreements like the ones negotiated with Dino Sajudin and Karen McDougal "hundreds of thousands of times" over the years.

This was a gross exaggeration that played well for Trump. Pecker mostly responded to Bove's effective rat-a-tat-tat with a quiet "yes," as if he was Grandpa sheepishly agreeing that the long story he just told at the dinner table was not entirely accurate.

Bove may have made a little headway convincing the jury that the June 2015 meeting at Trump Tower—on the eve of his campaign kick-off—was not a "conspiracy" (as the prosecution would have it) but just business as usual in "checkbook journalism."

After being reprimanded for confusing the witness, Bove walked Pecker through catch-and-kill tales about Arnold Schwarzenegger, Mark Cuban, Tiger Woods, and others. The jury learned about a transactional celebrity netherworld where, for example, Hollywood super-agent Ari Emanuel helped kill a steamy story about his brother Rahm Emanuel, just before his 2011 Chicago mayoral bid.

The defense didn't seem to care whether these stories were actually true. The point was to show jurors that Pecker's deals pumping birther conspiracies about Barack Obama in 2012 when Trump was considering a presidential race, or cutting a deal with Schwarzenegger, or buying off Dino the Doorman and Karen McDougal, were just SOP, thereby undercutting the importance of catching and killing the McDougal story.

Business as usual—that was a key defense argument.

But if Trump's defense lawyers thought they could turn a sleazy publisher into a sleazy liar, they were mistaken. By the end of his cross-examination, Bove seemed out of ammo.

On redirect, Steinglass established that the deals with Dino the Doorman and Karen McDougal were *not* business as usual at AMI. He drove home that AMI's largest prior payment to kill a story was $20,000 (compared to $150,000 for McDougal), and the standard checkbook journalism payment to sources was $500.

"Is it standard operating procedure having a presidential campaign's person [Cohen] weighing in on what parts of the [McDougal] contract ought to be amended?" Steinglass asked, his voice rising.

Pecker said no, and he explained why these deals were different from the "hundreds of thousands" of other NDAs and source agreements he had stumbled over earlier.

"On how many of those NDAs did the CEO of AMI coordinate with a candidate for president?" Now Steinglass was harshly crossing Bove's cross.

"That was the only one," Pecker said.

Bottom line: what might be "business as usual" in tabloid land was extremely rare in politics.

Bove had one final shot on recross and botched it. At what must have been Trump's direction, he then argued that Trump is a family man.

Pecker wasn't buying it and Bove quit while he was behind. He stepped away, silently indicating that he had finished his cross-examination. The judge told the witness that he could step down.

His testimony complete and largely intact, David Pecker now entered American history as a credible chronicler of the tawdry and corrupt life of Donald Trump—much more credible than many of the magazines he once published.

4/29/24
DEFINING DEVIANCY DOWN

Today, a judge held a former president of the United States in contempt of court and threatened him with jail time if he didn't stop attacking jurors and witnesses. Put that in your pipe and smoke it, as they used to say on *Rowan & Martin's Laugh-In*. At any other moment in American history, this news would have produced banner headlines, some with exclamation points. Now, it wasn't even the top story from the courtroom.

This era will be remembered for its numbness. A world-class deviant is "defining deviancy down," in the memorable formulation of the late Daniel Patrick Moynihan.

Day Nine of the trial seemed different from the start. Normally, when I arrive at the courthouse at 7:15 AM, I go first to the holding pen across Centre Street that is designated for protesters. That's in tiny Collect Pond Park, named for the sixty-foot-deep, eighteenth-century pond that collected nearby springs and provided drinking water for the Dutch inhabitants of Lower Manhattan.

On most mornings, there has been literally no one in the park. By lunch, five or six Trumpy protesters would gather with the hope of attracting the attention of the dozen or so TV news camera positions set up between the pen and the courthouse. And after adjournment, a few more might come by to shout at a slightly larger group of anti-Trump protesters.

On the eve of the trial, Trump had promised a "MASSIVE outpouring of peaceful patriotic support" and later complained that his people "are rudely and systematically shut down and ushered off to faraway 'holding areas.'" Big surprise: this is 100 percent bullshit.

Trump did make some adjustments over the weekend, putting out the word to his New York supporters that a photo op he had staged at a bodega wasn't enough. He needed more people to show up outside the courthouse. This morning, three dozen did, with two huge Trump flags.

And for the first time, Trump brought a family member with him to court—his devoted son Eric, wearing his usual clueless expression. Maybe that was after Lawrence O'Donnell pointed out on MSNBC that even Jeffrey Dahmer had family members show up for his trial.

Along with Boris Epshteyn and senior campaign officials Susan Wiles and Jason Miller, Trump again brought along Texas attorney general Ken Paxton. Trump now understands that he needs to fill up that row just behind him where the two Secret Service agents are. We'll see which stooges and whack jobs get the call.

PAPERWORK

Today is what lawyers call the "paperwork" part of the trial, where names, dates, transactions, and the like are nailed down. This is testimony that makes you understand why Trump is falling asleep. Reporters can't join him—we're too busy clacking away on our laptops—and the jurors seemed to be paying attention. Todd Blanche is meandering in his pointless cross-examination of paperwork witnesses.

As George Conway told me and Harry Litman over lunch, Blanche should have borrowed from *My Cousin Vinny* by asking the witnesses only one question—in this case, something like, "Did you ever see the name Donald Trump in any of these transactions?"—and sat down triumphantly. Instead, Blanche, who is under intense pressure from Trump to be aggressive, may have raised eyebrows in the jury box by going down time-consuming blind alleys.

DAPPER DAVIDSON

Keith Davidson, dapper attorney for both Karen McDougal and Stormy Daniels, did more on the stand than bolster the prosecution's narrative and pre-corroborate Michael Cohen's forthcoming testimony; he gave jurors a permission slip to believe Cohen's upcoming story even if they think he's a "jerk" (Davidson's description) and big-time liar.

Here's the key exchange of the day:

Prosecutor Josh Steinglass: "Even after he [Cohen] said, 'I'll just do it myself,' where did you understand the money would be coming from?"

Keith Davidson: "From Donald Trump or some corporate affiliation thereof."

That was Davidson's understanding based on all of his texts and calls with Cohen, and it will likely be the jury's understanding based on all of the evidence being amassed.

While Davidson is one step removed from Trump, the ground between them is now being covered by bank records, texts, videos, and emails that will make Cohen's firsthand account much stronger under cross-examination.

SHOW ME THE MONEY!

In the summer of 2016, both AMI and ABC News wanted the Karen McDougal story, but for different reasons: AMI wanted to catch it and kill it to protect Trump, while ABC News investigative correspondent Brian Ross wanted it because it was an explosive story about the man who had just won the Republican nomination for president.

Of course, a long affair with a Playboy Playmate when his wife was pregnant might not have ended Trump's candidacy any more than Clinton's dalliances ended his. The male MAGA base would have been fine with it; I have no confidence any more in my ability to assess Trump's Teflon. But it could well have made the later *Access Hollywood* imbroglio harder to survive.*

As McDougal's lawyer, Davidson was playing off ABC News against Cohen and Trump. After court adjourned today, I called Brian Ross, a legend in our business, to ask what happened. "We had it all set. We picked the date, camera crews, makeup," he told me. "Then she called and said, 'My family doesn't want me to do it.'"

Ross said he thinks the real reason this explosive story didn't come out was that ABC News, which doesn't pay for stories, became leverage: "In retrospect, they were using us to get to Trump for the money."

Davidson now turned his attention from the predicate—Karen McDougal—to the real crime: paying off Stormy Daniels, then covering it up.

Davidson testified that he developed pseudonyms to keep everything confidential. Stormy Daniels was "Peggy Peterson," and Donald Trump was "David Dennison," a name Davidson borrowed from a fellow player on his high school hockey team who, when he heard about it, was not amused. The text chains are peppered with "PP" and "DD."

With Davidson playing Cuba Gooding Jr. in *Jerry Maguire* ("Show me the money!"), Cohen dawdled. Davidson testified that Cohen missed an October 14 deadline for the hush money payment to Daniels, and he kept making excuses for why he hadn't ponied up the agreed-upon $130,000—he didn't have the wiring instructions (which Davidson sent three times), the office was closed on Yom Kippur, the computer system was "all fucked up."

* Dick Morris, who advised Clinton during the Lewinsky scandal before returning to the GOP, believes no sex scandal could have sunk Trump, just as Clinton maintained his popularity through all the sex scandals.

"To me, it was a situation we run into all the time . . . someone who didn't have the purse strings," Davidson said, teeing up Trump's direct involvement. "Michael Cohen didn't actually have the authority to spend the money."

When Cohen ran out of excuses, and it became clear Trump wouldn't pony up directly, Cohen told Davidson, "Goddammit, I'll just do it myself."

When he did—and when he got Trump to agree to reimburse him—the crimes at the heart of this case were set in motion.

MAY

5/2/24
BARON VON SHITZINPANTZ

I use my binoculars mostly on jurors. I briefly thought that one male juror had a MAGA-type shirt on, but then realized I have no idea what that even means. Maybe I should give the binoculars a rest.

Today, Merchan held another hearing on the contempt charges against Trump for violating the gag order. This means more humiliation for him—and more fun for me. Trump must sit silently in the courtroom without posting nasty rejoinders on Truth Social. He has no choice but to quietly endure a torrent of hate and ridicule, almost always in the voice of his own attorneys.

That's what happens when your lawyers argue that you are "just responding" to attacks. The court needs to hear exactly what those attacks were.

So today, with the jury out of the courtroom, the defense introduced five hundred pages of exhibits, most consisting of Cohen trashing Trump. Merchan, looking at his watch, only had the patience for a sampling.

When the jury returned, we all got an earful. After Todd Blanche read Cohen's tweet calling Trump "Baron von ShitzInPantz," you could hear stifled giggles in the courtroom, though not from the stone-faced jurors. That turned into laughter—immediately shushed by the humorless court police—when the overhead video screens displayed a Photoshopped fat

Trump as a bright-orange superhero named "Super Victim." Again, nothing to see on the faces of jurors.

Orange was a theme. I especially enjoyed the exhibit of Trump in an orange jumpsuit next to Nelson Mandela. (Trump recently dubbed himself a "modern-day" version of the anti-apartheid hero) and the line: "Keep messing with me Donald and I won't send anything to your commissary."

Trump doesn't react to the humiliating images of himself, but he is keenly sensitive to criticism of his businesses, and he stared grimly at the image on the video monitors of Barry Diller on CNBC's *Squawk Box* with a caption below: "Trump IPO is a scam."

Blanche complained that Cohen uses his podcast, *Mea Culpa*, to take vicious shots at his old boss, and that he is now shopping a TV show based on the trial.

"Everyone can say what they want in this case except President Trump," Blanche complained, his whine cellar smelling musty.

The judge was unimpressed: "They're not defendants in this case. That's a very significant issue you're overlooking."

When Blanche persisted, Merchan interrupted to remind him that Trump was the one approaching the microphones. "Nobody's forcing him to talk to the press in the hall. The entire area has been set up so that your client, who is a candidate for president, can exercise his political speech rights," Merchan said.

Blanche responded, "Judge, I agree with that."

At that point, Trump glared at Blanche. His orders to his attorneys are clear: Don't "agree" in court. Don't make nice to the judge. Don't give one inch.

The microphones to which Merchan referred are just down the hall from the courtroom, where—addressing the tiny press pool from behind a short metal barrier that fittingly resembles prison bars—Trump launches his morning fusillades against the judge ("corrupt"), the DA ("crooked"), and the trial ("rigged"). None of this is prohibited under the gag order.

The judge indicated that once again the most serious contempt charge stems from Trump's complaint about the jury, this time in an interview with Real America's Voice, a MAGA cable and satellite channel: "The jury was picked so fast—ninety-five percent Democrats. The area's mostly all Democrat. You think of it as a—just a purely Democrat area. It's a very unfair situation, that I can tell you," Trump said of the New York City borough where he lived for decades.

Merchan believes that's a flagrant violation of his gag order, which explicitly bars attacking jurors.

"He spoke about the jury. He said the jury was ninety-five percent Democratic," Merchan barked from the bench. "The implication was that this is not a fair jury."

When Blanche tried to distinguish between "the jury" that Trump attacked and individual "jurors," whom he spared, Merchan batted away the distinction.

Then Blanche, who knows better, claimed that TV commentators were allowed to comment on juries, so why couldn't Trump? Merchan thought this silly excuse—which sounded like something that the seventy-seven-year-old defendant himself came up with—was even weaker than the one Blanche used in the first hearing on the gag order.

Trump has also trashed Stormy Daniels, who is on the list of possible witnesses. This led Blanche to complain that Trump should be allowed to respond to President Biden's remarks at the White House Correspondents' Dinner last month. Blanche quoted Biden's quip, "Donald had had a few tough days lately. You might call it stormy weather."

The judge was incredulous, "Are you saying that he [Trump] cannot respond without saying, 'Stormy Daniels'?" Merchan said. "He can certainly respond to President Biden."

"The defendant is doing everything he can to make this case about politics," prosecutor Matthew Colangelo summarized. "It's not. It's about his criminal conduct."

DIRTY LOOKS

Trump is trying to sound chipper. On Wednesday, he posted on Truth Social, "Contrary to the FAKE NEWS MEDIA, I don't fall asleep during the Crooked

D.A.'s Witch Hunt, especially not today. I simply close my beautiful blue eyes, sometimes, listen intensely, and take it ALL in!!!"

When he opens his eyes and walks past me during breaks, his face is less defiant than a study in frustration. At the end of the day, he shot MSNBC's Lawrence O'Donnell a dirty look like the one he sent in George Conway's direction last week. All I get when I stare at him is a puzzled expression, as if he can't remember if he knows me from TV.

ROTTEN PEAS IN A POD

After Trump won the 2016 election, Keith Davidson texted AMI's Dylan Howard with what he called "gallows humor":

"What have we done?"

Howard replied: "Oh, my God."

As these texts are read in open court, it bolsters the prosecution's argument that those involved in the conspiracy (including Trump) intended to influence the election, an important element of the DA's case.

In December of 2016, Davidson was holiday shopping at a "strangely decorated" big-box department store when Cohen called and unloaded:

"Jesus Christ, can you fucking believe I'm not going to Washington after everything I've done for that fucking guy," a reference to his not being offered a big job in the White House. "I've saved the guy's ass so many times."

Cohen told Davidson, "That guy is not even paying me the $130,000 back."

Davidson testified that Cohen was "despondent" and feared he "would kill himself." Cohen had delusions of grandeur. He thought he should have been considered to be Trump's attorney general or White House chief of staff, and he was extremely disappointed.

This made me think about the assassination of President James A. Garfield in 1881. The assassin, Charles J. Guiteau, was routinely described in my history books as a "disappointed office seeker."

Defense lawyers aren't likely to make reference to Garfield, whom Trump surely remembers only as a cat. They don't need to. The jury learned from them that Cohen had a huge personal reason for seeking vengeance against Trump, and it landed. Now the prosecution will have to show he's not lying to get back at Trump for this.

Davidson exudes smug pride on the stand, and I'm beginning to think he and Cohen were two rotten peas in a pod. That won't help the prosecution, either.

EXTORTIONISTS

Trump might get off thanks to what could be called "the Sleazy Lawyer Effect." Davidson and Cohen were just sleazy lawyers trying to get some money out of a rich presidential candidate.

This was the theme of Emil Bove's blistering cross-examination: Davidson is basically an extortionist by trade. And it worked. After coming across reasonably well on direct, Davidson looked like Beverly Hills scum on cross.

The louche tabloid world that Trump has inhabited for half a century came alive in the courtroom, with lurid stories that took jurors far beyond tales of a Playboy Playmate of the Year and a porn star.

Davidson seems to have had a sub-specialty in sex tapes. In one highly publicized case, he "extracted" big money out of Hulk Hogan in exchange for not airing sex tapes. In another, he worked with a "sex tapes broker" to get $75,000 out of pro-Nazi reality TV star Tila Tequila.

Davidson represented a leaker at the Betty Ford Clinic who convinced TMZ to give her $10,000 in exchange for suppressing a story about Lindsay Lohan's addiction. And he extracted large sums from Charlie Sheen for a wide variety of bad behavior.

Bove pressed Davidson about his testimony that Stormy Daniels said to him, "If he [Trump] loses this election, we lose all fucking leverage."

This laid the groundwork for the defense to argue that Trump—for all of his shortcomings—was just the innocent victim of experienced extortionists.

5/3/24
WAS COHEN'S IPHONE TAMPERED WITH?

One of the biggest pieces of evidence in the case is the recording Michael Cohen made on his iPhone of Donald Trump discussing hush money for Karen McDougal.

Trump is not charged with anything related to McDougal, but the phone call is incriminating because it goes right to Trump's intent, which is crucial for the prosecution to prove. Trump can be heard on the call saying "150," a reference to the $150,000 that David Pecker paid in hush money to McDougal, with Trump's approval. Trump also says, "So pay with cash."

Unfortunately for the prosecution, the call ended very suddenly, which could raise questions in the jury's mind about the authenticity of the tape recording.

On cross-examination of a prosecution witness, Bove bored the crap out of everyone with his technojargon. But he did get the witness, Douglas Daus, to agree that the absence of a complete record of the chain of custody "presents risks."

Bove left the extent of the risk to the imagination of conspiracy-minded jurors, though he used innuendo in his questions to bring the FBI and Cohen under vague suspicion.

As the prosecution made clear on redirect, there is no record of Cohen, the FBI, or anyone else "manipulating or tampering with audio recorded on the phone."

ACCESS HOLLYWOOD TAPE

Neither side has released a full witness list, so we were all surprised when Hope Hicks strode into the courtroom, clad in a smart black suit and looking more than a little like her old friend Ivanka Trump, who got her doppelgänger a job at the Trump Organization when Hicks was only four years out of college. By the next year, Hicks was the communications director for a presidential campaign.

"I'm really nervous," she said at the beginning of her testimony, adjusting the microphone on the witness stand. But the nerves did not prevent her from being a compelling, appealing, and ultimately devastating prosecution witness.

Hicks described Trump as a boss who approved every tweet and press release, testimony that corroborated David Pecker's account that depicted Trump as a "micromanager." This will make it harder, though hardly impossible, for the defense to claim that Trump didn't know that the checks to Michael Cohen were reimbursement meant to cover up paying off Stormy Daniels.

Hicks recounted how David Fahrenthold of the *Washington Post* emailed her that the *Post* had learned of what would become known as the *Access Hollywood* story. He included a full transcript of Trump caught talking to Billy Bush about being able to "grab 'em by the pussy" among other disgusting comments.

The transcript—after much debate in front of the judge—is an exhibit. It was not read from today, but parts of it flashed briefly on the monitors, which all the jurors have in front of their seats. I didn't see "pussy," but I was able to quickly read Trump saying: "And I did try to fuck her. She was married."

When Hicks brought the transcript to Trump, "He said that that didn't sound like something he would say." In other words, Trump lied to her, which became clear later in the day when the tape itself was obtained.

Jurors might think that Trump is a liar based on their familiarity with him over the years. But this was the first time they heard direct evidence of it in court.

And they learned that his lying was contagious. After Trump lied to Hicks, she instructed her communications staffers to "deny, deny, deny." In other words, to "lie, lie, lie."

After the tape aired, Hicks testified that Paul Ryan, John McCain, Mitt Romney, and other Republicans jumped ship, and many Trump staffers thought the campaign was over. "The tape was damaging. This was a crisis," Hicks said, noting that the story was so big it pushed a Category Four hurricane out of the headlines.

Why is Trump's feverish reaction to the release of the *Access Hollywood* tape so important? Because it provides a motive for him to complete the transaction with Stormy Daniels that he broke the law to cover up.

"KINDNESS OF HIS HEART"

Hicks apparently knew nothing about Cohen's payoff to Stormy Daniels at the time, but she and Trump had a fateful—and incriminating—chat about it in 2018 in the White House.

In a rare piece of good news for the defense, she testified that Trump was worried about his wife: "He wanted me to make sure the newspapers weren't delivered to her residence that morning. He was worried about how this would be viewed at home."

But this testimony was undercut by what the jury heard next:

Hicks testified that when the payoff to Stormy Daniels became public in 2018, Trump told her that Michael Cohen had paid the porn star "out of the kindness of his heart and never told anyone about it."

The kindness of his heart?

Prosecutor Matthew Colangelo then asked a critical question:

Was this "consistent" with what she knew about Cohen?

Hope Hicks's tears watermarked her testimony (REUTERS/Jane Rosenberg)

"I'd say that would be out of character for Michael Cohen," Hicks told the jury. "I didn't know him to be an especially charitable person or selfless person," she said. To the contrary, Cohen was "the kind of person who seeks credit."

Hicks was basically saying that Cohen was such a putz he would never make a move without getting approval and credit from "the Boss." And she should know.

At the defense table, Trump showed no sign of realizing his defense had just sustained a body blow. Clueless, he smiled for the first time in a while when Hicks explained that Cohen's moniker, "Trump's fixer," had come from Cohen himself. He was a fixer, she testified, "only because he broke it so that he could fix it."

Of course, this just made her testimony doubting Trump's claim that Cohen had acted out of the "kindness of his heart" even more powerful.

Hicks went on to testify that Trump told her "It was better to be dealing with it now [in 2018], and that it would have been bad to have that story come out before the election."

This, too, was damaging testimony. Hicks was confirming that Trump was more concerned with the election than protecting his family.

On that high note, Matthew Colangelo ended direct examination.

With Hicks's testimony, the motive and criminal intent necessary for conviction have been reaffirmed by someone who worked closely with Trump, still admires him, and heard that motive expressed directly to her, not as hearsay testimony.

Trump may have wanted to spare Melania, but we have solid proof that his first priority was to interfere in the election.

TEARS OF TRUTH

It was now time for Emil Bove's gentle cross-examination. For a minute or two, he asked a subdued Hicks about her background.

Then she began softly crying.

This caused some brief confusion in the courtroom over what we were hearing. As the sobs continued, I could hear them from the back row.

After murmuring "Sorry" three times, Hicks asked, "Could I just have a minute?"

Bove requested a break, and the judge asked, "Do you need a break?" Between sobs that I could now hear from the second to last row of the courtroom, she said, "Yes, please."

After the break, Hicks mostly regained her composure, and Bove's easy cross continued in unmemorable fashion before petering out.

Hicks, who had not seen Trump in eighteen months, exited the courtroom by walking just three feet to the right of her old boss. She looked straight ahead; he looked away.

Trump should have been thinking this, but he has never shown any familiarity with Shakespeare:

"Et tu, Hope?"

WATERMARKED

Whatever her explanation, Hicks's tears watermarked the most devastating part of her testimony against her old boss.

She wept not at some hard-to-remember moment but shortly after strongly suggesting that Trump was lying to her in 2018 when he said that Michael Cohen paid off Stormy Daniels "out of the kindness of his heart" and without his knowledge.

For what it's worth, my take on her tears is that she retains her gratitude for everything Trump has done for her in the last decade. But when that gratitude and her close relationship with Trump came into conflict with her oath to tell "the truth, the whole truth and nothing but the truth," the oath won—and the pain followed.

BABY LOUISA!!!!

After court today, I took the subway up to Columbia Presbyterian Hospital to see Charlotte, Mark, and tiny Louisa Catherine Chiusano, who was born at 10:15 last night, May 2, 2024. It doesn't get any better than this!

Charlotte gave birth to [their first daughter] Rosie during Covid, and I wasn't allowed in her hospital room. So it's nice to see our second granddaughter where she was born. Super cute.

The happy parents asked about the trial, but we didn't really talk about it. This is a Trump-free zone.

5/6/24
JAIL TO THE CHIEF?

Today began with high drama when Judge Merchan warned Trump that his tenth violation of the gag order would be his last or he'd be sanctioned with jail time.

"The last thing I want to do is to put you in jail," Merchan told Trump. "You are the former president of the United States and possibly the next president, as well. There are many reasons why incarceration is truly a last resort for me."

Merchan told Trump that jailing him "would be disruptive to the proceedings" and he "worried about the people who would have to execute that sanction: the court officers, the correction officers, the Secret Service detail, among others."

"The magnitude of that decision is not lost on me," Merchan said. "But at the end of the day, I have a job to do, and part of that job is to protect the dignity of the judicial system and compel respect."

Trump's offenses, he noted calmly, represented "a direct attack on the rule of law, and I cannot allow that to continue."

We'll see if Trump gets the message. I think he will. He's a coward who fears having to squat over a low metal toilet and sleep under a low-thread-count sheet.

"JEFF, YOU'RE FIRED"

Today's first witness was Jeffrey McConney, a heavyset accountant with a gray mane and goatee who worked for the Trump Organization for thirty-six years, eventually rising to be senior VP and controller.

Seeing McConney on the stand took me back to when I first moved to New York in 1983. I snickered at Trump from the moment I saw him on television. His vulgar tabloid presence could be mildly diverting, but there was nothing funny about him destroying the superb Art Deco friezes on the old Bonwit Teller building or stiffing the undocumented Polish workers on his job sites.

McConney testified that he and his boss, Allen Weisselberg,* the former CFO and current resident of Rikers Island (on a perjury rap), had lunch every day for three decades. By quickly authenticating his old boss's handwriting—which he had seen for thirty-six years—McConney spared prosecutors from having to call a handwriting analyst to validate that the scrawled evidence was in Weisselberg's hand.

McConney had little direct contact with Trump, but he told a revealing story about his first year at the company. When he reported that the Trump Organization's capital balance had gone down after he approved payment to a vendor, Trump summoned him to his office and said, "Jeff, you're fired." Trump said he was joking but instructed him that he must never "mindlessly" pay any bill without negotiating down the price.

That was Trump's MO: stiff contractors, bleed them dry with legal expenses if they tried to sue for payment, and settle for fifty cents or less on the dollar.

"It was a teaching moment," McConney recalled. For the jury, too. McConney had inadvertently disclosed that the defendant was—as David Pecker, Hope Hicks, and others testified—a micromanager and a deadbeat.

Amid all of the stultifying but critical testimony authenticating the checks, invoices, and ledger entries, one number stood out for me: $130,000. That's the

---

* In 2022, Weisselberg pleaded guilty to tax fraud, grand larceny, and falsification of business records for not reporting as income the school tuition for his grandchildren, free rent for a Manhattan apartment, and lease payments for a luxury car that he received from the Trump Organization. The judge in that case, who reduced his sentence, was Juan Merchan.

number Weisselberg handwrote on a bank statement before "grossing it up" (his words, also scrawled) to $420,000.

That $130,000 is the same amount the jury now knows was paid from Michael Cohen to Stormy Daniels through her attorney, Keith Davidson. The handwritten evidence proves that the amount was first doubled to $260,000 to save Cohen the roughly 50 percent he would have otherwise paid in taxes.

Prosecutor Chris Conroy asked, "Are you aware of any other expenses doubled to account for taxes?"

"No," McConney said, essentially confirming the part of the cover-up intended to make it seem as if Cohen was being reimbursed for expenses, which are not tax deductible.

Cohen wrote on every monthly invoice he sent to Trump, Weisselberg, and McConney: "Pursuant to the retainer agreement." But McConney testified that there never was any retainer agreement.

To further the cover-up, the reimbursements (McConney used that incriminating word) to Cohen were coded "legal expenses" in the Trump Organization's computerized ledger.

Even as the prosecution was cementing its case against him, Trump basked in the accolades from loyal employees on the witness stand, especially after all of the attacks he has endured in the courtroom, with more to come.

On cross, Emil Bove elicited even more praise, but McConney hurt Trump's case when he reemphasized his direct testimony by admitting that "Most personal legal expenses are not deductible for tax purposes." Oops. That gives the DA's office an opening to make tax fraud one of the additional crimes it needs to bring into the case.

AUNT BEE

The next witness was Deborah Tarasoff, an older woman in sensible shoes who resembles Aunt Bee on the old *Andy Griffith Show*.

Tarasoff still serves as the Trump Organization's accounts payable supervisor. She's the one who cut the checks to Cohen and brought them to Rhona Graff,

Trump's assistant, who arranged to FedEx them to Washington for Trump's signature. She confirmed that the "accounts payable" and "accounts receivable" stamps were real, and that it was her initials on various incriminating documents.

Todd Blanche's gentle cross mostly consisted of preparing the jury for an argument that during the transition and his early presidency, Trump was too busy to know anything about the real purpose of the checks he was signing.

Zzzzzzz . . .

I noticed a couple of drowsy jurors. But there was a metronomic majesty to the redundancy of validating all thirty-four of the invoices, ledger entries, and checks that make up the thirty-four counts in the indictment.

Andrea Bambino, an Italian correspondent for Agence France-Presse (AFP), told me he thought the most moving part of the trial so far was hearing the "Yes, ma'am" of Trump Organization witnesses confirming for a prosecutor that it was Donald Trump's (surprisingly artistic and vertical) signature on nine of those checks. Of course his fingerprints are on them, too.

I imagine that after court adjourned, the jurors went home and told their spouses or friends that they couldn't talk at all about the trial but vaguely mentioned that it was boring as hell today. They could not in good conscience share that the foundation of the prosecution's case was now firmly in place.

Bottom line: the former controller of the Trump Organization and current accounts receivable supervisor, both still getting their legal expenses paid by Trump, authenticated the checks, ledger entries, and invoices that make up the bulk of the charges against him.

5/7/24
PINCHING PENNIES

The first witness of the day was Sally Franklin, an editor at Penguin Random House called to validate exhibits that the prosecution believes are incriminating, namely two of the books Trump wrote about himself.

The books are *Trump: How to Get Rich* and *Trump: Think Like a Billionaire.* After establishing that the use of a ghostwriter did not lessen Trump's responsibility for his words, the prosecution asked the publishing executive to read from some of them.

In print, Trump explained that you must pay attention to details "down to the paperclips." He advised, "When you're working with a decorator, make sure you see all of the invoices . . . When you sign a check yourself, you're seeing what's going on in your business."

Trump noted, in a line that may stick in some jurors' minds: "Even in high-end shops, I bargain," often offering $2,000 for a $10,000 item.

Another example of Trump skewering himself: In a chapter of *Trump: Think Like a Billionaire* entitled "How to Pinch Pennies," Trump recounted that his editor, Jonathan Karp, ribbed him for being so tight that he used space heaters in Trump Tower.

Trump explained in one book how *Spy* magazine, a wickedly funny publication of the 1980s, famously sent him a check for fifty cents to see if he'd deposit it. Sure enough, he did. *Spy* didn't think this made Trump look so good. The magazine routinely referred to him as "the short-fingered vulgarian."

The point of all this testimony is to show that Trump knew exactly what the checks he signed were for—and that "grossing up" the money he paid Cohen as part of the cover-up was out of character for the cheap bastard, so he must have had a damn good reason to do it.

Beyond this case, it's great to see Trump's bad character revealed by a good source—himself. This is the part of the trial where he's consistently hoisted by his own petard. Omen for November? The best way to beat Trump has always been for him to beat himself.

The gentle, literary Trump wrote that sometimes you have to "screw people" and instructed that "When someone hurts you, go after them as viciously and violently as you can."

This cuts against the defense's argument that he was merely the victim of an extortion scheme.

"All the women on *The Apprentice* flirted with me, consciously or unconsciously," he wrote, because he possessed "a sexual presence." More like sexual entitlement, as we will soon learn from Stormy Daniels.

STORMY ON THE STAND?

The day began with a motion offered by Susan Necheles, a slight, savvy sixty-four-year-old defense attorney with a good rep in the New York bar for "pulling rabbits out of hats."

I'm told that she and Trump have a frosty relationship, in part because she refused to sign pre-trial motions she considered frivolous and damaging to her reputation.

More fundamentally, Necheles, a registered Democrat, had the balls to confront Trump. In 2023, Trump called her "a loser" for failing to convince a jury to acquit Allen Weisselberg. Necheles was pissed and told Trump that Weisselberg lost because he was guilty.

Necheles has handled many cases but may be best known for her defense of the late Genovese crime family underboss Venero ("Benny Eggs") Mangano.

To help her latter-day "Benny Eggs" beat the rap, Necheles wanted to keep Stormy Daniels off the stand. Without the jury present, she argued to Judge Merchan that any talk of sex in Daniels's testimony would be "unduly prejudicial" to her current client.

The judge was concerned about prejudicial testimony, and he asked prosecutor Susan Hoffinger how much detail she needed. Hoffinger—the dark-haired, matter-of-fact chief investigator of the DA's office—agreed that "certain details are too salacious" but stressed that a full explanation of the conversation between Daniels and Trump in the hotel penthouse was essential.

As for the sex act, Hoffinger promised that it would be "very basic without any descriptions of genitalia."

Necheles insisted there was no need to bring up sex at all because "this case is about records." If so, the defense may have lost it on Monday when two Trump Organization accountants confirmed the records' accuracy.

The judge ruled that he would allow Daniels's testimony about the sexual encounter because she "has credibility issues" that she should be permitted to address. But he added: "We don't need to know details about intercourse."

WICKED PICTURES

Just after 10:30 AM, a medium-sized buxom woman, clad in black palazzo pants, a black tunic, and a black hoodie, walked with purpose into the courtroom, her sensible glasses propped on her head. She looked like a Texas mother and small business owner on her way to the funeral of a much older man she despised. At least, she hoped it was his funeral.

As she settled into the chair, I focused on . . . the hair. This constitutes observatory growth for me. I'm normally so oblivious to hair that I was the last to learn how often Hillary Clinton changed her look. But after my success in closely examining Trump's bald scalp, I now use my binoculars to determine that Stormy Daniels wears her hair—blonde in front and dark brown in the back—with the kind of informal claw clip a female reporter next to me said was what a woman would wear to the gym.

Daniels, who is forty-five, did not come across as a porn star. She seemed like a younger, hipper, saucier Claire McCaskill—if McCaskill had chosen strip clubs over the Senate.

She doesn't seem to have had a lot of face work, but she wore plenty of eye makeup and bore a tattoo that I couldn't identify on her right forearm. On the stand, she came across as a smart and ambitious woman, accomplished in her field, whatever one thinks of it. She apparently disregarded the standard advice to witnesses—which is to mostly answer "yes" or "no" and leave it at that. Daniels has a dark story to tell, and she's damn well going to tell it.

At the outset, the witness said she preferred to be called Stormy Daniels, not by her real name, Stephanie Clifford.

She grew up in Baton Rouge, where her parents split up when she was four years old. She attended a "very Christian, very strict elementary school," took part in 4-H, and wanted to be a veterinarian. She said she was an editor of her high school newspaper, danced in a Baton Rouge ballet company, and graduated in the top 10 percent of her class, adding that she received a full scholarship in veterinary medicine from Texas A&M but took a year off and never went back.

I met someone outside the courthouse who knows Daniels and says she simply made bad choices at this time in her life, as she was trying to escape a mother she described on the stand as "very neglectful." Instead of becoming a vet, she left home at seventeen and started stripping.

Daniels testified that, at twenty-one, she did nude modeling for a magazine, and at twenty-three, she was offered a contract with Wicked Pictures, where she was proud to say she wrote and directed as well as acted. Daniels says this was not supercheap, unscripted porn but "actual movies that have sex." She said she was the youngest feature director in the adult film industry, with more than one hundred credits.

Daniels mentioned bit parts in movies but did not specify her roles. My intensive investigative reporting reveals that she was "Lap Dancer #1" in *Knocked Up* and the porn actress Steve Carell's character is watching on TV in *The 40-Year-Old Virgin.* Bit parts, to be sure, but in iconic American films about sex.

Trump, then sixty, and Daniels, then twenty-seven, met at a 2006 celebrity golf tournament in Lake Tahoe. Wicked Pictures sponsored "a hole," which Daniels said she found "very funny." She had her now-famous picture taken with him as her boss introduced her as "contract star and director, Stormy Daniels."

"Oh, you direct, too, you must be the smart one," Trump said, according to Daniels. She had never seen his TV show but heard something about his involvement in professional wrestling.

Later, they spoke in the gift room. Daniels didn't know Trump's age, but "I knew he was as old or older than my father."

She testified that Trump was with another gentleman who told Daniels, "Mr. Trump would like to know if I wanted to have dinner with him." That was Keith Schiller, his bodyguard and procurer for years.

I heard recently that Schiller—who left the White House early on to start his own security business—has no interest in testifying, and it's easy to see why. He'd either have to betray his old boss or perjure himself defending him. Neither the prosecution nor the defense seemed to want to bet on which it would be, so he was not subpoenaed.

At this point, Hoffinger asked if the person under discussion was in the court. Daniels said yes and grimly gestured at Trump before saying, "Navy-blue jacket—at the table." Trump scowled.

Here, I wrote a note to myself: "Doesn't look or sound sketchy, but like a smart, uninhibited businessperson."

Daniels testified that she only agreed to go out to dinner with Trump because she didn't want to eat with her female coworkers. "Catfight stuff," she explained.

Her manager, identified only as Mike, told her eating with Trump could maybe help her get good business advice or an agent. "What could possibly go wrong?" she recalled Mike saying, to laughter in the media overflow room. Reporters in the courtroom knew we risked ejection if we laughed.

Trump was staying across town at Harrah's, and Schiller instructed her to take an elevator to the penthouse, and they would then go down to dinner. When she arrived, she said, Schiller was standing outside the door, which was cracked open, and he told her to "Go on in."

Daniels remembered many details about the huge suite ("three times the size of my apartment"), from the flowers on a big wooden table to the black-and-white tile pattern on the floor of the foyer, the latter of which the judge later used as an example of excessive detail in her testimony.

Trump emerged wearing silk-and-satin pajamas.

Daniels, unintimidated and apparently never at a loss for words, made fun of him: "Did Mr. Hefner know you stole his pajamas?"

The line was unforgettable and it offered an early glimpse of Stormy's cheeky wit. It also placed Trump in his proper cultural time element. The "great" that Trump wants to bring "again" is Hef's world, only Hefner was an ardent liberal.

"I told him to go change, and he obliged very politely," Daniels recalled. He came back wearing a dress shirt and dress pants.

After pleasantries and questions about where she went to school, brothers and sisters (none), whether she was married, had a boyfriend or kids (no, no, and no), Trump asked about the adult film business, with questions about unions, how performers were paid, and "how often tested." At the time, it was every thirty days.

"Have you ever had a bad test?" Trump asked.

She replied that she "never tested positive for anything," before explaining to the jury that Wicked Pictures was a "condom mandatory company" where even in later years when she and her then husband had sex on camera, they were required to use a condom.

She told Trump, "Yes, some adult films have real scripts and are real movies, not just, 'Oh, I am sorry, Mr. Pizza Boy,' which is very offensive to me."

I'm not sure the jury buys that she never imagined what Trump had on his mind, especially after he responded to her question about whether he was married with, "Oh, don't worry about that. We . . . actually don't even sleep in the same room."

But the five women jurors are likely to be sensitive to depicting Daniels as eager to have sex just because of her choice of occupation.

I want to continue with Daniels' testimony not because it's so germane to the case but because it's more evidence of what a louche loser the forty-fifth president has always been.

Daniels reports that Trump began bragging about all the magazines he was on the cover of and showed her one. Daniels was not impressed. "It was not like I made a habit of reading financial magazines. I was just a twenty-seven-year-old stripper."

"It was almost like he wanted to one-up me—which is really hilarious when you think about it—to talk about himself."

At this point, Daniels "had enough of his arrogance" and decided to take him on. "So I said, 'Are you always this rude, arrogant, and pompous? You don't even know how to have a conversation,' and I was pretty nasty. I snapped. And he seemed to be taken aback."

Referring to the magazine, "I said, 'Someone should spank you with that.'"

He rolled it up and "gave me the look that he dared me. So, I took it from him and said, 'Turn around.' So, now I kind of had to." She testified that she swatted him on the butt and that after that he was "much more polite."

Trump, awake at the defense table, appeared to mutter the word "bullshit" under his breath.

The judge called a sidebar and said, as we later learned: "I understand that your client is upset at this point, but he is cursing audibly, and he is shaking his head visually—and that's contemptuous. It has the potential to intimidate the witness and the jury can see that."

Merchan added. "You need to speak to him. I won't tolerate that." Blanche conveyed the message to Trump.

I didn't think the spanking story was bullshit, but I was concerned that it sounded flirty and could harm her credibility.

Daniels now started testifying about her business opportunities. As Trump dangled a possible appearance on *Celebrity Apprentice*, he said, "You remind me of my daughter because she is smart and blonde and beautiful and people underestimate her as well."

Were the jurors creeped out by the idea of Trump wanting to have sex with someone who reminded him of his daughter? Sorry, but I couldn't tell.

When Daniels said she wasn't a businesswoman and was worried about losing badly on *Celebrity Apprentice*, Trump told her the show could be rigged a bit so her team did relatively well. Daniels said that he told her something along the lines of, "You could go on the show and prove you aren't just the dumb bimbo."

Daniels testified that she began thinking about how Trump might help her career. "I have no shame. That's who I am, but I also wanted to direct other, bigger things. They have bigger budgets and better catering." That's Stormy Daniels in a nutshell.

Daniels said she called a friend named Alana, who we learned outside the trial was Alana Evans, another porn star. Evans didn't believe Daniels was actually meeting Donald Trump. Daniels put her on speakerphone and won her bet.

Was Trump hoping for a three-way? I'll take those odds.

During the break, the judge told prosecutor Susan Hoffinger that "this degree of detail is just unnecessary"—an admonition that would later prove important.

When Daniels resumed her testimony, she explained that in the suite she excused herself to go to the bathroom. She said she wasn't proud of it but she snuck a look at Trump's toiletry bag and saw a gold manicure set with gold tweezers, Old Spice, and Pert Plus.

I'm an Old Spice guy myself—or was until I found out Trump uses it.

"WHAT DID I MISREAD?"

I want to take you through Daniels's testimony about the sex in some detail because it's critical to assessing Trump's motive for paying the hush money.

Trump wanted to suppress untrue stories, too, like that of Dino the Doorman. But it was the thought of Daniels telling a true and convincing story on TV just after the *Access Hollywood* tape and just before the election that must have terrified candidate Trump. To win the case, the prosecution must drive this point home.

I'm convinced that if Daniels had gone on TV in late October of 2016 and told her detailed and convincing story, it would have pushed James Comey and "laptops" out of the headlines and elected Hillary Clinton.

Here's the story she told in court eight years after she was paid not to tell it to millions:

"When I opened the bathroom door to come out, Mr. Trump had come into the bedroom and was on the bed, basically between myself and the exit" wearing boxer shorts and a T-shirt, Daniels testified.

"At first, I was just startled, like a jump scare. I wasn't expecting someone to be there, especially minus a lot of clothing. That's when I had that moment where I felt the room spin in slow motion. I felt the blood leave my hands and my feet and almost like if you stand up too fast, and everything kind of spun, that happened too. Then I just thought, 'Oh, my God, what did I misread to get here?' The intention was pretty clear, somebody stripped down in their underwear and posing on the bed, like waiting for you."

"And I went to step around. I laughed nervously, and, you know, tried to make a joke out of it, and step around and leave. Even though I was moving like I was in a funhouse, like slow motion. I thought to myself: Great. I put myself in this bad situation."

"He stood up between me and the door, not in a threatening manner. He didn't come at me. He didn't rush at me. He didn't put his hands on me or anything like that. I said, 'I got to go.' He said, 'I thought we were getting somewhere, we were talking, and I thought you were serious about what you wanted.'"

Daniels paraphrased Trump to devastating effect: He was basically saying, "If you ever want to get out of that trailer park . . ." Daniels testified. "I was offended because I never lived in a trailer park."

Here, the defense objected. Judge Merchan sustained the objection and instructed Hoffinger, "Move along."

Daniels then testified, "I just think I blacked out. I was not drugged . . . I never insinuated that I was on drugs. I was not drunk." I saw Trump whispering to Blanche.

The witness's next lines would prove especially contentious. "I did note there was a bodyguard right outside the door. There was an imbalance of power for sure. He was bigger and blocking the way."

Daniels made sure to add, "I was not threatened verbally or physically," but the overall context recalled the stories that E. Jean Carroll and other women have told about Trump.

Next came the sex act itself, which the judge had ruled could not be discussed in detail.

"The next thing I know, I was on the bed, somehow on the opposite side of the bed from where we had been standing. I had my clothes and shoes off. I believe my bra, however, was still on."

When she added, "We were in the missionary position," the judge sustained the defense's objection and had the line stricken from the record.

The sex was brief and afterward, Daniels remembered, "I was staring at the ceiling. I didn't know how I got there. I made notes like I was trying to think about anything other than what was happening there." After sex, "he was just up on the bed like this," Daniels said, indicating with her body that he was leaning back.

She concluded this part of her testimony by describing, "Sitting on the end of the bed, noticing that it was completely dark outside now and that it was hard to get my shoes on, my hands were shaking so hard. I had on tiny strappy gold heels with little tiny buckles . . . I was having a hard time getting dressed."

"He said, 'Oh, great. Let's get together again, Honeybunch. We were great together.' I just wanted to leave."

Daniels went on to chronicle several nonsexual encounters with Trump, starting on the next day of the golf tournament when he introduced his "little friend Stormy" to "Big Ben," Pittsburgh Steelers quarterback Ben Roethlisberger.

Later, she appeared at an event promoting Trump's vodka brand, where Daniels said Trump introduced her to Karen McDougal.

So to keep this all straight: Trump introduced his mistress to the woman he had cheated on her with.

In the years that followed, Daniels talked to Trump several times by speakerphone, within earshot of several others, and met him at Trump Tower. He finally told her that some senior NBC executive had vetoed her appearance on *Celebrity Apprentice* because she was a porn star, though Jenna Jameson later appeared on the show.

Daniels described a 2011 incident in the parking lot of a Las Vegas shopping mall when she and her infant daughter were en route to a Mommy and Me exercise class. She said an unidentified man approached her and "he threatened me if I continued to tell my story." Daniels said she didn't call the police or tell her ailing and alcoholic husband, who also knew nothing of her sexual encounter with Trump.

A lawyer friend advised her that she would be safer if her story was known, and her agent, Gina Rodriguez, began shopping it. When she learned that Michael Cohen, on behalf of Trump, was interested in buying and burying her story, she felt "that was the best thing that could happen because then my husband wouldn't find out, but there was still documentation of a money exchange and a paperwork exchange, so that I would be safe and the story wouldn't come out."

How did Stormy do on the stand? I didn't trust my own reactions and wanted the reaction of women journalists. For weeks, this no-lingering-in-the-hall-except-in-line-to-the-bathroom thing was lending a single sex, non-coed vibe to the breaks that I didn't appreciate. Women bring different lived experiences and—in many cases—superior intuition, and I felt deprived of their analysis of how her testimony was going. I feared that I was missing some very shrewd takes in the women's restroom.

Unfortunately, some women—and plenty of men—are touchy about sharing their views outside of their news organizations. I missed the old days of talking shop at the courthouse.

5/9/24
STORMY FLUSHES TRUMP ON CROSS

Today should have been a good day for the defense, and not just because it had a chance to break Stormy Daniels on cross-examination.

I could see from Trump's less-frustrated expression that he liked feeling a little love in the courtroom. When he swaggered out during a break, a young Orthodox Jewish guy, one of six early bird spectators allowed in the courtroom that day, loudly whispered, "Stay strong!"

Trump pointed at him with his closed-mouth smile. The spectator was pulled from the room and tongue-lashed by a court police officer for breaking the strict rules we've all learned to abide by.

Senator Rick Scott, the Florida Republican, was in the courtroom for ninety minutes or so, showing his moral support for his famous new constituent.

Scott came to New York to peddle the asinine and ass-backward idea that the real election interference isn't January 6 but Trump being tried in the New York trial.

As the day began, the Trump legal team also had a small tactical advantage. After direct examination, the defense team had all day Wednesday (an off day) to pore over Stormy Daniels's direct testimony and pick new holes in it.

When defense attorney Susan Necheles began her cross-examination two days prior, on Tuesday afternoon, I immediately sensed that Daniels was actually more effective on cross than on direct—less canned (she has told her story often) and self-justifying, and her oversharing was now under control. On cross, Daniels was combative and cheeky without being defensive. It worked.

Right off the top, Necheles accused Daniels of "acting in pornography" out of greed. "It's that simple. You wanted more money, right?" Daniels didn't miss a beat: "Don't we all want to make more money in our jobs?"

Then came the argument that Daniels was just "out to get" Trump:

Necheles: "Am I correct that you hate President Trump?"

Daniels: "Yes."

Necheles: "And you want him to go to jail, right?"

Daniels: "I want him to be held accountable."

Necheles introduced into evidence a tweet from Daniels: "I don't owe him shit, and I'll never give that orange turd a dime." Daniels stood by that odorous description and would do so again later in her testimony. She said she was just responding to Trump "because he made fun of me first."

This playground tussle makes each look squalid and small, of course, but only one of them is a former president running for president again. Daniels's feisty point that she was just returning fire undermined a good chunk of Necheles's cross. Trump, just a dozen feet away, could only glare.

Necheles barked up every fruitless tree. She tried to make Daniels out to be a liar over slightly conflicting accounts of whether she left the Mommy and Me workout class in 2011 after being confronted by a "supposed threat" in the parking lot.

At least some jurors must figure that threats like these are issued not just in movies but in real life. By this time, Daniels didn't have to accuse anyone in particular for a few jurors to perhaps assume the guy in the parking lot was a Trump thug.

As on direct, Daniels's level of detail—which the judge thought excessive—made her more believable.

Necheles is like a scary high school principal who is damn well gonna kick you out of school for something.

She scored some points by identifying Daniels's conflicting public accounts of whether the sex happened. But did she get any jurors to move from thinking maybe Daniels exaggerated her story a bit to believing she made it up out of whole cloth? Not likely.

Self-protective denial of having sex is neither uncommon nor that big a deal to most voters. This is a fact of modern life that helps both Daniels and Trump. The sex only hurts Trump because it goes to his motive for breaking the law to keep Daniels from talking and blowing his chance of winning the presidency.

Necheles now leaned heavily into the extortion argument that had worked well when Keith Davidson was on the stand.

Necheles: "You were looking to extort money from President Trump, right?"

Daniels: "False!"

Trump's essential argument is that Daniels and her lawyer were extorting him with an untrue story, like the one about the love child peddled by Dino the Doorman.

Necheles: "Your whole story is made up, isn't it?"

Daniels: "No, none of it is made up . . ."

A dodgy Daniels should have just copped to being an aggressive capitalist. After endless wrangling, she finally said cutting the deal with Cohen and Trump, then going public, was "a chance to get the story out *and* to make some money." She should have said that early and stuck with it.

But the prosecution benefited because Necheles was off her game. She called author Jeff Toobin "Jeff Daniels" and twice referred to Daniels's agent, Gina Rodriguez, as "Geena Davis."

"YOU CAN'T UNRING THAT BELL"

When cross resumed on Thursday morning, Daniels arrived in court dressed better than two days before. She wore a black robe almost like that of a judge over a modest green dress, and her strappy stiletto heels clicked on the grimy floor. Her hair—no longer two-toned—was parted in the middle, and she sported a simple pearl-and-ruby necklace, apparently made by her teenage daughter.

Defense attorney Susan Necheles cross-examines Stormy Daniels (REUTERS/Jane Rosenberg)

Like most defense attorneys on cross, Necheles drilled in on perceived inconsistencies. Daniels had occasionally said one thing to one magazine or TV host and another to someone else. Nothing seemed to land.

At one point, Necheles asked questions related to Jacob Weisberg, one of my oldest friends. In the fall of 2016, Jacob—then the editor of *Slate*—had heard rumors about a sexual relationship between Trump and a porn star. Jacob interviewed Daniels at length and was ready to print the story whenever she put it on the record.

"He was my backup," Daniels testified. "I stopped talking to Weisberg because of the NDA [non-disclosure agreement]." In the end, Trump paid, while *Slate,* like most reputable publications, could not.

Besides fishing for inconsistencies, Necheles focused on sex. This was a bad move. By trying to show that Daniels had changed her story about the encounter being consensual, Necheles gave the jury a chance to hear Daniels's testimony all over again that she "blacked out" and "didn't remember how she ended up in bed."

I ran into George Conway during a bathroom break. He was much more damning than on TV: "Literally the worst cross I've ever seen." He thought that, like the cross of Keith Davidson, Necheles should have asked Daniels if she had any knowledge of Trump's business records, emphasized her "no," and sat down.

Later, when Trump's lawyers moved for a mistrial, admission of Daniels' prejudicial sexual testimony was their main argument. Merchan rejected the motion, but they will use it on appeal.

Those appeals will almost certainly not be heard until after the election. In the meantime, Trump's lawyers are succeeding in making their client look worse. With the jury out of earshot, Todd Blanche told the judge: "You can't unring that bell." Good.

To make matters even bleaker for the defense, Necheles may have erred by trying to shame a stripper and porn star. It wasn't slut-shaming, but close, and the women jurors I watched did not seem to be buying it.

Referring to Daniels's work as a porn screenwriter, she said, "You have a lot of experience in making phony stories about sex appear to be real," in a tone indicating that she was passing judgment on the witness's career choices.

Daniels responded with a drop-the-mic moment: "The sex in the films is very much real, just like what happened to me in that room."

This would have been a rough road to tread for a defense attorney any time in the last thirty years, but it was an almost suicidal one today when even prostitutes are carefully referred to as sex workers.

It got worse. You've "acted and had sex in over 200 porn movies, right?" Necheles said contemptuously. And "there are naked men and naked women having sex in those movies . . . But according to you, seeing a man sitting on a bed in a T-shirt and boxers was so upsetting that you became light-headed and almost fainted?"

"Yes," answered Daniels. "When you're not expecting a man twice your age, yes."

It felt as if Trump's side was arguing that porn stars, like women wearing short skirts, are asking for it all the time. Not a good look to a jury in 2024.

The only time I felt Necheles got any traction was when she confronted Daniels on whether she had eaten dinner with Trump or not. In an unpublished interview with *In Touch Weekly*, the gossip magazine, Daniels said she had talked at length with Trump in the hotel suite "before, during, and after" dinner. But Daniels testified on direct that they hadn't had dinner. Now, she said she clearly remembered being famished. "I'm very food motivated, and in all of these interviews, I would have talked about the food" if there had been any.

That was as good as it got for the defense.

Even if the defense had scored more heavily on conflicting accounts of why Daniels denied the story or on Daniels dabbling in the paranormal ("You claimed you lived in a haunted house and that a spirit attacked your boyfriend, correct?"), Daniels's details of her encounter with Trump were so extensive that Necheles's efforts to portray her as a fantasist went nowhere.

At one point, when Necheles once again accused her of making the whole thing up, Daniels deadpanned, "If [my] story was not true, I would have written it to be a lot better."

I was pounding away on my laptop but the reporters on either side of me spotted jurors visibly stifling laughs.

There was one moment when I feared that Necheles might blow Daniels out of the water. She began pushing Daniels on the details of the foyer of the hotel penthouse.

Here it comes, I thought. Daniels had testified earlier that the foyer had a black-and-white tile floor, and the judge had earlier used the tile floor as an example of her being too detailed.

Now, I was sure the defense would produce an exhibit with the décor plan or a photo from Harrah's proving the floor tile was not black and white, but—I don't know—orange and blue. Nope. No such exhibit was produced. For me and—I predict—jurors, this confirmed that Daniels was indeed in the suite and not making the whole thing up. Otherwise, how would she have known the color of the tiles? It was hardly a big leap from that to concluding that Trump, who has denied even knowing her, clearly had his mind on more than conversation.

I lost track of how many times Necheles took a big swing and missed. It seemed as if Trump was using his defense attorney to tarnish Daniels for the kinds of dopey promotions and branding opportunities (Trump Steaks, anyone?) that have defined much of his own career. Only these were at his expense.

So Necheles showed the jury images of the *Political Power: Stormy Daniels* comic book, the Stormy, Saint of Indictments candle, and posters from Daniels's "Making America Horny Again Tour."

When Necheles expended a huge amount of time on all of Daniels's efforts to monetize her fame, she replied with a simple and devastating, "Just like Mr. Trump."

This landed.

Trump's history of projection—accusing others of doing what he does—may have finally caught up with him.

Jurors had seen tweets on their individual screens where Trump calls Daniels "horse face" and a "sleaze bag," and now it was *Daniels* who was out-of-bounds on social media? This didn't fly.

Necheles asked, "Isn't it a fact that you keep posting on social media how you're going to be instrumental in putting President Trump in jail?"

Twice, Daniels outdueled an experienced trial attorney. From the witness chair, she demanded: "Show me where I said I would be 'instrumental in putting President Trump in jail.'"

So Necheles offered on the video monitor a tweet from Daniels describing herself as "the best instrument to flush the orange turd down."

Orange turd?

Daniels said she was merely responding to Trump's toilet talk.

Necheles then proved Daniels's point by entering into evidence Trump's Truth Social post, "Michael Cohen and Stormy Daniels a/k/a the human toilet are their star witnesses."

Yes, this is what it has come to in American public life.

Necheles then dug a deeper hole for herself: "So when you said you were 'the best person to flush the orange turd down,' you weren't saying you were going to be instrumental in causing him to be convicted of a crime?"

"I am pretty sure this is hyperbole," Daniels said, seeming to enjoy the exchange. "If somebody calls me a 'toilet,' I say I can 'flush' somebody. See how that works?"

At this point, she gestured directly at Trump and said: "It goes around."

Yes, what goes around, comes around—this time landing in court.

Let's hope that it continues doing so, though in a less scatological fashion.

Redirect and recross were uneventful and after nearly seven hours of testimony, Daniels stepped down from the stand. Her testimony had nothing to do with falsifying business records but it was significant nonetheless. Stormy Daniels established that Donald Trump is a liar—not just generally, but in this case. That will make it much harder to prove that Michael Cohen—the key witness—is not telling the truth.

5/13/24
WHERE'S WEISSELBERG?

For the first three weeks of this trial, we've heard one constant theme: a play on Ray Romano's old TV show *Everybody Loves Raymond*. In this case, it's, Everybody Hates Michael. In their testimony, David Pecker, Keith Davidson, Hope Hicks, and Stormy Daniels all trashed Michael Cohen.

This was not bad for the prosecution because, in toto, it made it hard to believe Cohen would pay hush money out of what Trump called "the kindness of his heart" without checking with the boss. But prosecutors were irritated with Cohen for persisting in trashing Trump on social media after the trial was underway. This gave ammunition to the defense.

Judge Merchan instructed prosecutors to tell their witness that he had to knock it off. They said they had tried to do so, but Cohen wouldn't listen. So Merchan directed the prosecution to tell Cohen that *the judge* was telling him to STFU, though not in so many words. On the advice of his skillful lawyer, Danya Perry, Cohen finally zipped it.

The first order of business today was the judge's ruling in favor of the defense. Because Merchan is a fair man, he sometimes does so. This time, the judge gave the Trump team a break by not allowing Allen Weisselberg's $750,000 severance package from the Trump Organization to be entered into evidence.

Prosecutors had wanted to use Weisselberg's golden parachute to show there was a reason they haven't subpoenaed him from Rikers Island to testify. They fear he might risk another perjury charge by lying on Trump's behalf, which he has done often, at great personal expense.

The defense, meanwhile, doesn't want Weisselberg to testify because if the seventy-six-year-old accountant pleads the Fifth Amendment, it would make it seem as if a crime had been committed, even though jurors are always told not to hold invoking the Fifth against witnesses and defendants.

So, at the trial's end, when the jurors are sent to deliberate, they'll wonder: "Where's Weisselberg?" My bet is that jurors in the habit of reading the news before being selected will know the answer: Rikers.

COHEN LANDS SOME BLOWS

Michael Cohen is a cross between a Damon Runyon character and Sammy "the Bull" Gravano, the squat mobster who brought down John Gotti.

Trump says Cohen is a "rat." My family and I don't like that term because when we lived at 111th and Amsterdam thirty years ago, the empty lot across the street was the most rat-infested place in New York, according to *Spy* magazine. Rats are a thing with Alters.

So I prefer stool pigeon or stoolie.

Until he flipped in 2018, Cohen wasn't just Trump's fixer and enforcer, he was one of the biggest pricks in New York. Who can forget the tape that my old *Daily Beast* colleague Tim Mak made of a 2015 call he had with Cohen. "I'm gonna mess up your life for as long as you're on this frigging planet," Cohen told him. "Frigging" instead of "fucking" was Cohen's idea of playing nice.

We won't hear that phone call in this case. The defense won't use it because it concerned a story Mak was working on about the late Ivana Trump accusing her ex-husband of raping her when he was enraged about the failure of a hair transplant, a charge she later retracted. It's a good bet she walked that one back with the help of some Benjamins.

I last saw Cohen in October of 2023 when I interviewed him on stage at Cooper Union as part of an anti-Trump conference sponsored by the *New Republic,* where I had first been published forty-three years earlier by the great Michael Kinsley, another major figure in my life. On stage, Cohen reamed Trump but refused to talk about his coming testimony in either the civil or criminal cases. This suggested to me that he might be a more disciplined witness than some people expected.

And he was.

When Cohen quietly took the stand, thinner than he was a decade ago but still in the Trump Organization Paul Stuart uniform, he almost sat down before taking the oath. But as he raised his right hand and pledged to tell "the truth," he seemed to me to mean it. Whether it would turn out to be "the whole truth and nothing but the truth" remained to be seen. My guess was that, even now, he would lie on a few small things but not flagrantly enough to wreck the prosecution's case.

I also thought that certain details of his story would help him, especially the fact that he never cut a deal with the government to testify against the president.

From the start, Cohen was all low-key "Yes, ma'am" and "No, ma'am" with prosecutor Susan Hoffinger, who led him through a by-the-book, uninspired but competent enough direct examination. It's clear we are going to spend time with a very different Michael Cohen than the over-caffeinated person we see on cable TV, hear on podcasts, and read on social media.

Cohen grew up in Lawrence, Long Island, one of the "Five Towns," long an area of striving middle-class Jewish families. In one of his books, he describes himself as a sleep-deprived atheist who stole from his parents' liquor cabinet to calm himself down. His father was a Holocaust survivor who became a doctor in a family of doctors and lawyers. Cohen hoped to work on Wall Street, but his grandmother wanted him to become a lawyer, and after attending American University, he took her advice.

As a young attorney in private practice, Cohen bought a 50 percent interest in a taxi medallion company (his wife's family was in the business), and he made lucrative real estate investments. After helping the Trump family oust a condo board, he came into contact with the man himself and began to worship him.

Cohen loved working for Trump for most of the ten years he spent at the company. He was executive VP and special counsel, reporting directly to Trump from an office just down the hall. With a bonus, he made $525,000 a year.

Cohen recounted how happy he was to win Trump's praise by paying the vendors of the failed Trump University—a scam that ripped off struggling people—twenty cents on the dollar. He said his job was to help Trump with "whatever concerned him, whatever *he* wanted," from arbitration at the Miss Universe pageant to dealing with insurers when the fresco in Trump's bathroom was damaged in a flood.

He and Trump talked several times a day, either in person or on the phone, in part because Trump didn't use email or texts. "Too many people have gone down as a direct result of having emails," he quoted Trump as saying.

The MO at the Trump Organization was consistent: "When he would task you with something, [Trump] would say, 'Keep me informed about what's going on,'" which meant "you would report straight back." Trump needed constant "updates," a word Cohen used almost as a talisman of incrimination.

Cohen admitted to being a bully for Trump. "The only thing on my mind was to accomplish the task, to make him happy."

These self-abasing portions of his testimony made the former fixer seem like a pathetic, needy stooge. Still, they were important to hear because they conveyed the core of the relationship that's at the core of this case.

Cohen testified that, in 2011, he told Trump that he was the choice of 6 percent of Americans for president and should consider running. He created a site, TrumpShouldRun.com, as "further proof of name recognition."

Six percent! If it had stayed at that level we could have avoided this long national nightmare.

Trump didn't want to run in 2012. He had several large real estate projects underway and a contract for another season of *The Apprentice*. "You don't leave Hollywood, Hollywood leaves you," he explained.

In 2015, Cohen helped with the down-the-escalator announcement of Trump's presidential candidacy at Trump Tower and was part of the inner circle, though never officially on the campaign staff. He later claimed to have ordered the first MAGA caps, which were mostly made—big surprise—in Vietnam.

"Just be prepared," Trump told him before the announcement, according to Cohen's testimony. "There's gonna be a lot of women coming forward."

This reminded me of what Bill Clinton said to his people in Arkansas in 1991. They were always on the lookout for what were then called "bimbo eruptions" but didn't pay to prevent them. I guess I should check that one with Mike Isikoff.

One thing I know Clinton didn't do was make up shit out of whole cloth about Paul Tsongas, Bob Kerrey, George Bush, or Bob Dole.

Cohen recounted some of the tabloid lies about Trump's rivals that Trump had gleefully embraced: Hillary Clinton's brain injury (complete with a super-unflattering photo), Ted Cruz's father conspiring with Lee Harvey Oswald, Marco Rubio hanging out at a pool with buff men on a supposed drug binge, and more.

When Cohen would see an AMI cover trashing one of his boss's opponents with lies, he "immediately showed it to Mr. Trump so he knew David [Pecker] was loyal, on board, and doing what he said he would do." Trump's reaction: "That's fantastic! That's unbelievable!"

My reaction: That's awful! That's disgusting! Imagine any other president signing off on that kind of thing—or senators of an earlier era kissing up to someone who has slimed them this way.

Do Rubio and Cruz and the rest of them have any pride? Any self-respect? The questions answer themselves.

Cohen said he told Trump about all of his dealing with David Pecker "so he knows David is going to do exactly what he said he would. And for credit." Always the "credit" from the boss for the bully bootlicker.

When Cohen told Trump that Karen McDougal was shopping a dangerous story, his first response wasn't concern but braggadocio: "She's really beautiful."

Here, the trial descended into further authentication of documents we have mostly seen. Cohen's texts with Keith Schiller, Trump's bodyguard, are important because they show Schiller connecting him to Trump to report "the updates I received on the Karen McDougal matter." With this slower, more precise explanation, the puzzle pieces of the prosecution's case began fitting together.

SECRETLY TAPING TRUMP

All the texts and other back-and-forth about McDougal didn't interest me much. What caught my attention was the timing: Instead of concentrating on his campaign or—God forbid—preparing to be president, the Republican nominee was still knee-deep in his native habitat, tabloid muck. And he would continue to wallow in it as president-elect, president, and former president. There's a reason this is called the Trumpiest of the Trump trials.

But the silencing of McDougal is important in this trial because of the tape, which Cohen says he recorded on the Voice Memos app on his iPhone in his pocket. The motive for making this important recording is murky and will no doubt be exploited by the defense. I'm not convinced by Cohen's story that he hit record to prove to Pecker that Trump would eventually pay him back. But the tape is nonetheless incriminating.

When the bombshell tape was finally played for the jury, the first voice you hear is Cohen saying, "I need to open up a company for the transfer of all of that info regarding our friend David [Pecker]" and "I've spoken to [Trump Organization CFO] Allen Weisselberg about how to set the whole thing up." The jury had first heard the tape weeks ago, when it was authenticated, but this time, Cohen unpacked every line.

We hear Trump say from a distance, "So what do we got to pay for this? 150?" If that wasn't harmful enough, the man who would soon be elected the forty-fifth president of the United States added: "Pay with cash." Then, we hear Cohen quickly explain the need to use a company (instead of cash) for the payments.

"Pay with cash" reminds me of Richard Nixon saying on the White House tapes, "No problem, we could get the money" to pay Watergate burglars for their silence.

The defense has wasted huge amounts of time trying to raise suspicions about how the tape cuts out at the end—and will do so again on cross.

In earlier testimony, the prosecution used extensive phone records to show that this was no big deal, hardly evidence of the recording being doctored. We learned that the abrupt cutoff happened because another call came in on Cohen's phone.

On the stand, backed by phone records, Cohen convincingly testified that the incoming call was from the branch manager of one of the banks he used for unrelated purposes.

After the secretly taped meeting, Cohen and Weisselberg met in Weisselberg's office to discuss how to launder the money. Weisselberg said it could not be sent to McDougal through a Trump Organization entity. That's when they came up with creating a shell corporation, eventually renamed "Essential Consultants LLC."

LOCKER ROOM TALK

Cohen was in London on vacation with his family when the *Access Hollywood* story broke. He quickly jumped into damage control. We learned for the first time that Trump said it was Melania Trump who came up with the effective spin that Trump's banter with the show's Billy Bush about grabbing "women by the pussy" was "just locker room talk." Whether or not Melania is a political genius, this line—and the press's willingness to let the debate shift back to Hillary's emails—essentially saved the Trump campaign.

Oh, another thing saved it, too: making sure Stormy Daniels's story did not come out before the election. When Dylan Howard of AMI told Cohen that Daniels was again peddling her story, Cohen understood that would be "catastrophic—horrible for the campaign."

"I immediately went to see Trump," he testified. "I asked him if he knew who she was. He said he did."

Cohen reminded his boss that in 2011, he had worked with Daniels's lawyer to suppress the story when it appeared on the tabloid website dirty.com. He told him he could bury it again.

"Absolutely. Do it, take care of it," Trump said, according to Cohen. "He said he was playing golf with 'Big Ben' Roethlisberger, a famous football player, and they had met Stormy Daniels and others." Referring to himself in the third person, Trump said Daniels "liked Trump, and women prefer Trump over Big Ben."

Trump, as usual, wanted it both ways: he was a bigger stud than the Steelers quarterback but didn't have sex with her.

So far, Cohen's testimony has struck me as fully believable. I can't think of one portion of it that feels made up.

On October 10, 2016, just three days after the *Access Hollywood* story broke, Cohen spoke to Davidson about purchasing Daniels's life rights and told Trump about it. "That's what I always did—keep him abreast of everything."

"Trump was really angry with me," Cohen said.

"I thought you had this [Stormy Daniels] under control," Trump raged. "I thought you took care of this!" After all, he had handled the story when it was briefly posted on dirty.com five years earlier. "Just take care of it!"

Trump went on, in a line that goes directly to his motive: "This is a disaster, a total disaster. Women will hate me. Guys, they think it's cool [sex with a porn star], but this is going to be a disaster for the campaign."

At the time, Cohen said, Trump was polling very poorly with women. This, coupled with *Access Hollywood*, spelled real trouble. Trump told Cohen again, "Get control over it."

Trump instructed him to work with Pecker to secure Daniels's life rights: "Just get past the election," he told Cohen. "If I win, it'll have no relevance when I'm president. And if I lose, I don't really care."

DUMPING MELANIA

Cohen brought up Melania with Trump, wondering, "How's this gonna go upstairs?" (in the Trump Tower apartment). "He goes, 'Don't worry. How long do you think I'll be on the market for? Not long.'" Cohen—like Pecker and even Hope Hicks—testified, "He wasn't thinking about Melania. It was all about the campaign."

"He wasn't thinking about Melania" is a critical prosecution point in a case about election interference. But Trump *was* thinking ahead to possibly ditching wife number three for someone "better" the fourth time around, soon to be available "on the market."

This is Trump at his core and something far beyond Cohen's powers of imagination to make up.

For the first time in the trial, jurors shed their poker faces in favor of some movement in their chairs and maybe even a little emotion. They were, at least metaphorically, on the edges of their seats.

I tried to "think in time" about it. Imagine Jack Valenti or George Stephanopoulos or Reggie Love (not that I'm comparing these close presidential aides to Michael Cohen) testifying on the eve of the convention that their boss wanted to divorce Lady Bird Johnson, Hillary Clinton, or Michelle Obama in favor of hot new wife number four?

Might there be a headline or two about it? Nowadays, there aren't.

COHEN DETAILS THE DEAL

This case is about sex and lies but also non-disclosure agreements and home equity loans.

Susan Hoffinger drew out Cohen on the NDA with Daniels and the frenzied negotiations around it. She produced documents with the key figure in the case—$130,000—and the staggering $1 million Daniels would owe Trump for every time she mentioned their fling. It was Cohen's idea to have punitive damages in the deal, and, once again, Cohen told Trump about it to get credit with him.

With the election approaching, Keith Davidson was worried about losing his leverage. So he set a deadline of October 14 for completing the deal, but Cohen blew right through it, bending to Trump's desire to get past Election Day (November 8), after which Trump would no longer care whether the story came out. That way, Trump could save $130,000. Thanks to exhibits of books authored by Trump with chapter headings like "Penny-Pincher," the jury needed no convincing that the self-described billionaire would do what he could to save $130,000.

Given the post–*Access Hollywood* political climate, Trump wanted the money paid—just not by him.

That's when Davidson, representing an antsy Daniels, turned the screws on Cohen. According to Cohen's testimony, Davidson didn't mention the looming *Slate* article, but he did hint that the *Daily Mail*—which often pays for stories—was interested.

Right before lunch, Hoffinger missed an opportunity. "I tried to push it past the upcoming election," Cohen testified. "I was following directions."

My row of courtroom spectators was dismayed that Hoffinger didn't immediately ask, "Whose directions?" Cohen has done a good job on the stand tying everything to Trump, but the more examples of direct contact on the hush money, the better. We all hoped she would return to this question in the afternoon, but she didn't.

Julie Blackman, a top jury consultant and friend from Montclair who was in the courtroom for the day, explained that good direct examination should be like a symphony, where you tell a story—usually in chronological order to make it compelling. The soft music is the often-familiar interplay of the voices. Then, on critical points, you should "reach a crescendo" that the jury remembers.

Hoffinger wasn't doing any of that, perhaps because of her background as a defense attorney whose clients, if they testify at all, do so only grudgingly. It was a missed opportunity.

After lunch, Cohen testified that in late October, he spoke with Trump again about the payment to Daniels. "[Trump] stated to me that he had spoken to some friends, some individuals, very smart people, and that: It's [only] $130,000. Just pay it. There is no reason to keep this thing out there. So do it. And he expressed to me: Just do it. Go meet up with Allen Weisselberg and figure this whole thing out." So Cohen went to Weisselberg's office to figure out how to pay for and hide the transaction.

Cash, Trump's suggestion, was much too risky, and schemes involving a high-end golf club membership and even a bar mitzvah were impractical. Weisselberg said he had grandchildren and bills and couldn't pay himself. So he fobbed the whole thing off on Cohen, who said he'd pay for it.

"Don't worry about it," Cohen quoted Weisselberg. "I'll make sure you get paid back."

I thought I saw a juror give a "Where's Weisselberg?" look.

I was sitting with my new friend Norm Eisen, the canny and ebullient legal analyst and former ambassador to the Czech Republic, and Julie Blackman, who comforted me by saying that based on a few hours in the courtroom and forty years of experience, she didn't spot any "rogue jurors," including one that Norm and I had suspected. And she told me that in the hundreds of cases she has been involved in, Senator Bob Menendez's trial in 2017 was one of only about fifteen that ended in a hung jury. "They are actually rare," she said, as are sequestered juries, which have gone out of fashion in most parts of the country, including New York.

Hung juries are rare. Now that was something that might help me sleep better.

Under Hoffinger's questioning, Cohen's narrative of the scheme continued: On October 14, three weeks before the election, he told Trump he was moving forward to fund the deal. What he didn't tell him or others was that he was doing it by tapping his HELOC—home equity line of credit. He couldn't just take it out of the bank because of his wife. "The CEO of the household would ask me [about it], and I clearly could not tell her. So I elected to use the HELOC." He figured: "When I got money back from Mr. Trump, I would deposit it, and nobody would be the wiser." I made a mental note that Cohen was still married.

The next day, Davidson told Cohen, "We gotta get this done. She's going to the *Daily Mail*." Apparently *Slate* was no longer in contention. Cohen made one final effort to get Pecker to make the payment. Pecker's response: "Not a chance."

Then Cohen testified that he called Trump again before he wired his own money to Davidson: "I wanted to make sure that once again, he approved it." Trump wanted it done "to assure it didn't appear in the *Daily Mail* or somewhere else." Cohen testified: "Everything required Mr. Trump's sign-off. On top of that, I wanted the money back."

Cohen repeated his "taking credit" point several times because he knew it was necessary to establish the constant connection to Trump—especially on the money for Daniels—that is essential to a conviction.

The jury will have to consider whether hearing updates are enough to convict. I'm wondering if the prosecution will return to the hit man analogy in its closing argument. To me, it's like the hit man who tells the underboss, "We know what street he lives on." Then later: "We know his route to work." When the hit man completes his assignment, is the mob boss liable? Yep.

On October 18, Cohen said he reported to Trump that "this matter is now completely locked down and under control." He told Trump that the documents had all been finalized, though not yet signed. He updated him with more details on October 24 and October 28.

On November 4, four days before the election, the *Wall Street Journal* ran a story with the headline, "National Enquirer Shielded Donald Trump From Playboy Model's Accusation." The story described how catch-and-kill arrangements with celebrities worked. Trump's affair with McDougal was not confirmed, and Daniels was mentioned only in passing.

Cohen called Davidson to ensure that McDougal and Daniels "didn't go rogue." He was angry at Davidson. "I expected he would have this under control," Cohen testified. "I wanted to make sure that Mr. Trump was safe."

Davidson and Daniels sent a denial to the *Journal* to "appease me" and "more important, Mr. Trump." Cohen then called Trump, which, like all calls between them, is confirmed by phone records, though the content is not. "I told him exactly who I had spoken to," Cohen testified, "I had Dylan Howard on board and [said] we will do anything in our power to protect" him.

Cohen testified that "Trump was angry . . . It was another story that could impact the campaign in terms of women." But after Cohen and Hicks worked overtime refuting it, they were pleased to learn that only six news organizations had picked up on the *Wall Street Journal* story.

In seeking credit from Trump for his great spinning, Cohen clearly didn't understand that most news outlets are wary of late hits in a campaign, although the one that week about reopening the investigation into Hillary's emails from FBI Director James Comey is obviously a huge and tragic exception.

The bottom line on the most disastrous election in American history? Trump and his minions lied their way to victory.

"ABOUT MY EGO"

When the trial resumed after a break, we heard about Cohen and Trump in the days following the election. Davidson testified that Cohen was bitterly disappointed at not getting a big job like chief of staff or attorney general. This was important because it might give the defense a motive for Cohen to lie.

Cohen said he was disappointed he didn't get the chief of staff job but admitted that he wasn't qualified for it and "didn't believe the role was right for me," though he wanted to be considered. He said, "It was more about my ego." With his new, low-key style on the stand, it was almost—*almost*—possible to believe his ego was now in a little better check.

Cohen pitched another role for himself—"Personal Attorney to the President"—and Trump gave it to him.

This title has never existed before, for any president. The personal attorneys of American presidents have been, without exception, prominent members of the bar already associated with major law firms. But Cohen loved the title and it had the added benefit of allowing him to stay in New York with his family, which had no interest in moving to Washington.

Cohen described his plan to "monetize" his connection to Trump. Selling access is a big business, and word of Cohen's close ties to Trump got around. "You've been here ten minutes; he's been here ten years," Cohen claimed Trump said to his first chief of staff, Reince Priebus, about Cohen. In Washington, that ten-year relationship with the incoming president was convertible to cash.

Cohen said he didn't discuss pay with Trump because "I didn't expect to be compensated." This sounded strange but became clear the next day when he explained how much money he was making selling access. He didn't even have to lobby—just peddle a little influence.

In the meantime, Cohen expected a big bonus for taking care of Trump's dicey personal situations. He didn't get one. When Rhona Graff, Trump's long-time assistant, distributed bonus checks in Christmas cards, Cohen said he did a double take. Trump had cut his bonus by two-thirds—from $150,000 to $50,000.

This struck me as one of the stupidest things Donald Trump ever did, which is saying something. If he had properly rewarded his fixer for doing his dirty work for him, none of this would have happened. But Trump couldn't admit to himself—then or now—that he had anything to cover up, and he blamed the guy who kept reminding him of the pickle he was in.

Cohen described himself as "beyond angry" about being shorted on his bonus. "I was truly insulted. Hurt. It made no sense after all I had gone through."

Cohen expressed to Weisselberg "how truly pissed off and angry I was." Cohen noted that "I used quite a few expletives." He told Weisselberg, "You didn't lay out money. I did."

Now, we were getting even closer to the crime and the cover-up.

"Take it easy," Cohen said Weisselberg told him. "You know that Mr. Trump loves you. Go enjoy vacation. Relax."

Cohen thought his anger had an impact "given all the things I'd resolved."

Trump called him right after New Year's from Florida. "Don't worry about that other thing," he told him in his usual mobster code, which has helped keep him out of trouble over the years. Trump said he had spoken to Weisselberg and "I'm gonna take care of you when I get back."

The smoking gun scheme that Weisselberg, with Trump's approval, developed is right there in the authenticated handwriting, as we have seen since early in the trial. The bank statement from First Republic, which Cohen used to set up the shell company, went up on the video screen again.

On the left side of the page, jurors can see, in Weisselberg's hand, $130,000. Then he writes "grossed up" to $260,000 to save Cohen on taxes and ends up with $420,000, which included restoring $60,000 of Cohen's bonus, reimbursement for fees and expenses, and $50,000 to pay a tech company called Red Finch that used algorithms to rig the results of a CNBC survey of popular business leaders.

Cohen thought he would get the $420,000 in one lump sum but would soon learn otherwise. He testified that at a three-way meeting in Trump's office shortly before the president-elect left for his inauguration, Weisselberg told Cohen that he would be paid in monthly installments of $35,000 so that it looked like legal services rendered. Cohen said he later made up fake invoices to make the "retainer agreement" that never existed on paper look legit.

At the Trump Tower meeting, Trump, according to Cohen, approved the hush money arrangement and said of his impending move to Washington: "This is gonna be one heck of a ride."

I tried to think of an historical parallel to an incoming president arranging to pay off his mistress shortly before taking the oath. The only ones that occurred to me were Franklin D. Roosevelt's arranging for his old (and future) mistress, Lucy Mercer Rutherfurd, to have a car and driver and seat at his 1933 inaugural, and John F. Kennedy on the night of his 1961 inauguration going upstairs with actress Angie Dickinson at a Georgetown after-party.

Would they and other cheating presidents have been capable of using illegal subterfuge to cover up their affairs? Yes. Would they have faced severe consequences if their reckless activities had been exposed? Without question.

TOADIES

Until now, Donald Trump has been trapped almost alone inside the decrepit courthouse. When Trump wasn't shivering, as he claimed, he napped—or maybe he shivered and napped at the same time. Or, more likely, he just napped, because according to a legal reporter who brought a thermometer, it hadn't been chilly in the courtroom in three weeks and was currently a comfortable 72 to 74 degrees. That left Trump's much-repeated "icebox" line just another lie.

One day, I sat just behind the row for reserved guests of the defendant, and all the seats were empty except the one occupied by Boris Epshteyn, the Moscow-born Trump attorney who faces indictment in Arizona for masterminding the fake electors plot. That was embarrassing, so Eric Trump and his wife Lara, who now runs the Republican National Committee like it's a family business; incompetent former Trump attorney Alina Habba; impeached-but-not-removed Texas attorney general Ken Paxton; and a few other supporters started coming to 100 Centre Street.

Then the GOP clown car pulled up and disgorged a pathetic and dangerous collection of flunky politicians assigned to keep "President Trump" company.

Sometime last week, Trump realized that if he wanted to avoid being jailed for contempt, he needed surrogates to violate his gag order for him. Senator J. D. Vance, the Ohio Republican, who, before he got high on his ambition, derided Trump as "cultural heroin," figured that his new surrogate father (see *Hillbilly Elegy* for how Trump fits this twisted role in his life) was "a little bit lonely" and he flew in.

Vance's visit kicked off a scramble to audition for the role that nearly got Mike Pence hung. By Tuesday, I spotted North Dakota governor Doug Burgum, Florida representative Byron Donalds, and over-caffeinated entrepreneur Vivek Ramaswamy, sporting his patented lean-and-hungry look. Vivek seemed to be looking down and taking notes as if he and he alone could crack the case and mount a plausible defense for Trump. But when I sat directly behind him in the afternoon, I could see that he and others in Trump's entourage were actually peering at their phones. For some reason I don't understand, guests—but not the defendant or reporters—are allowed to do so.

Beyond the VP wannabes, all the toadies showing up in court were also auditioning for a different role: the one originally played by Michael Cohen. Like Cohen, they want "credit" for prostrating themselves before the would-be dictator.

Standing in line, I had a great convo with Chris Hayes, the MSNBC anchor, and Harry Litman, the law professor and legal commentator, about this crowd and power.

Chris pointed out that high-level Trumpsters enjoy denouncing Democrats as communists, but they are the real latter-day Marxists. Back in the day, those lefties argued that liberal democratic institutions are just a cover for elites to use their power to exploit the people. Now this worldview has infected the right; J. D. Vance and his ilk have no ideology but power.

I like to think of them as Bolsheviks in the vanguard of the MAGAteriat, preparing, with the help of former KGB officer Vladimir Putin, to subvert the "Deep State" (i.e., Congress, the judiciary, the bureaucracy) once Trump is reelected. Steve Bannon cops to something similar on his podcast.

The presence of House Speaker Mike Johnson outside the courthouse today has drawn criticism, but most of it involves his almost comical hypocrisy—a guy who says a literal interpretation of the Bible guides his every decision staunchly defending a con man (tenth commandment) who covets not just his neighbor's wife but a porn star and *Playboy* Playmate (ninth commandment).

This is garden-variety GOP behavior. What's much scarier is seeing Johnson, third in line to the presidency, traveling to New York and using his office to attack the integrity of the courts. This is a form of constitutional obstruction of justice that's straight from the playbook of authoritarians all over the world: trash impartial judges, then replace them with Aileen Cannon types, who only answer, as Cohen once did, to the Dear Leader.

For all its faults, the American judicial system has been the jewel in our constitutional crown for 235 years. Now, even the pretense of honoring the rule of law is gone for the kowtowing, apple-polishing, bootlicking suck-ups gathered in their red ties outside 100 Centre Street in Lower Manhattan.

"IN ORDER TO PROTECT MR. TRUMP"

With Cohen back on the stand and Trump's cronies in their seats, we learned that three weeks after the inauguration, Cohen visited Trump *in the Oval Office* and discussed his criminal reimbursement. "He said, 'I can get a check [right now].' I said, 'No, I'm OK,'" Cohen recounted. "He said all right, just make sure you deal with Allen."

That was incriminating, but otherwise the testimony had begun to get boring, and mercifully, the trial moved on to pre-butting the Trump team's argument that Cohen was indeed doing legal work for Trump. All told, Cohen testified, he did "less than ten" hours of legal work for Trump in all of 2017. "Did the $420,000 have anything to do with that minimal work?" Hoffinger asked. "No," Cohen replied.

Hoffinger turned to an important point. Cohen's claim that he took no money for being "Personal Lawyer for Donald Trump" seemed to stretch credulity. Why hadn't he?

It turned out that five corporate clients wanting access to or favors from President Trump paid him $4 million in consulting fees. Plus, he snagged another half a million just for allowing his name to be on the letterhead of Patton Boggs, a powerful law firm specializing in lobbying.

Charlie Peters once wrote a book called *How Washington Really Works*. Now we know.

When asked one more time why he had lied about Stormy Daniels and encouraged Keith Davidson to do so as well, Cohen replied:

"In order to protect Mr. Trump."

To me, that is an all-purpose explanation for everything bad Michael Cohen did before 2018. And it lands.

Amid this, Cohen testified about what he described as "the worst day of my life"—when, in 2018, the FBI knocked on his door at 7 AM and seized from multiple residences his cell phones, computers, tax books, and other documents.

With a small catch in his throat, Cohen said that he was frightened.

Trump called to say, "Don't worry. I'm the president. There's nothing here. Stay tough. Everything's going to be fine. You're going to be OK."

That was the last time Donald Trump and Michael Cohen ever spoke. In court, when he's awake, Trump often glares at Cohen, who never seems to glance in his direction.

"I MADE A DECISION NOT TO LIE ANY MORE"

When court recessed for a break, I was close enough to glimpse Cohen just after he walked through a side door. When he thought no one could see him, he heaved a huge sigh as if badly wrung out.

After the break, we heard the story of Robert Costello, a sleazy lawyer enlisted by his close friend Rudy Giuliani to keep Cohen from flipping. Trump had his eyes closed, but mine were wide open for this cloak-and-dagger testimony.

Costello was presumptuous in assuming that Cohen would hire him as his lawyer and partial to platitudes aimed at keeping Cohen in the fold: "Sleep well tonight, you have friends in high places."

Cohen described his decision to flip as personal and connected to his family. "I decided it was about time to listen to them—to my wife, my daughter, my son, and my country." He added: "I made a decision not to lie anymore."

In August 2018, Cohen had pleaded guilty to several crimes, including five counts of tax evasion, false statements to a financial institution, and one count of violating campaign finance laws. Cohen owed $1.4 million in back taxes and paid two $50,000 fines—one for crimes related to paying off Stormy Daniels and one for campaign finance violations.

For complex legal reasons, the full details of Cohen's plea deal were not explained to the jury, which was obliquely told that campaign finance violations were among his crimes but that this fact could not be considered by them in assessing Trump's guilt.

Jurors did see, for the second time, Trump's old tweet on the video screen: "Anyone looking for a good lawyer I would strongly recommend you not to retain Michael Cohen."

As Hoffinger ended her direct examination of Cohen, it seemed to me that it had gone reasonably well. Cohen had stayed cool and rational throughout.

5/16/24
COHEN ON CROSS: THE CLIMAX

The cross-examination of Michael Cohen is being billed as the central moment in this trial—and it will be. If Trump's defense attorneys are going to destroy Cohen's credibility so he looks like a liar bent on revenge, they must do it now. It's Trump's only chance to win.

Todd Blanche seems from afar to be a nice, smart guy. But his inexperience shows in his meandering cross.

As a prosecutor, you usually have a lot of facts on your side, making cross of defense witnesses easier. As a defense attorney, you usually have to not just ding the key witnesses but blow them up. It isn't easy. In courtrooms across the country, defendants are convicted every day based on the testimony of liars and sometimes killers who have turned state's evidence and still managed to keep it together under cross.

Right from the top, Blanche tried a gambit that a more seasoned defense attorney would have known was silly: "On April 23, you went on TikTok and called me a lying little shit, didn't you?"

Cohen replied: "Sounds like something I would say."

A courtroom artist sitting next to me, Isabelle Brourman, kept score of the three other times in one morning that Cohen would use "Sounds like something I would say." I know my kids will want to give me the T-shirt.

The judge rebuked Blanche for making his cross about *him*, so Blanche resumed cataloging Cohen's insults of Trump, to little effect. The jury was unsurprised to learn that Cohen believed in vengeance just as much as Trump and that he repeatedly trashed Trump on his podcast. It got a little dicey for Cohen when Blanche got Cohen to concede that he was leaking things about the prosecution's strategy when he went on Don Lemon and other cable shows. After long stretches of his insults airing in court, Cohen finally said: "I do have a First Amendment right to speak." In this, of course, he was echoing Trump.

I know Blanche's job is to throw everything against the wall and see what sticks. But this part of his attack didn't seem to be working. He was almost wasting the time of the jury, which was no doubt concluding that these two, Trump and Cohen, deserve each other.

Having said that, I enjoyed some of Cohen's barbs, all of which were repeated in Trump's presence, though who knows if he was awake for them. "You referred to President Trump as a dictator douche bag," Blanche said. Duly noted.

I also liked Cohen's newer tweets featuring Trump in an orange jumpsuit, and I'm tempted to buy some of Cohen's merch (e.g., a coffee mug reading "Send him to the big house, not the White House"). These are plenty childish but seem mild next to Trump's toilet humor.

Blanche asked about the years when Cohen was "in the fold" and "obsessed" with Trump. Cohen said, "I admired him tremendously" and admitted, "At that time, I was knee-deep into the cult of Donald Trump."

After quoting some of Cohen's slobbering lines about Trump, Blanche said, "And you were telling the truth [then], right?" Cohen said yes. It was as if Blanche wanted his client, Trump, to see how he got Cohen to admit that he was telling the truth about the greatness of his old boss.

And Blanche reminded Trump's sycophantic guests in the first two rows of the courtroom just how far their loyalty must go. You said you "would take a bullet for the president?" Blanche asked. "I did say that, yes," Cohen replied.

Finally, Blanche got to Cohen's lying to authorities, which is his best shot at discrediting him. After the FBI raid, Cohen met with federal prosecutors. Did he lie about the Trump Tower Moscow project?

"The information I gave to them was inaccurate. I don't know if I'd characterize it as a lie," he said, about misstating the number of times he and Trump spoke about investing in Moscow. Moments later, he testified, "Sure, I'll say it's a lie."

Blanche elicited that Cohen had made $3.4 million from two books, one titled *Revenge*. This scuffed Cohen, but only a bit. Blanche lost the thread when he returned to the insults.

On his first *Mea Culpa* podcast—the name was chosen in part because of the initials "MC"—Cohen called Trump a "boorish cartoon misogynist." He kept the animation theme with one of my personal favorites: "Cheeto-dusted cartoon villain."

I glanced at Trump. No orange crumbs on his blue suit.

Blanche kept going with the *Mea Culpa* trash talk: "President Trump needs to wear handcuffs and to do the perp walk." Then: "I truly fucking hope this man ends up in prison."

These jibes were getting a little tiresome. I found myself relieved that Blanche spared us "Baron von ShitzInPants."

That may have been Blanche's only smart move of the day, but he'll have all day Thursday and beyond to bring up his game and improve Trump's defense.

5/17/24
MATT GAETZ'S WIDOW'S PEAK

For the first seventeen days of the trial, I wore the same blue jacket with the nice purple lining over the inside breast pockets. Today, I broke my superstition and accidentally wore another coat. The consequences for the prosecution were devastating.

Before everything went to hell, Thursday started propitiously enough. Recalling that all of the sycophantic wannabe VPs on Tuesday had worn the same white shirt, red tie, and blue suit as their Dear Leader, I made a point of checking out who Trump took with him to court today and how they were dressed. Lauren Boebert and Matt Gaetz were in the courtroom, on their best behavior, if that concept has any meaning for them. They were not wearing red ties, signaling that they were not running for vice president.

Unfortunately, reporters have no way to interact with Trump's guests. They enter and exit down the center aisle with their monarch while the rest of us must cool our heels in "lockdown" inside the courtroom. During lunch and breaks, Trump and his entourage retreat to private but still dingy rooms, where 1970s-era fluorescent lights illuminate Gaetz's Eddie Munster widow's peak.

I had no interest in talking to Boebert or Gaetz, whose Truth Social post "LFG Juror #2!" ("Let's Fucking Go!") was the beginning and end of his knowledge of the case, though I would have liked to have a word with Jeffrey Clark, who slipped out of the back row of the courtroom before I could reach him.

On some days, the courthouse seems like a convention of cable news anchors. In recent weeks, I've run into MSNBC colleagues Chris Hayes, Chris Jansing, Rachel Maddow, Ari Melber, Andrea Mitchell, Lawrence O'Donnell, Joy Reid, and Lisa Rubin, as well as Kaitlan Collins, Anderson Cooper, and Jake Tapper from CNN. Most borrowed a courtroom pass for half a day.

Beyond sitting with a pleasant representative of Steve Bannon's website one day, the closest I've come to reaching across the divide—like British and German troops exchanging small gifts in no-man's-land between trenches at Christmas in Belgium in 1914—was when I chatted amiably with Fox News anchor Laura Ingraham in the line for the fifteenth-floor metal detector.*

I took my seat in the courtroom at about 8:45 AM. Right around that time, Gaetz, proud to be a Proud Boy congressman, posted on social media: "Standing back and standing by, Mr. President."

Forty-five minutes later, Todd Blanche resumed his cross-examination of Cohen when he introduced an exhibit that brought Cohen's loud, obnoxious voice into the courtroom—a voice (on his podcast) much at odds with the quiet one we're hearing from the witness stand.

It's hard to know where this is taking the defense. In that sense, it resembles a lot of the lawyering in this case, which ain't great so far.

The two main legal adversaries are both fish out of water and playing roles on a huge stage for which they have little experience. *Prosecutor* Susan Hoffinger is an expert on cross (the specialty of *defense* attorneys) while *defense* Todd Blanche is better on direct (where *prosecutors* can usually elicit friendly testimony backed by voluminous evidence). Whoever does better in the new uncomfortable role will have an advantage.

* In 1996, MSNBC's first year on the air (also the first year of Fox News), the cable network's founder, Andy Lack, created a short-lived discussion format for a dozen young opinionated journalists—including me and Ingraham—inspired by the hit NBC show *Friends*. I was no Ross or Chandler, and Laura was no Rachel or Phoebe, but it was fun for a while.

LYING TO JUDGE PAULEY

Blanche is trying to build a case that Cohen simply has a vendetta against Trump. To do so, he once again read vicious Cohen quotes about his client, who must sit quietly and listen, doze, or read his packet of clips by bootlicking columnists.

We hear Cohen on his podcast say, "Picturing Donald Trump having his mug shot taken fills me with delight." On TikTok, he said he had "mental excitement" about Trump's impending trial. He admitted that he wanted Trump to go through things he went through (his home raided, jail); he called him "Dumbass Donald"; and he said on a podcast from Otisville prison, "Revenge is a dish best served cold."

This all reminded me of Trump's tit for tat with Stormy Daniels. It was hard to see any of it moving the jury beyond amusement and/or disgust.

Blanche scored better by focusing on how often Cohen lied under oath. After cataloging that Cohen had testified seven times under oath before Congress, which led to two guilty pleas, he walked him through a dizzying series of lies he had told in federal court. It was haphazard and lacked the rhythm of a good cross, but it proved effective nonetheless.

With the jury's full attention, Blanche leaned in: "And each time you met with the federal agents, you were told that if you made a false statement, that that was a felony, that was a federal crime. Correct?"

"Yes, sir."

Cohen had testified on direct that he lied to Congress in small ways to protect his boss on the Trump Tower Moscow project, so the added scrutiny today didn't hurt much. Nor did it seem to hurt when he admitted to lying for Trump as part of a "joint defense agreement" crafted by Trump's lawyers. Any lies he may have told on seeking (though not receiving) leniency got lost in the often-confusing back-and-forth.

But the lies were now piling up. Blanche drilled in on the home equity line of credit (HELOC) that Cohen testified he had tapped to pay for the hush money so his wife wouldn't find out. In eliciting testimony about how Cohen's partner in his New York taxi medallion business had flipped on him, Blanche forced Cohen to walk through the specifics of his guilty plea on federal tax evasion and on making a false statement to a financial institution when applying for a HELOC.

Blanche scored heavily by focusing on Cohen's past claims that the guilty plea had been "induced."

"I asked whether you said, 'No,' under oath to Judge Pauley, that nobody had threatened or induced you to plead guilty?" Blanche asked.

"Correct," Cohen said.

"That was a lie?" Blanche pressed.

"That was not true; correct," Cohen said.

Either of Trump's other more experienced defense counsels, Emil Bove or Susan Necheles, would have borne down hard now on lying to the judge. But Blanche was too inexperienced, and he lost momentum with wordy and vague questions before getting to the right ones:

"You say you want the truth to come out that the prosecutors in the Southern District of New York were corrupt and knew it, right?"

"Correct," Cohen replied, who had said on TikTok in April that his case was "the most corrupt prosecution in at least 100 years."

After establishing that Judge Pauley was deceased, Blanche asked:

"Do you believe that Judge Pauley was in on it?"

"I do," Cohen said.

This was a devastating admission—that Cohen believed, as he has said in the past, that the SDNY *and the judge* were "in on it," i.e., corruptly conspiring against him.

If Trump had tapped Bove or Necheles for the big cross, either would have gone to town and pounded away on this "in on it" point.

Blanche settled for "You called the Southern District of New York prosecutors and Judge Pauley fucking animals." This sounded tough, and it followed Trump's instruction never to leave an insult untouched. But it missed Cohen's true vulnerability—not insults but promoting a far-fetched conspiracy involving a federal judge.

But once again, Blanche got sidetracked, this time by developing an elaborate and confusing point that rejected Cohen's view of the difference between "accepting responsibility" and "lying." Did the jury really care about these semantics? Did it help build "reasonable doubt"? I didn't think so.

And it gave Cohen, reeling under Blanche's blows, a chance to fight back. He explained that he felt coerced because federal prosecutors gave him only forty-eight hours to plead guilty or his wife would be included in his taxi medallion tax fraud indictment.

Blanche pressed the argument that Cohen had also lied when he said he took responsibility for the crimes. Cohen retorted: "No, sir . . . I take responsibility, but I did not believe that it was . . . a crime I should have been charged with."

I didn't think Blanche scored much on the refusal of the feds to offer Cohen a cooperation agreement; the jury might just go: "Duh, the Department of Justice was controlled by Trump." And I wasn't sure jurors would care much about Blanche's repetitive claim that Cohen was again lying when he said he never wanted to be White House chief of staff.

I thought Blanche failed to show that Cohen was lying to his daughter about his job prospects when they exchanged emails. And he missed the human element: Many people who fail to get a big promotion or job deny afterward that they ever wanted it. No biggie.

But by this point, Cohen looked dazed. Each time Blanche said, "Well, let me see if I can refresh your recollection," I knew there was trouble ahead for Cohen. He was bearing up without losing his cool, which was critical, but it was hard to gauge the jury's reaction. Over the course of three hours, he had admitted to lying under oath—with the oath repeatedly emphasized—to Congress, federal prosecutors, a federal judge, and on bank paperwork, and acknowledged thinking that prosecutors and the judge were in cahoots to get him. Whoa.

And then, just twenty minutes or so before lunch, Day 18 went from very good to terrific for Donald Trump.

A FOURTEEN-YEAR-OLD PRANK CALLER

Suddenly, Blanche brought up a call Cohen made to Trump on October 24, 2016, two days before Cohen said he moved the hush money from his home

Defense attorney Todd Blanche blisters Michael Cohen on cross-examination (REUTERS/Jane Rosenberg)

equity line of credit to his shell corporation and wired it to Keith Davidson and Stormy Daniels.

Cohen had testified on direct earlier in the week that at 8:02 PM on the twenty-fourth, he called Keith Schiller, Trump's body man, and said he needed to talk to Trump about the Daniels matter.

First, Blanche established that Cohen didn't remember whether Schiller handed the phone to Trump or put the call on speaker; conversations with Trump could happen both ways, Cohen said. Then, he got Cohen to admit that he had not brought up the October 24 call in his grand jury testimony.

After a sidebar conference, it was clear something big was coming but I couldn't figure out what it would be.

Blanche asked Cohen if he remembered "a bunch of ongoing and continuing harassment phone calls" on October 22, 23, and 24.

Cohen—with a blank expression—said he did, but when Blanche asked, "Do you remember that on the twenty-fourth, at around seven o'clock at night, the person who was harassing you forgot to block the number, and you got the number—do you remember that?"

Cohen, blindsided, said no. Blanche produced a text to the number from Cohen, who told the person on the other end that his or her number had been given to the Secret Service to investigate.

The return text read: "It wasn't me, my friend told me to call, I am sorry for this. I won't do it again."

It was clearly from a kid.

Cohen texted back that there had been dozens of harassing calls, that he would continue contacting the Secret Service, and that "If you are a minor, I suggest you notify your parent or guardian."

The person texted back: "I didn't do it, I am fourteen, please don't do this."

Cohen again told the kid to have a parent or guardian contact him. Then he texted Schiller: "Who can I speak to regarding harassing calls to myself and office, the dope forgot to block his call on one of them."

At 8:02, Schiller texted Cohen: "Call me."

Cohen immediately called Schiller, and the call lasts for one minute and thirty-six seconds. The length of the call is highly relevant to the outcome of this whole case.

Blanche reminded Cohen that on Tuesday, he had testified that he called Schiller—not to talk to *him* but to candidate Trump about moving forward on the hush money payments to Stormy Daniels.

At this point, the jurors were looking intently at the witness. Some of the rest of us knew by now that prosecutor Susan Hoffinger had messed up big time by not including these texts about the prank caller when prepping Cohen for her direct examination of him.

By now, Hoffinger knew that she had missed key texts in her prep and that her witness had been blindsided—never a good thing—but she stayed cool and tried to stop Blanche's rhythm with objections. It didn't work.

Blanche had Cohen on the run:

"When you testified on Tuesday that you had a specific recollection that that one-minute-and-thirty-six-second phone call on October twenty-fourth was not with Keith Schiller, that you called Keith Schiller and he passed the phone to President Trump, you finalized the deal with Stormy Daniels and you said, 'We're going to move forward,' and he said, 'Yes,' because you kept him informed all the time . . ."

Blanche spit out his words: "That. Was. A. Lie."

Now Blanche was yelling. "You were actually talking to Mr. Schiller about the fact that you were getting harassing phone calls from a fourteen-year-old, correct?"

Cohen responded feebly: "I always ran everything by the Boss immediately. And in this case, it could have just been saying everything is being taken care of; it's going to get resolved."

A dazed Cohen neglected to point out that the call was long enough for him to talk to both Schiller and Trump, each on different matters.

Blanche bore in: "That was a lie!" he shouted a second time, as if he was inhabiting the role of the triumphant defense attorney in some old movie he half-remembered. "You did not talk to *President Trump* on that night. You talked to *Keith Schiller* about what we just went through. You can admit it!"

"No, sir, I can't," Cohen said, almost meekly. "I am not certain that is accurate."

Then he testified, "Based upon the records that I was able to review, in light of everything that was going on, I believe I also spoke to Mr. President Trump [sic] and told him everything regarding the Stormy Daniels matter was being worked on, and it's going to be resolved."

Now came the best exchange of the trial for Trump's defense team. In what many in the courtroom viewed as a *Perry Mason* moment, Blanche shouted:

"We are not asking for your *belief.* This jury doesn't want to hear what you *think* happened."

Hoffinger objected again and the objection was sustained, but the damage was done.

Blanche then got Cohen to admit that in preparing him to testify, the prosecution had never shown him the texts with Schiller. He left the impression that Cohen testified to things based more on prompting by the prosecution in prep than on his memory.

When the trial broke for lunch, we emerged from the courtroom a little shell-shocked. In the line to the bathroom, I asked retired judge George Grasso, my go-to spectator on this case because of his many years on the bench, how serious a blow had been landed. "Very serious," Judge Grasso said. "For the first time, this planted real doubt."

In the elevator, reporters were talking about the Judge Pauley being "in on it" moment and the fourteen-year-old prank caller. How would the jury react? Cohen's other lies were not about the facts of this case. If he was making this up, how about his other renditions of his conversations with Trump? Would jurors believe them?

Norm Eisen, an ethics lawyer and co-counsel to the House Judiciary Committee during Trump's first impeachment trial, had the best take. The prosecution would try to fix this on redirect. Even if it couldn't, jurors rarely decide based on one exchange, no matter how bad.

I worried that maybe I had been suffering from confirmation bias—only absorbing the material that hurt Trump's case. I resolved to try harder not to let my feelings about Trump color my sense of whether jurors of good faith could have reasonable doubt about his guilt. If the prosecution delivered more blows like that one, they might. That could mean a hung jury or even—yikes!—an acquittal, which would in turn mean Trump getting reelected, thanks to this boneheaded move by Susan Hoffinger.

After lunch and back on the stand, Cohen was forced to reveal more about the way he operated. He had made ninety-six secret recordings on his phone over ten years, many of them of conversations with reporters. Cohen was constantly quoted; Maggie Haberman of the *New York Times* put his name in thirty-eight stories, usually when seeking a response to something related to Trump in the news. Blanche was trying to show that Cohen operated independently of Trump and lied about it, but the line of attack was boring and didn't land.

Blanche tried to poke holes in arguably the most important piece of evidence in the case—Cohen's tape of Trump saying "150" about the $150,000 in hush money that David Pecker wanted reimbursed. The prosecution had damaged if not obliterated the defense team's innuendo and conspiracy theories about the sudden end of the call by producing phone records showing that Cohen hung up—thus ending the tape—to take a call from a banker at Capitol One.

Why did Cohen take the call when he was taping Trump? Cohen testified that he wasn't certain, but he thought the Capitol One representative was calling him back about his being the target of identity theft.

Cohen being Cohen, I'm not sure I believed that. But there had to be some reason he took the call, so I guess that one is plausible. The tape ends at this point so there's no way to know for sure.

Blanche also tried to explain that when Trump used the incriminating word "cash" on the tape, he wasn't talking about actual green bills, just about financing a project without borrowing. This was silly and went nowhere.

At the end of the day, the secret tape of Trump saying "150" and "cash" was very much intact as a key piece of evidence against Trump. So was critical Exhibit 35—Weisselberg (barely mentioned by Blanche all day) scrawling "130,000" and "grossing up" on Cohen's bank statement.

And if there were more contacts between Cohen and Trump that were like the October 24 call—critical conversations that were a figment of Cohen's fervid imagination—where the hell were they? Blanche hadn't produced them. Would he do so on Monday?

After the jury was excused, the defense team tried hard to convince Judge Merchan to allow a possible defense witness, Bradley Smith, former chair of the Federal Election Commission, to testify about why campaign finance laws were not applicable in this case. Merchan said Smith could testify but not offer the jury instructions about interpreting the law. That was *his* job. So, Smith is unlikely to testify. That means, with Trump not taking the stand, the defense won't likely put on any case at all.

There's a cliché about the man who "lies every which way to Sunday"—Sunday being the day for redemption and forgiveness. Has Michael Cohen reached his Sunday with the jury? Will they accept his confession of past sins and buy his redemption? We'll find out soon enough.

I feared that the prosecution had blown it. "That lucky bastard!" I raged at Emily on the phone after court, from a little park near the courthouse. "He's the luckiest guy in the whole wide world!!" Emily talked me off the ledge, reminding me that there was plenty of time in the ninety-six-second call for Michael Cohen to chat with the bodyguard about the fourteen-year old prankster and *then* to tell Trump about the payments to Stormy Daniels.

God, I hope she's right.

5/20/24
MONA LISA JURORS

I knew it would be a weird day in court when I saw that Chuck Zito was in the house. Zito is the Hells Angels hell-raiser and gang leader from HBO's *Oz* who served time in the real world on drug conspiracy charges, attended his friend John Gotti's wake, and punched out Jean-Claude Van Damme—among other qualifications for being in Donald Trump's entourage.

Zito was wearing cool, pointy, blue suede boots. That made me prefer him to Alan Dershowitz, who told the row in front of me during a break that "this is the weakest case I've seen in sixty years of teaching." Sure, Alan.

Trump still hasn't said whether he'll take the stand in his own defense. Nobody who has kept tabs on Trump—or on this trial—believes he will. There's much too much he'd have to answer for.

That doesn't mean there will be no defense. Trump's team still seems obsessed with getting Bradley Smith, the former FEC chair, on the stand.

Before the trial began, Merchan had ruled that Smith—now a law professor—was welcome to appear but he could testify neither that this case involved a "novel" interpretation of campaign finance laws nor about its similarities to the case of John Edwards, a reach into another case that judges routinely reject. Now, Todd Blanche wanted to revisit the issue.

Blanche was practically pleading for the judge to let Smith give the jury his very conservative take on campaign finance laws, which basically comes down to anything less than passing a bag full of cash is kosher.

Merchan properly underscored that *he* was the judge and only *his* instructions on the law would be delivered to jurors. Once Trump's lawyers understood that their witness would not be allowed to bring right-wing legal spin into the courtroom, they scrapped his appearance, and their chances to win a reversal on these grounds—much-touted by conservative TV analysts who have read or heard none of the motions—are slim.

This morning, I was sitting up close on the far right side and had my best view yet of how many jurors were taking notes. Most held identical white legal pads and scribbled things down sparingly, like students who don't want to be overwhelmed by too many notes when studying for the final.

I'd say the jurors have Mona Lisa smiles but that would be inaccurate. They don't smile; they don't frown; they don't give anything away beyond the occasional sigh or eye bulge. For the most part, they're conscientious jurors from central casting.

THE TAXI KING OF NEW YORK

Before long, Blanche resumed his cross of Cohen, which—after a terrific morning last Thursday—had gone downhill when he failed to crack the incriminating recording Cohen had made of Trump with an iPhone in his pocket.

His first line of attack today was to make Cohen out to be a tool of prosecutors. Blanche established that after turning on Trump, Cohen had held about twenty meetings with the DA's office, most recently on May 11. Cohen acknowledged that Daniel Goldman, a former federal prosecutor, helped prep him for his congressional testimony.

If Blanche's aim was to make Cohen seem like the puppet of Democrats, I'm not sure he succeeded. Goldman is now a popular congressman from New York.

Then Blanche returned to one of the key periods in the case—October 2016, when Cohen was completing the hush money deal with Keith Davidson, the attorney who represented Stormy Daniels. Blanche tried to show that Cohen—like Trump—was just too busy in late October to worry about something so minor as Daniels going public and blowing the Trump campaign sky-high.

After all, Cohen was involved in a $7 million real estate deal with his brother; handled the endorsement of Trump by a niece of Martin Luther King Jr.; worked with David Pecker and Marc Kasowitz (a Trump attorney) on an investment in a company called I Payments; and helped Tiffany Trump when she was subjected to a ham-handed extortion attempt. And, of course, there were those prank calls from a fourteen-year-old. How could such a busy aide possibly have time to worry about a ticking time bomb in the form of a free-wheeling porn star?

On redirect, the prosecution will contend none of this activity would have prevented Cohen from *also* keeping Trump updated. But as usual, Cohen was caught lying about some of the details.

In prior testimony, Cohen had, for some reason, described a taxi medallion acquisition proposal as a real estate deal. On the stand, Cohen had to stick to that lie so as not to be accused of lying again, and predictably, Blanche busted him for it.

I wish we'd heard even more details of the wildly profitable and now nearly worthless New York taxi medallion business and the story of the late Evgeny "Gene" Freidman, the flamboyant entrepreneur long known as New York's fabled "Taxi King," who ended up ratting on Cohen's underpayment of taxes. As the surging rideshare industry sent the value of medallions plummeting, Freidman's checks to Cohen bounced, and his marriage was in trouble. Cohen explained the volume of his communication with Freidman during this period as part of his efforts to find Freidman a lawyer and a place to live and to help "bring him and his wife back together."

I was sitting next to Janon Fisher of *Newsday*, who deadpanned: "Michael Cohen, marriage counselor."

Unfortunately, the prosecution didn't prep Cohen to disclose that he also talked to Trump about a few other matters in late October. But it may be that Cohen was telling the truth when he testified that "My recollection is I was speaking [to Trump] about Stormy Daniels because that's what he tasked me with taking care of," Cohen testified.

This didn't look good because October was also when Trump was celebrating the opening of his new Washington hotel in the Old Post Office building, and Cohen had taken an active role in Trump's hotel projects for years. Blanche dinged Cohen in this stretch, but it was not—thank God—another fourteen-year-old prankster moment. The defense seemed out of fresh ways to directly discredit Cohen's testimony about his critical conversations with Trump during this period. Phew.

$42,000 AN HOUR

The cross-examination turned to Red Finch, a mysterious tech company we had heard of but wouldn't get the full story on until redirect. Cohen was friendly with the owner of Red Finch. So when Allen Weisselberg, the Trump Organization CFO, was figuring out what should go into "grossing up" to the $420,000 that was used to compensate Cohen and cover the $130,000 payment to Daniels, Cohen suggested $50,000 should go to compensate Red Finch for helping Trump rig the CNBC poll.

Then Cohen did something stupid and criminal. He covered what he said were Red Finch's expenses by giving the owner $20,000 in a "small brown paper bag" when he came by the office—and pocketed the other $30,000. This made Cohen look like a common thief, though it came in the context of classic Trump narcissism that the jury would soon learn about.

Later, MSNBC's Lawrence O'Donnell—who started his career writing about trials in Boston and comes to court much more often than the other day-tripping cable anchors—made a good point. He said that in closing arguments, the prosecution wasn't likely to let the defense have it both ways: nailing Cohen for stealing from the Trump Organization while simultaneously arguing that the $420,000 that Trump paid Cohen—which included the Red Finch money he stole—was just for "legal expenses."

Blanche thought he was scoring when he said, "In the middle of that conversation [about the cover-up], you lie to Allen Weisselberg about how much you're owed on that [Red Finch] transaction."

Amid Blanche's barrage of questions, I had one for him: So, Todd, did "that conversation" take place or not? I thought your whole argument was that it was a figment of Cohen's imagination.

Cohen testified that while he had never had a retainer agreement with Trump in their eleven years together, he did need some kind of agreement.

"Why would you have had to prepare an agreement to get paid monthly?" Blanche asked.

"To get the $35,000," Cohen replied.

Blanche pressed: "And why would Don Jr. and Eric approve your payment?"

Cohen explained that the kids were trustees of the Trump trust, from which the first two payments to Cohen were drawn.

Don Jr. wouldn't show up in the courtroom until the last day of testimony, but Eric was sitting in the second row on the left for most of the trial, wide awake and in the direct line of sight of several jurors. Aren't some of them wondering why neither son testified on their father's behalf?

Blanche then turned to Cohen's announcement that he would be "Personal Attorney for President Trump," which Cohen printed on business cards and trumpeted on every show from *Hannity* to TMZ.

Cohen had testified on direct that he did only about ten hours of legal work in all of 2017 and billed Trump for none of it. I thought that sounded suspicious at the time, but Blanche inadvertently strengthened it on cross—a boneheaded move that almost certainly came at Trump's urging.

Cohen testified again that he did almost no legal work for Trump in 2017 beyond briefly reviewing Melania's contract with Madame Tussauds and a small handful of other things adding up to only ten or so billable hours. This account was convincing enough (and unimpeached), and it may have left jurors wondering why Trump—a self-described "penny-pincher"—would pay him $420,000 in 2017 for so little work.

Here the defense was essentially doing the prosecution's bidding. If jurors did simple math and divided $420,000 by ten hours of legal work, it would come to $42,000 an hour, about fifty times more than Trump normally pays his lawyers.

Blanche then made it worse for his client. The phony monthly invoices Cohen sent Trump said "for services rendered," but without a retainer agreement, did not preclude him from billing further, especially for the work he did in 2018. Cohen would have been loath to do that, of course, partly because it would have pissed off Trump. But he didn't have to. He was making big money as an influence peddler.

Instead of ignoring that, Blanche, for some reason, walked Cohen through his six corporate clients, who paid him a total of $4 million to do very little real "consulting."

In the scummy world of Washington lobbying, the companies weren't necessarily going to use Cohen to get to Trump on some issue, but they could brag to their boards that they had better access to the very top than their competitors did.

I loved this part of the trial because it offered a peek into how the influence industry works when a new president is elected. Charlie Peters would have appreciated the anthropological look at lobbyists who are paid so much for doing so little.

Trump had introduced Cohen to the CEO of AT&T, which paid him $600,000 in 2017 for what turned out to be only twenty "communications" (mostly emails). Novartis paid him $1.2 million for only six communications. Were jurors thinking that's $200,000 per email? BTA Bank paid Cohen a $150,000-per-month retainer, Kia paid $100,000 per month, and Columbus Nova paid $80,000 per month.

I felt like checking to make sure none of the mutual funds I own have invested in these companies, but I declined to do so after reasoning that the damage this testimony did to the defense was worth any pangs of conscience.

REVENGE IS A DISH BEST SERVED COLD

As Blanche meandered down blind alleys, his client napped, not just occasionally, but much of the time, as he has for weeks. Over the course of Day 20, I used my binoculars more than a dozen times to focus on the video monitor that showed Trump and the lawyers from the front. Each time, Trump had his eyes closed, though I was never sure if he was actually sleeping. Regardless, he was not listening to the cross-examination of Michael Cohen, which the whole world knew was the most important part of his case.

Some of it was helpful to Trump. Blanche brought up the many interviews Cohen did after the Stormy Daniels story broke in 2018 in which he said, as

Cohen told the BBC, that there was "no way [he] would have told Trump about [the hush money] at the time."

He walked Cohen through the April 2018 FBI raid and his meeting a week later with Robert Costello to discuss Costello possibly representing him, which the defense is deciding to make an important part of its case.

While they only met twice, "You were in touch seventy-five times," Blanche said. "You spoke for over nine hours over the course of a few months with Mr. Costello."

I wracked my brain to see what the defense could be driving at with this guy Costello and came up empty.

We learned that last year, a TV studio shot a pilot for a show called *The Fixer* based on Cohen's career, but it hasn't been picked up, and that Cohen is considering a run for Congress because "I got the best name recognition out there."

When Blanche suggested that was because he was exploiting his relationship with Trump, Cohen mildly replied, "My name recognition is because of the journey I've been on."

This was the sad-sack Cohen, in contrast to the histrionic Cohen we heard on a couple of audio clips from his podcast. I'm sure the defense hoped it might provoke an outburst of that frenzied Cohen on the stand, but it never did.

Cohen admitted he had a financial interest in the outcome of the case, but he put a surprising spin on it: "It's better [financially] if he's not [convicted], for me, because it gives me more to talk about in the future."

Of course his preference was clear. When asked about using the line, "Revenge is a dish best served cold," he replied squarely: "I meant it then and now."

Blanche ended strong: "When you lied to Congress, you said you lied out of loyalty." Cohen tried to stall a line of questioning that he knew could be damaging with the jury.

"It's true you will lie out of loyalty, correct?"

"Yes, sir," Cohen replied.

This was a mistake. Cohen should have said something like: No sir, I lied out of loyalty *in the past*.

HAVING IT BOTH WAYS

Susan Hoffinger, the chief of the Manhattan DA's investigation division, began her impressive redirect by straightening out that Cohen didn't lie to Congress in 2019 (when Daniel Goldman helped prepare him) but in 2017 on the Trump Tower Moscow deal.

Then she turned to the elephant in the room—the October 24, 2016, call to Keith Schiller to discuss the fourteen-year-old prankster, the very evidence she had neglected when prepping Cohen for direct. This could be deadly for the prosecution if it were part of a pattern of Cohen talking to Schiller and Trump about matters other than Stormy Daniels. That's why Blanche on cross had focused on the Tiffany Trump extortion plot, the opening of the Trump Hotel in the Old Post Office building, and other things that kept Cohen busy that month, though Cohen convincingly testified that they did not.

Crucially, Blanche had failed to present any evidence challenging Cohen's testimony about the more incriminating call on October 26, two days after the discussion with Schiller of the harassing prankster call. Hoffinger now focused on that October 26 call.

"You testified that you didn't have a specific recollection about talking about other matters . . . But you did have a specific recollection about talking [on October 26) about Stormy Daniels's payoff to Mr. Trump?" Hoffinger asked. "And that is because it was important to you at that time, correct?"

The new, subdued Cohen gave her his patented: "Yes, ma'am."

She continued, with a crisper style than she had earlier: "Is it possible that other matters may have been discussed on those calls, but you are sure that the Stormy Daniels matter was discussed?" Cohen replied, "Yes."

Hoffinger: "Were you pretty busy all the time or just in October?"

Cohen: "I was busy."

Hoffinger: "Were you too busy in October of 2016 to finalize the Stormy Daniels payoff with Mr. Trump?"

Cohen: "No, ma'am."

Hoffinger: "Were you too busy to get his approval to make that payoff?"

Cohen: "No, ma'am."

At that moment, I wished she had explained the prankster episode more directly, but the prosecution turned out to have a card up its sleeve on that one that we would learn about later.

Hoffinger then turned to the critical question of whether Cohen's cover-up agreement with Weisselberg constituted a legal retainer.

Cohen said no, and he explained that he never sent Weisselberg a retainer agreement because Weisselberg told him to send invoices for reimbursement instead.

Hoffinger: "Was the $420,000 payment that you were owed as reimbursement—did that have anything to do with a retainer agreement?" Cohen issued another "No, ma'am" and explained that his work for Trump in 2018 had no connection to the $420,000.

RED FINCH RIGS A DIGITAL POLL

Redirect now moved to the touchy subject of Red Finch and the brown paper bag of cash, which turned out to be a quintessential Trumpy story.

In 2014, CNBC.com launched a self-promotional digital poll to determine who readers thought were the "Top Business Leaders of the 20th Century." Trump "was polling towards the very bottom [of one hundred names], and it upset him," Cohen testified. So Cohen hired a company called Red Finch that used an algorithm that miraculously made Trump rise to number nine. That wasn't good enough for Trump; he thought he should be number one. So he stiffed Red Finch.

He rigged the election, then stiffed his vendors. Sound familiar?

Cohen testified that he knew Red Finch's CEO and felt bad about not paying Red Finch something. He tried and failed to explain why he paid Red Finch only $20,000 (in a "small brown paper bag") and pocketed the other $30,000: "I was angered because of the reduction in the bonus, so I just felt it was almost like self-help."

It's just a guess, but I'm not sure the pathetic and prophetic Red Finch episode hurt Cohen's credibility with jurors as much as the defense assumes.

In fact, when I glanced at the jury box, I saw disgust in a few sets of eyes as they heard details of the rigged CNBC survey. Trump could have blown his case right there. Jurors might just side with the monetizing chiseler over the "Biggest Con Man of the 20th and 21st Centuries," a fantasy list Trump would easily top without having to cheat.

Over the weekend, the prosecution prepared a good rejoinder to the Cohen-Schiller prankster text messages they had not been prepared for. Prosecutors found a screenshot from C-SPAN video dated October 24, 2016, which showed Trump with Keith Schiller at a campaign rally a mere five minutes before the pivotal phone call. This supported the idea that Cohen could have both talked to Schiller about the fourteen-year-old harasser *and* to Trump about Stormy Daniels in the ninety-six-second call.

After some debate, the C-SPAN screenshot was admitted.

"YOUR HONOR, THE PEOPLE REST"

After lunch, when Cohen returned to the stand, Hoffinger asked: "How has telling the truth affected your life?"

"I lost my law licenses, my businesses, my financial security," Cohen said. "To name a few." At this point, his voice seemed to catch a bit, and the jury noticed.

It was a good way to end the direct examination of Michael Cohen.

On recross, Todd Blanche made one last stab at destroying Cohen's credibility.

"Was losing your law license President Trump's fault?" Blanche asked, arguing that tax fraud and lying on records shouldn't be blamed on Trump. "And is one of the reasons why you lost your license to practice law because of those felonies?"

Cohen fought back, in part to remind the jury he had also gone down on campaign finance violations: "No, because of the totality, including the campaign finance violations, two counts, as well as the . . . lying to Congress."

The point of slipping in the campaign finance violations was to remind the jury that Cohen took the fall for Trump on the Stormy Daniels hush money.

Blanche kept slinging spaghetti against the wall to see what stuck. Nothing did. After the judge sustained an objection, Blanche said he was done and slunk back to the defense table.

The cross of Cohen—the most important part of the trial for the defense—ended with a whimper.

At 3:12 PM, Josh Steinglass from the DA's office stood and said, "Your Honor, the People rest."

BIG-EGO NEW YORKER

At this critical juncture, the defense made a mistake, the magnitude of which will remain unknown until the verdict. If Trump's lawyers had left it there, they would have had a clean and simple argument that this case was so ridiculous that no defense was necessary. This would have made Trump's decision not to testify in his own defense seem perfectly sensible, not a slippery and hypocritical invocation of the Fifth Amendment.

Instead, the Trump team ended with a horrible witness who would at best leave the jury wondering *Is that all they got?*—and at worst, do real damage to the defense.

Trump was egged on by Fox Nation, but this gambit was his doing: Last Wednesday, Robert Costello, the Giuliani buddy, testified before a friendly Republican House subcommittee and denounced Cohen as a liar. I learned from a good source that Trump loved that and ordered his defense team to scramble and put Costello on the stand.

The first defense witness was Daniel Sitko, a young paralegal in Blanche's law office assigned to assemble a summary chart of all the calls between Cohen and Costello.

Sitko dutifully confirmed the defense's number—seventy-five calls—but backed off when pressed by Hoffinger on cross about whether he was sure of the accuracy of that figure, which included numerous very short voicemail messages from Costello, several at a time he was worried about "pestering" Cohen. A total bust for the defense.

Regardless of the number of calls, it wasn't clear what the defense was driving at, though it seemed to have something to do with letting Costello dump more slop on Cohen's head.

It's hard for me to express just how arrogant and smug a witness Robert Costello turned out to be.

From the moment he took the stand, this well-groomed, ruddy-faced, silver-haired, self-appointed master of the legal universe embodied everything I have come to despise about a certain kind of big-ego New Yorker, proud of his toughness and ability to push other people around.

Costello is a former federal prosecutor—never forget that!—who has defended the likes of arrogant Yankees owner George Steinbrenner and Leona Helmsley (the "Queen of Mean" hotelier and Trump friend who believed that "only the little people pay taxes") and borrowed a bit of his nasty affect from each. Add a dollop of Giuliani and Trump and you got a real Gotham delicacy.

It was no surprise to learn—after he first tried to deny it—that Costello is close to Rudy, though he's annoyed at him now for not paying him the legal fees he owes.

On direct, Costello testified that after the FBI raided Cohen's apartment in April of 2018, he and his law partner, Jeff Citron, met for two hours with Cohen at the Regency, where he found Cohen "manic."

The reference to this hotel brought me up short because it was just outside the revolving doors of the Regency where in 2017 I first met—accosted is more accurate—Michael Cohen. I tried to ask him questions about Russian collusion (everyone forgets that it actually happened, according to the Mueller report) and he rudely brushed me off. When I reminded him of that last year just before I interviewed him onstage at Cooper Union, he laughed and warmly apologized.

Early in his testimony, Costello said that he told Cohen at the Regency that the entire situation "would be resolved by the end of the week" if he had "truthful information" about Donald Trump. This clanged for me. The only way he could get Cohen's situation "resolved" so quickly was a pardon from Trump.

But the defense felt it set up their money line—the "kill shot" that had earlier led several Fox hosts to insist that Costello must testify:

"I swear to God, Bob, I don't have anything on Donald Trump . . . I don't understand why they're trying to put me in jail for fucking NDAs," Cohen supposedly told him at the Regency. Costello added: "He [said] he did this on his own, and he repeated that numerous times."

It was too early to know how damaging this might be. In the meantime, Emil Bove's direct examination of Costello kept getting interrupted, which seemed to annoy Costello.

"CLEAR THE COURTROOM!"

The trouble began after a sidebar and a series of objections, some sustained and some overruled. After a prosecution's objection was sustained, Costello answered the question anyway, even though after a long career in the courtroom he surely knew that was forbidden.

Hoffinger for the prosecution asked: "Can the answer be stricken from the record, Your Honor?" Merchan ruled: "That answer is stricken from the record." Then he turned to the witness and said politely, "When I sustain an objection, you don't need to answer it."

The next ten minutes were among the wildest anyone present had ever seen in an American courtroom.

When Hoffinger objected to a question about Giuliani, Costello said, with total disregard for the court, "Jeez." Merchan sustained the objection and the one that followed. At that point, Costello said something almost unfathomable: "Strike it."

Who did Costello think he was—the judge? The real judge calmly said, "Counsel, let's take a minute. Can the jury please step out?"

We all rose while the jurors hustled out of the courtroom. They must have known something had angered the judge they clearly respect. It was easy to imagine that some jurors asked spouses what happened. Experts on juries say that they almost always try hard not to look at any news in high-profile cases but usually slip a bit.

"Mr. Costello, you remain seated," Judge Merchan said.

Costello tried to say something, but Merchan wasn't interested. Now, His Honor was hacked off. Instead of staying quiet, the witness said, "I'm sorry, go ahead," as if he was the judge.

"Mr. Costello, I would like to discuss proper decorum in my courtroom," Merchan said.

"I understand what you're saying." Costello replied, though it was not clear that he did.

"So, when there is a witness on the stand, if you don't like my ruling, you don't say, 'Jeez,' OK? And then you don't say, 'strike it,' because I'm the only one that can strike testimony in the courtroom. Do you understand that?" This was said in a firm, judicial way.

Costello said he did, but Merchan was now irate: "And if you don't like my ruling, you don't give me side-eye, and you don't roll your eyes. Do you understand that? Do you understand that?"

At first, that seemed to be the end of it. But as soon as Merchan said, "Let's get the jury back," he noticed something. He realized that this Trumpist witness—accustomed to getting his way in the world—was trying to intimidate him. "Are you staring me down right now?" Merchan said with a tone of incredulity.

Then: "Clear the courtroom."

For a moment, the press and spectators were stunned. Suddenly, everyone started talking, which under normal circumstances we were told not to do. The chief court police officer, a burly six-foot, three-inch redheaded lieutenant I'd taken to calling Gingerbeard (not to his face), said: "Step outside, please. Step out and step to the side, please. Step out, please. Quiet, please. Step out, please."

The court police officer nearest me on the right side of the courtroom was more abrupt: "Get your belongings and go! Go!" I complied and rushed into the hall, where we were wrongly told that a court officer would soon brief us on what was happening.

Inside the courtroom, several reporters—maybe ten out of fifty-four—refused to go. "Your Honor, may I object on behalf of the press? Your Honor, our lawyer is objecting. The press lawyer is objecting," one shouted. "We have a right to remain here."

Gingerbeard answered for the judge: "This is not an open forum. We will answer all questions in the hallway. Please step out. This is a [state] supreme court courtroom. Step out!"

The arguing grew loud enough for us to hear from the hall. "You can't throw us out!" Frank Runyeon, a legal reporter distantly related to Damon Runyon, shouted. "Our lawyer has a question. This is a public forum. Why do we need to step out?"

When Gingerbeard repeated, "Everybody step out!" someone in Trump's entourage said, "We are guests. Why do we have to leave?"

It turned out most of them didn't. Chuck Zito left, perhaps to help handle security in the hall; he once owned a security business offering muscle to celebrities. I spotted those pointy blue suede boots again and hoped he wouldn't stomp me with them, Hells Angels–style.

I didn't see where Joe Piscopo and Sebastian Gorka went. Alan Dershowitz stayed, and later said on Fox, "Shame, shame on that judge. He ought to be taken to the woodshed by the bar association." On TV, Dershowitz tried to make a normally calm and wise judge seem like Travis Bickle in *Taxi Driver.* "You lookin' at me? You lookin' at me?" Dershowitz said in his lousy DeNiro imitation.

While we were in the dingy hall, the judge apparently addressed the remaining reporters in a conciliatory tone. I was willing to cut him some slack. Merchan said he understood the press needed to do its job and thus would provide a transcript of everything that happened after we were removed. This will prevent a reversal on appeal that Dershowitz kept bloviating about on TV. Then he addressed Costello:

"Sir, your conduct is contemptuous right now. I'm putting you on notice that your conduct is contemptuous."

Merchan seemed to be searching for some reason for what he had just done, and he found it sitting in the witness chair.

The judge told Costello: "If you try to stare me down one more time, I will remove you from the stand."

He turned to the defense table: "I will strike his entire testimony—do you understand me?" Emil Bove said he understood. Now, Merchan directly addressed Costello again:

"Listen to the question and answer the question."

Instead of backing down, Costello, incredibly, said: "Can I say something, please?" Because I was out of the courtroom, I can't characterize Merchan's tone, but I can conjure it:

"No! No! This is not a conversation." Then, he politely told the court officer to bring the press and jury back in.

When the trial resumed, Bove had a series of questions for Costello about Giuliani and retainer agreements, but it seemed as if no one was listening. Even Trump was napping again as the very long day wound down.

I busied myself thinking about Emily's Theory of Has-Been-itis. Her notion is that aging has-beens like Robert Costello, Rudy Giuliani, and William Barr are so adrift at home on the couch watching Fox News all day that when Trump calls them back into action they are so grateful for a return to relevance that they will say and do anything on their boss's behalf.

After Merchan excused the jury, he began a hearing. Like every competent defense attorney at every trial, Blanche asked for an order of dismissal—a directed verdict by the judge, just as Professor Jonathan Turley, a newcomer to the courtroom who pretended to be on top of all of the evidence, including evidence he had not heard, had been arguing for on Fox and in the *New York Post*.

Earlier in the day, I tried to act friendly toward Turley in the line inside the men's room. We don't really know each other but are both Jonathans who grew up as Cubs fans a few blocks from Wrigley Field. We agreed that raising our kids as Chicago sports fans built character. He seems like a nice guy but doesn't know what the hell he is talking about when it comes to this case—or the Trump impeachments, for that matter.

For days, Turley has insisted that the judge should grant a motion to dismiss the whole case because Michael Cohen is a liar—a standard, if applied to snitch or rat testimony generally, that would reduce the number of criminal convictions in the United States to roughly zero.

But Trump and Blanche moved forward with the Turley gambit anyway, just to lay down a marker for their whining after the verdict.

"You're asking me to find Mr. Cohen not credible as a matter of law?" Merchan asked Blanche, incredulous. "You want me to take it out of the jury's hands so that, as a matter of law, his testimony should not be considered by the jury."

"Yes," Blanche replied, with his dozing client by his side.

Even Alan Dershowitz apparently didn't think much of this motion.

He was on his phone.

5/21/24
HOFFINGER DESTROYS COSTELLO

For a week and a half, MAGA World had been clamoring for Robert Costello to testify, and yesterday, he finally did. I sensed from the start that his arrogance left a poor impression on jurors, even if the judge sent them out of the jury box before tongue-lashing the witness, then clearing the courtroom. But if Costello was an obstreperous witness on Monday, he wasn't yet a serious liability to Trump as the trial moved toward its conclusion.

That changed today with Trump's disastrous decision to call Robert Costello as his only real witness. It blew up in Trump's face like a mob hit gone bad.

Prosecutor Susan Hoffinger was responsible for the fourteen-year-old prankster setback and will be seen as the goat if there's an acquittal or hung jury. But if the DA's office wins a conviction, her brisk and deadly cross-examination of Costello will be taught in law schools as one of the GOAT. To change species for a moment, Hoffinger has evolved from the awkward duckling into the graceful swan of this trial.

I realized that until now, I have mostly viewed Hoffinger from the back, where her curly black hair obscured her. Reporters are very familiar with the defense team's appearance and demeanor because Trump's lawyers and sycophants walk dutifully behind him every time he rolls up or down the center aisle—usually eight times a day.

The prosecutors, by contrast, linger by the defense tables and exit by a side door far to the front. So beyond distant shots on the grainy monitors and a few glances when she returned from sidebar conferences, I had to look up Hoffinger online for a closer view of the face the jury sees nearly every day. She is fiftysomething and looks like your poised and businesslike friend from the office.

On Monday afternoon, Hoffinger's cross had seemed standard. She established that Costello was dodgy when he said he wasn't anxious for Cohen to hire him. And she proved that Cohen had gone with a different lawyer, Guy Petrillo, much earlier than Costello indicated on direct—undercutting the white-haired attorney's claim that Cohen was a bad guy for stringing him along.

Prosecutor Susan Hoffinger destroys Robert Costello on cross-examination (REUTERS/Jane Rosenberg)

Costello claimed in an email that he didn't want "to pester" Cohen about signing a retainer agreement, but that's exactly what he was doing. "Please cease contacting me as you do not and have not represented me in this or any other matter," Cohen finally wrote to him after ignoring many of his attempts to be in touch.

The most intriguing moment had come when Hoffinger asked Costello about what he had described as Cohen's "manic" and "suicidal" behavior at the April 17, 2018, meeting at the Regency, the only time they ever met.

Suddenly, Costello barked at Hoffinger as if he was addressing an intern: "Talk into the microphone, please."

Had Costello learned nothing from the judge's smackdown earlier that day? As Costello knew perfectly well, it's for the judge, not the witness, to say "Strike it" or "Talk into the microphone, please."

The jurors knew that, too. During Costello's mic comment, I was clacking away on my laptop and didn't peer at the jury box, but several reporters saw two jurors turn in their seats and look at each other in surprise as if to say, *What the hell was that?*

The rest of us didn't have any difficulty comprehending what it was: Costello was still a political witness whose motive was impressing Trump by trashing Cohen and at least trying to intimidate the judge and prosecutors. Trump's folly is to assume such behavior might let him beat the rap. MAGA surrogates may or may not help him outside the courthouse, but they indisputably hurt him here.

As Hoffinger coolly said, "I'm sorry," and resumed her questioning, she turned slightly to her right, and I could see a small wry smile directed at the jury.

It had been a long, tumultuous day, and Hoffinger's cross was cut short to let the jury go home at 5 PM. She told the judge she would resume for just a half hour more on Tuesday morning.

So here she was again, bright and early, and suddenly, her cross was working beautifully. Cohen had testified that in mid-2018, it gradually became clear that he needed a different lawyer because Trump had assigned Giuliani and Costello to ensure he didn't spill his guts to the feds. Now Hoffinger got Costello to say again that no, of course, he had nothing like that in mind. He claimed over and over that he didn't even want Cohen as a client.

Like a pleasant executioner, Hoffinger produced email after email showing Costello to be a liar, and his lies were more menacing than Cohen's.

Costello had repeatedly testified that he didn't play up his connection to Giuliani when he and his law partner met Cohen at the Regency. But Hoffinger produced an email in which Costello wrote to Cohen two days after that Regency meeting, "I told you [of] my relationship with Rudy, which could be very, very useful for you." Then he emailed Citron, his law partner, that Cohen would be smart to hire him "because of my connection to Rudy Giuliani, which I mentioned to him in our meeting."

In another email, Costello wrote to Citron, "Our issue is to get Cohen on the right page without giving him the appearance that we are following instructions from Giuliani or the president."

If I was on the jury, I'd be thinking: *Cohen should have run away from these witness-tampering thugs much sooner than he did.*

On direct, Costello had arrogantly denied that he sought to open a "back channel" from Rudy to Cohen and attributed that to Cohen. The emails "speak for themselves," Costello said.

Now Hoffinger, with an even tone that contrasted well with Blanche's shouting when he thought he had nailed Cohen on the fourteen-year-old prank caller, produced an email in which Costello reported that Giuliani said, "Thank you for opening this back channel of communication and asked me to keep in touch." In another, Costello wrote that Giuliani was "thrilled and said this could not be a better situation for the President or you."

Hoffinger: "And the email 'speaks for itself,' right, sir?" Ouch. But she wasn't done yet.

Hoffinger offered into evidence an email in which Costello writes to his law partner, "He [Cohen] continues to slow play us and the President. Is he totally nuts??? I'm in a golf tournament early tomorrow and again on Sunday. What should I say to this asshole? He is playing with the most powerful man on the planet."

Suddenly, Tom Hagen had become Luca Brasi, and the thug who wrote this email had become a perfect match for the man we were looking at on the stand—a man, of course, who undertook his witness tampering at the direction of Don Vito Corleone from the White House.

Hoffinger moved in for the kill: "Now, that email certainly 'speaks for itself'; does it not, Mr. Costello?"

"Yes, it does," Costello replied, dead man sitting.

"You had lost control of Michael Cohen for President Trump," Hoffinger concluded.

"Absolutely not," Costello replied, lying again. It was hard to imagine jurors believing him.

Hoffinger ended her eviscerating cross by pointing to Costello's testimony five days earlier on Capitol Hill.

"It was an effort by you, wasn't it, to try to intimidate Michael Cohen while he was testifying here. Isn't that correct?"

"I was intimidating him?" Costello snapped as if he felt insulted for having been caught using the MAGA playbook. "That's ridiculous."

"Nothing further," Hoffinger told the judge. If she'd been in stand-up, she would have dropped the mic.

Susan Hoffinger had completed a satisfying comeback after the humiliation of the fourteen-year-old prankster setback, and was now on the cusp of an historic victory for the People.

On redirect, Emil Bove tried and failed to paint Michael Cohen as a sleazy client who was using Costello's legal counsel without paying for it. Costello recalled again that he emailed his son two days after the April 18 Regency meeting to brag that a senior Trump aide—Cohen—had told him, "I am on the team." He testified that a couple weeks later—on May 3—Jeff Citron gave Cohen a draft retainer agreement that he put in his briefcase.

On recross, Hoffinger, who like most good litigators believes less is more, took less than a minute to clarify that at the time Cohen was supposedly "on the team," he was not. He had a retainer agreement dated April 22 that he never signed, and he never paid Costello a nickel. Costello's story didn't fly.

With that, Hoffinger sat down, and Costello left the stand.

ORANGE JUMPSUIT

Instead of discrediting Michael Cohen, Robert Costello had essentially become a witness *against* Trump by showing that Cohen lied to him for a good reason—to make sure the president of the United States and the former mayor of New York City didn't fuck with him from the White House. La Casa Blanca meets La Cosa Nostra.

But it turned out that Rudy and Bob botched the job of keeping Cohen in the Ravenite Social Club, the John Gotti hang out.

Having called just two witnesses—both of whom were massacred on cross-examination—the defense rested. Trump's team had no one else to call: no Schiller, Weisselberg, no Eric and Don Jr., no "President Trump" himself.

With the trial winding down, Trump went out into the hall and raged for eleven minutes. I'm not going to report much about this because it was the same old crap he's slung a couple of times a day for five weeks from behind the now-familiar bicycle rack barriers.

Those of us with golden tickets almost never see this live because we are in lockdown inside the courtroom until he leaves the hallway. But today, we were in line for the fifteenth-floor metal detectors after lunch, and he came out suddenly. So even though we were stopped by security one hundred feet down the hall and around the corner, we could hear him whining.

After he finished his diatribe against Biden, Trump said the DA, the judge, and the Democrats are turning the United States into a "banana republic" and a "fascist" state. This guy's tiresome projection knows no bounds. But I also heard something I hadn't heard before. He called the trial "a very serious situation."

Is he scared he might lose? Maybe so. As he turned to leave, he was asked by the press pool: "Are you nervous about conviction?" "Why didn't you take the stand?"

Trump didn't answer either question. Leaving court for the afternoon break and at the end of the day, he still had that alpha male swagger, but he looked troubled, as if the thought of some time in an ankle bracelet had crossed his mind.

To *my* mind, the proper punishment from Merchan—either for contempt or if Trump is convicted—would be thirty days of community service picking up trash in an orange jumpsuit. Given his age, he should be issued one of those long sticks so that he can make sure he gets all of the coffee cups, crumpled old newspapers, and used condoms.

Unfortunately, retired judge Grasso told me in the line to the bathroom that outdoor community service would be impossible because the Secret Service could not secure the windows and rooftops of buildings in the area. Oh, well.

5/24/24
BRONX CHEER

Trump campaigned last night in Crotona Park in the Bronx, where I wish I could say he was greeted by what used to be called a "Bronx Cheer"—catcalls. There were a few from counter-protesters but he mostly won a surprisingly warm reception in a borough where he carried only 16 percent of the vote in 2016. This was scary, and not just because it reminded me of when he said "the Blacks—they love me" long before he went into politics. Even a slight increase in Black and Latino support could make the difference in a close election.

5/28/24
ROBERT DENIRO, PROPHET

Before the courthouse opened, I heard from a Trump-connected source that his legal team said over the Memorial Day holiday, "We're fucked." Apparently, Robert Costello was their last shot and when that failed, they realized it was all over, though they continued to lie to credulous reporters that they were confident of a hung jury. Their odds of saving their case in Blanche's closing arguments are slim.

Inside the courtroom, we hear that Robert DeNiro and former Capitol Hill police officers Michael Fanone and Harry Dunn are outside raising hell. Good for them.

DeNiro told reporters, "I don't mean to scare you. No no, wait, maybe I do mean to scare you. If Trump returns to the White House, you can kiss away these freedoms that we take for granted, and elections, forget about it . . . He will never leave."

DeNiro is not only right; he is consistent. When I interviewed him in 2017, I could barely get him to talk about the subject at hand. He raged the whole time about Trump and predicted even then that he wouldn't leave if he lost in 2020. DeNiro and Bill Maher were well ahead of the curve on that.

LINE SITTERS

I spoke today to some lucky people allowed into the courtroom as spectators. An affordable-housing advocate from Idaho flew in from Cancun, where she was vacationing, and camped out for two nights to snag a seat. In order to catch closing arguments, a retired man got in line on the Friday before Memorial Day—four days ahead. Another spectator, a student at Clark University, slept in a friend's car.

News outlets pay plenty to cut in line to obtain seats in the overflow room, where it's first-come, first-served each morning for the press passes. A line-sitting business called "Same Ole Line Dudes," which has a near monopoly in New York, does brisk business with the press. For the overflow room, the "line dudes" charge $300–$500, depending on the appeal of the day's testimony. Passes for the courtroom itself can go for $1,000 or more, though on many days they aren't available because spectators (who have waited at least fifteen hours) want to use them, not sell them.

I met R.J. Partington, a part-time teacher from Long Island, who slept on his father's old rolled-up blanket inside a sleeping bag he had bought for a trip to Mongolia. "It's one of the most fantastical experiences of my forty-three years of life," he said of the half dozen times he's gotten a seat in the courtroom, though waiting in line can be stressful and contentious.

Tina Johnson, a Black retired office worker from Westchester County, has become the unofficial organizer of the spectator line for those who want to get in, not sell their tickets. When I met her, she had been sleeping in a lawn chair or on a bench for four nights in a row, in part to save places for the regulars, including a retired judge from California and a UN representative from Australia. Tina, who ran a tight and sometimes manipulative ship in her self-appointed role, is pro-Trump but said most of the spectators are not.

Tina tells me that spectators generally get along well across party lines. Even so, fights have broken out in the middle of the night between regulars and homeless people brought over from the Bowery to wait in line in exchange for a few bucks offered to them by a bearded pro-Trump ticket-selling entrepreneur named John.

I ran into Eric Shawn of Fox News, who described what it was like being on the air while seeing the guy set himself on fire a few weeks ago. The experience left him shaken. In 2004, Eric broke the story of Frank Sheeran, whose claim that he killed Jimmy Hoffa was the basis for the movie *The Irishman*. Eric never interviewed Hoffa, but we agree that the rumor that Hoffa is buried beneath what is now the end zone at Giants Stadium is bullshit.

Eric knew Jimmy Breslin and he remembered that I'm from Chicago so we got into a fun LeBron-or-Michael discussion about Breslin and Mike Royko. He asked which one I thought was the GOAT local columnist. I told him I had grown up on Royko and thought he was funnier, but I finally settled on Breslin because he was a great writer *and* a great reporter.

It's nice talking warmly with someone from Fox News. As Lincoln said of Confederates after 620,000 Americans died in the Civil War: "We are not enemies, but friends."

CLOSING ARGUMENTS

This is getting exciting!

I'd arrived at court this morning feeling more confident of a conviction because Trump's case—such as it was—ended on such a self-destructive note. Trump would have been so much better off not putting on any defense at all.

If he hadn't, he could have ended the trial cleanly, with the burden not just legally but psychologically on the prosecution. Once Trump forced his lawyers to put Robert Costello on the stand and Susan Hoffinger quietly blew him away on cross, it began to get harder to see how he could win. Trump's lawyers had taken a big swing and whiffed.

The Former Guy brought family today—Don Jr., Eric Trump, Lara Trump, Tiffany Trump, and son-in-law Michael Boulos. Nobody expected Melania and Barron, but how about Jared and Ivanka? They haven't shown up once.

As usual, the defense closes first, followed by the prosecution. This is the law in New York State, but Trump told the press it was some kind of conspiracy against him.

THE DEFENSE CLOSES

Todd Blanche delivered his team's closing argument from an inconspicuous lectern toward the right side of the courtroom. New York law does not permit an attorney to stroll up and down the jury box.

He began with the same line he used in his opening argument: "President Trump is innocent. He did not commit any crimes, and the DA has not met their burden of proof. Period."

Here are just a few of the other "periods" Blanche used to cover a slim argument:

"The payments were compensation to him—period."

"There is no falsification of business records—period."

"Cohen was President Trump's personal attorney—period."

"There is no way that you can find that President Trump knew about this payment at the time it was made without believing the words of Michael Cohen—period."

Oh, did I forget to mention it? Blanche also called Michael Cohen a "liar" more than thirty times. I liked those moments when Blanche would take a break from "liar" and say something fresher about Cohen, like, "He's the human embodiment of reasonable doubt."

Blanche's voice always has the same studied urgency, as if he's somewhere between pleading legally and pleading literally. Now, he was pleading with the jury to understand just how humongous a liar Cohen was.

"You cannot just minimize the lie and say, 'Well, maybe he made a mistake,'" Blanche said, as if he was the captain of the parsing police. "A lie is a lie." I mean, he's literally an MVP of liars. He lies constantly." Blanche was inspired by popular culture: "Have you guys heard of a GOAT, like the GOAT, the greatest of all time? . . . Michael Cohen is the GLOAT. He's literally the greatest liar of all time!" Clever, Todd.

The only part of Blanche's argument I responded to was when he talked about the Trump Tower "conspiracy." He tried an Occam's razor approach without labeling it as such ("In life, usually the simplest answer is the right one") and argued, "There was no conspiracy."

I must admit I bought this a bit—or thought the jurors might. "It doesn't matter if there was a conspiracy to try to win an election. Every campaign in this country is a conspiracy . . . a group of people who are working together to help somebody win."

There's some truth to this, and campaign operatives have been "interfering in elections" for centuries. I imagine some jurors are a little jaded about politicians and the press and figure all of us in the news media get together on coverage all the time. We don't, but you can certainly find plenty of evidence for this kind of thing in American history, from party-sponsored newspapers in the election of 1800 slamming Thomas Jefferson for his affair with his slave, Sally Hemmings, to the *Los Angeles Times*' hand-in-glove relationship with Richard Nixon in the mid-twentieth century, to Roger Ailes's advisory relationship with George W. Bush while running Fox News in the twenty-first.

Blanche argued that catch and kill was just a variation on all of this and was "nothing unusual." And catch and kill has, in fact, been used before in politics. But the "nothing unusual" stuck in my craw. The vast majority of American journalists don't pay for stories or use sleazy means to get someone elected. Part of what Trump's team was trying to do was to normalize the ethical and journalistic sins of the *National Enquirer*—make it seem to be just another publication that's representative of the press in general. It's not. So, working with AMI really did constitute some kind of conspiracy, especially when catch-and-kill payments were made specifically to impact the 2016 election, thus constituting campaign finance violations.

Blanche also wasted a lot of time trying to make the *Access Hollywood* tape into a small bump in the road—something like finding out that Trump had slipped two points in Michigan or the *New York Times* had criticized him for lying. It was just one of those things "that happens all the time in campaigns," Blanche said.

This was a ridiculous Trump-level lie and I bet the jury knew so. Anyone old enough to vote in 2016—meaning all twelve jurors—understood that the tape was a huge deal.

Earlier, I expected the defense would introduce evidence that Cohen performed more than ten hours of legal work for Trump in 2017, the year Trump gave him $420,000. If he had—if Cohen had done, say, one hundred hours of legal work—then even a cheapskate like Trump might have paid him $420,000 for a combo of extensive legal work, delayed bonus, and reimbursement for the Red Finch expenses. That could have spelled a hung jury or even an acquittal.

But the jury never saw any records proving Cohen did significant legal work on the Summer Zervos case (she charged Trump assaulted her on the set of *Celebrity Apprentice*) or much of anything else beyond spending an hour or so reviewing Melania's contract with Madame Tussauds wax museum.

Blanche discussed the checks, invoices, and ledger entries that are the physical evidence in this case. Don Jr. and Eric Trump signed the first two checks to Cohen. "They [the prosecution] called Michael Cohen, and they did not call Don or Eric," Blanche said in his tinny tenor tone of phony triumph.

This would have sounded OK if the defense had mounted no case. But now, it looks weak. Last week, Trump summoned Robert Costello—a guy he barely knows—to defend him on the stand but not his own sons. If Dad was innocent, his boys would be defending their father, testifying that those checks were for legitimate legal expenses. But they aren't testifying because they don't want to perjure themselves.

Blanche also tried to say there was no way Cohen would work for free as "President Trump's personal lawyer." But that argument could only work before we learned that Cohen made $4 million as an influence peddler. He didn't need to risk billing the man who was already his golden goose.

When Blanche got to Exhibit 35—the "smoking gun" bank document on which Allen Weisselberg scrawled his "grossing up" details—he gamely offered, "The point of this document is that it contains lies."

But it doesn't, which is the heart of Trump's problem. Documents don't lie.

On cross, Emil Bove had done a decent job of challenging the chain of custody of the phone and throwing sand into jurors' eyes on whether there was something nefarious about the call ending suddenly. The conspiracy mongering was in bounds (if a little desperate).

But it was just plain stupid for Blanche to tell jurors in his closing statement to listen to the tape for themselves and figure out if they heard the incriminating number "150" (for the $150,000 to pay Karen McDougal) come out of Trump's mouth.

When they deliberate, jurors will have access to all exhibits, including the tape. What will they hear when the volume is turned up? They'll clearly hear "150"—and dispense with much of Blanche's argument.

At the end, Blanche got sneaky. "You cannot send someone to prison based on the words of Michael Cohen," he said, in a bid to make jurors think it was *their* role to decide if a president should be incarcerated. But that IED blew up in his face.

"Saying that was outrageous," the judge told Blanche after the jury left for lunch. Mentioning sentencing to gain sympathy with jurors who have no say at all in punishment but might not know it "is simply not allowed," he said. Merchan added that given Blanche's long experience, it was "hard for me to imagine how that was not intentional."

After lunch, the judge turned to the jury and told them to disregard Blanche's comment. Not a good final look for the defense.

THE PROSECUTION CLOSES

If I walked you through all of Josh Steinglass's five-and-a-half-hour closing argument, I would have to revisit every day of the last five weeks. Steinglass showed why he has been, from the start, the best attorney in the courtroom. He went at least an hour too long, but there was little likelihood that jurors would punish him for their fatigue. The head of the prosecution team acknowledged "trading brevity for thoroughness," but it paid off. And late in the day, he won jurors over by joking about "beating a dead horse."

Steinglass is an effective litigator and true public servant who has worked in the DA's office for twenty-six years. He began by explaining that the prosecution's "mountain of evidence" was incomplete. Landlines, for instance, which Cohen sometimes used to call Trump, are not included in the call records. The same, of course, is true for Cohen's Signal encrypted communication.

After all the phone, email, and text records we've seen, my only reaction is: Phew! Glad we didn't have to endure more.

Steinglass walked through all of the defense's arguments about Stormy Daniels, Keith Davidson, and Dylan Howard being involved in a celebrity extortion racket. It sure sounded like one from their testimony. But then he made a simple and convincing point:

"Extortion is not a defense to falsifying business records."

I finally began understanding why the 2015 Trump Tower "conspiracy" meeting was so important. Pecker's damning testimony about Trump's direct involvement, Steinglass said, means "you don't need Cohen to prove [they were] intervening in the election."

As for Stormy Daniels, "We don't have to prove sex took place . . . but Mr. Trump knew what happened, and that reinforced his incentive to buy her silence." Steinglass told jurors: "It makes you uncomfortable to hear [the discussion of sex], but that's the point." They "didn't want the American public to pay attention to it."

After Clinton, we know that sex stories aren't decisive for the American voter. But they sure don't help in the closing days of a campaign.

"Stormy Daniels is the motive," Steinglass said as the pieces of the prosecution's case moved firmly into place. "He [Trump] wouldn't pay $130,000 grossed up just because he took a photo [with Daniels] on a golf course."

Steinglass explained how Hope Hicks confirmed that Trump was more worried about the election than Melania's reaction—a central point for the prosecution to prove. Steinglass repeated Hicks's incriminating testimony: "Mr. Trump's opinion was that it was better to be dealing with it now and it would have been bad to have that story come out before the election."

In the bathroom, I mentioned to Adam Klasfeld, one of the best reporters here, that Steinglass had forgotten to use my favorite part of Hicks's testimony, which was when she quotes Trump telling her that Cohen was acting on his own and without Trump's knowledge "out of the kindness of his heart." Hicks on the stand then demolished this by saying Cohen would never do anything like that because he wasn't a "charitable" or "selfless" person. Besides, who takes out a home equity loan out of "kindness"? This piercing logic for why the old Cohen would never make a move without the boss's approval did as much as anything to seal Trump's fate.

I need not have worried about Steinglass deftly deploying Hicks's testimony. Not long after the break, he gestured to his left toward Trump and rammed that "kindness of his heart" line right down his throat.

Cohen's decision to pocket part of the Red Finch owner's cash like a petty thief presented a delicate problem for Steinglass. But he solved it with the nifty little argument I had first heard from Lawrence O'Donnell: "The defense is trying to have it both ways," denying that the $420,000 was a reimbursement at all. If the money was for a legal retainer, as the defense argues, "There was no theft," Steinglass said. And if Cohen did steal the money, as he admitted on the stand? "It's not a defense from falsification that one of the conspirators was stealing from another."

By this time, I sensed that whatever else they thought, the jurors knew damn well that the $420,000 was a reimbursement. Even Trump admitted as much in a civil deposition in Stormy Daniels's California NDA suit, though for complex legal reasons this could not be directly introduced into evidence.

One of the best moments of the entire trial was when Steinglass did schtick in the courtroom. It was a risky but clever way to defuse the October 24, 2016 call.

That call was the single best argument for the defense. On Blanche's cross a couple of weeks ago, Cohen had been blindsided by a chain of texts that seemed to show he was calling Keith Schiller about a fourteen-year-old prank caller who was harassing him, not Trump about Stormy Daniels. This was where Blanche had shrieked at Cohen: "You're a liar!" The prosecution helped limit the damage by deploying the C-SPAN screenshot showing Trump and his bodyguard together at a campaign rally five minutes before the call. That helped, but a bit more repair was now necessary.

Steinglass cradled an imaginary phone in his ear and set a timer. "This is a little experiment," he told jurors with a puckish smile. "I will be Cohen." Then he began imitating Cohen, without the New York accent:

"Hey, Keith. How's it going? It seems like this prankster might be a fourteen-year-old kid. If I text you the number, can you call and talk to his family? See if you can let them know how serious this is. It's not a joke. Uh-huh. Yeah. All right. Thanks, pal. Hey, is the Boss near you? Can you pass him the phone for a minute?" Steinglass then told the jury he would wait for a couple of seconds until Schiller handed Trump the phone.

"Hey, Boss. I know you're busy, but I just wanted to let you know that that other thing is moving forward with my friend Keith and the other party that we discussed. It's back on track. I'm going to try one last time to get our friend David to pay, but if he's not, it's going to be on us to take care of. Aha. Yeah. All right. Good luck in Tampa. Bye."

"Forty-nine seconds."

Having proven that Cohen could talk to both Schiller *and* Trump in forty-nine seconds (the real call lasted ninety-six seconds), Steinglass apologized to the jury: "Sorry if I didn't do a good job."

In fact, the half smiles I glimpsed on the faces of at least three jurors suggested that he had done so. If the prosecution wins, Steinglass's playacting will be discussed in law schools for years.

As we had learned earlier in the trial, Cohen updated Trump many times on the progress of the complicated hush money negotiations and the most incriminating call came two days later—on October 26, when Cohen got the final OK from Trump just two hours before he went to the bank to wire the money.

Throughout, Steinglass would lapse into too-long rehabilitations of Cohen. But some were helpful. "We didn't pick up Michael Cohen at the witness store," he said with a touch of irony, but Cohen could be a "good tour guide" as the jury reviews the evidence.

On the question of whether Trump et al. were truly interfering in an election, Steinglass made a point I hadn't focused on. The *National Enquirer*'s reach extends far beyond its circulation of 350,000. The headlines trashing Hillary Clinton and boosting Trump were seen by anyone at a supermarket checkout or a Walmart. That's tens of millions of voters.

This brought me up short: the 2016 election that changed the world was close enough that it could have been determined by all this tabloid shit. Scary.

Steinglass ended with the "IF YOU GO AFTER ME, I AM COMING AFTER YOU" tweet and a selection of the especially nasty things Trump has said about people—and they had said about him—that were admitted into evidence by one side or another for differing reasons. I love that Trump has to sit and listen to some of this abuse for the third or fourth time.

But the jury, after watching Steinglass in rapt attention for more than four hours, was getting restless. The judge sustained objections from the defense when Steinglass said that after Trump posts something incendiary, there are "throngs of followers who interpret that as a call to arms." This is obviously true in the outside world, but inside a courtroom, it is considered "prejudicial." After a sidebar, the judge instructed him to tell the jury: "I'm not saying it was his intention to get his throngs involved."

Steinglass overreached again by urging jurors not to let Trump get away with "shooting someone on Fifth Avenue." These were Trump's own words, of course, but prejudicial and irrelevant in this context. Not long after that objection was sustained, Steinglass wrapped up and court finally adjourned.

It was dark outside. I saw Trump sharply pull his jacket down with both hands before he passed me on the aisle, in what looked to be a moment of frustration. His campaign manager, Susie Wiles, and a few others in his entourage looked as if they were at a funeral. They had been so busy attacking the judge and Cohen and Stormy Daniels that they didn't seem to realize how strong the case against their leader had turned out to be.

5/29/24
JURY INSTRUCTIONS

I made a point of watching Donald Trump roll in heavy with his sorry (i.e., pathetic, not apologetic) entourage. Because I've seen him swagger up and down the center aisle more than 150 times over the last six weeks—if you count coming and going for morning and afternoon breaks, as I do—I've grown a bit blasé and sometimes have my head over my laptop and miss it. Not today.

I also wanted to make sure not to miss my favorite part of the trial: when jurors enter and exit a few feet from him and look straight ahead, soldiers for justice. I wanted to see if Juror #2, the one some people think might go rogue, nodded at Trump, as others (not me) say they have seen him do in the past.

My own experience with Juror #2 was to see him glaring at me from the jury box when he saw me focus my binoculars on him. Now I was training my binoculars on the spot where the jurors would pass the defendant.

But just after I raised them, Gingerbeard commanded me to take them down. Gingerbeard was normally cordial, with a really hard job that he performed well. This was the first time I had been busted by him, so I protested mildly that I wasn't looking at anyone's screen. But he had a point: I could see Trump's screen between me and where the jurors passed. "Down!" Gingerbeard said, and I hastily complied.

Moments later, the Honorable Juan Merchan began one of the most important parts of the trial:

"I will now instruct you on the law," he told the jury in a measured and winning way. "The level of my voice or intonation may change, but that is only to help you understand," he said. "You are the judges of the facts."

Unlike many other states, New York does not allow the jury to have a written copy of the judge's "charge"—his instructions. Lawmakers didn't want smarty-pants jurors to use them as a way to lord themselves over their fellow jurors. Same for notes. Merchan told jurors that any notes they took during the trial or now could not be used to override what other jurors remembered.

The facts of this case are overwhelmingly on the prosecution's side, but the law that jurors must apply to the facts is murky. So, this will be an unusually complex charge.

Essentially, jurors must decide if they can cross a narrow bridge that I think of as two attached causeways. They will have to find that Trump intended to cause the conspiracy to interfere in the election, then caused the falsification of business records and "other crimes" (unspecified in the statute) to conceal what he and his posse did.

Republicans have seized on this vaguely written law to try to discredit the case. But as Jimmy Breslin said in 1984 after Bernhard Goetz ("the Subway Gunman") shot three unarmed Black teenagers in the back, and most of Phil Donahue's TV audience thought he hadn't broken the law: "You're wrong! It's in a book—a law book!" Same thing here. There's a law, whether Fox types like it or not.

Merchan is from Queens, but his similarity to Breslin or Trump ends there. In dulcet tones, he said, "Remember, you have promised to be a fair jury" and must not "permit bias on account of race, origin, age, or sexual orientation."

That was standard fare, but Merchan's repeated references to "stereotypes" were specific to this case and valuable to the defense. The judge reminded jurors to be "mindful of any stereotypes about people or groups of people . . . We all hold unconscious views that may come from stereotypes and may influence a very important decision about another member of the community." He wasn't done yet:

"Make sure your verdict is based on the evidence, not on stereotypes or attitudes. Justice requires no less." Then: "You must set aside any biases you have in favor or against the defendant."

Not exactly the words of the imaginary judge Trump fulminates about: a "bad man" who is "biased" and "corrupt" and running a "rigged" trial.

Merchan instructed the jury on the meaning of the word "inference." To explain that one can infer "based on proof from other facts," he made an analogy. He told jurors to imagine they woke up and it wasn't raining, but they saw people with umbrellas: "It's an inference that it rained while you were sleeping." He told them to use "reason, common sense, and experience" to infer.

The section on his "limiting instructions" included specific references to David Pecker's non-prosecution agreement with the government, the Federal Election Commission's investigation of the Stormy Daniels payment, and Michael Cohen's plea deal on violating campaign finance laws. Merchan said these facts were admitted into evidence "for context [in assessing] Michael Cohen's credibility." But he stressed a few times that they must not be used as "evidence of the defendant's guilt." The same went for clips from the *Wall Street Journal.*

I saw Juror #2—the one Trump hopes will hold out for him—taking notes on the limiting instructions. Did that mean anything? Probably not, but staring at #2 is a sign of how nervous people are.

Most of Merchan's instructions did not differ from the norm. His definition of reasonable doubt was . . . reasonable. "It is an actual doubt, not an imaginary doubt . . . Very few things we know with absolute certainty . . . It is not sufficient to prove a defendant is probably guilty . . . the decision must not rest on speculation."

The judge seemed to be speaking directly about Cohen on the stand when he said, "It is the quality of the testimony that is controlling . . . You may disregard the entire testimony [of a witness] or accept it if you find it truthful and accurate." He added, "If a witness had a motive to lie . . . you may consider it." Even so, "you are not required to reject testimony if a witness has lied."

One might think this would interest Trump, but of course, it didn't. I trained my binoculars on the video monitor that showed him from the front and noticed he had been asleep or at least resting his eyes for twenty minutes, which is typical for him. He finally woke up and asked Emil Bove for water, and Bove produced a bottle of Poland Spring.

Merchan now turned to Cohen specifically. "Under our law, Michael Cohen is an accomplice," the judge said, which means "you cannot convict the defendant solely on [his] testimony" unless corroborated.

"Our law," Merchan said, referring to the New York State criminal code, covers "acting in concert." I guess he figured using the term "accessorial liability" was too wonky, so he quoted from the relevant definitional portion of the code directly:

"When one person engages in conduct which constitutes an offense, another is criminally liable for such conduct when, acting with the state of mind required for the commission of that offense, he or she solicits, requests, commands, importunes, or intentionally aids such person to engage in such conduct."

My guess is the jury will go with "commands."

With this criminal liability and "state of mind" illuminated, Merchan said, "The extent or degree of the defendant's participation in the crime does not matter." He is "as guilty of the crime as if the defendant, personally, had committed every act constituting that crime."

This was bad news for Trump, not because the judge is biased against him but because in New York (and other states), you don't get acquitted if you've hired and paid a hit man to kill your wife but didn't pull the trigger yourself.

After court, an old friend of mine—a smart, moderate Republican—started repeating GOP talking points to me about how Merchan was messing with the need to be unanimous. But Merchan's instructions are straight out of the New York penal code:

"Your verdict on each count you consider, whether guilty or not guilty, must be unanimous. In order to find the defendant guilty, however, you need not be unanimous on whether the defendant committed the crime personally, or by acting in concert with another, or both."

Trump enablers pretend this is just a minor bookkeeping misdemeanor. But as Josh Steinglass explained on Tuesday, the Manhattan DA's office brings more than one hundred cases a year under this falsification of business records statute—most of them felonies—because adherence to it is essential to the order and transparency on which all business in New York depends.

Forest Reinhardt, a professor at Harvard Business School, later told me that our entire financial system rests on this prosaic idea. Without it, we'd have Russia's unproductive crony capitalism.

One of the key words in the statute is "intent." Merchan instructed the jurors that "intent does not require premeditation or advance planning . . . Intent may exist only at the moment he acts . . . Intent can be inferred . . ."

In assessing intent, Merchan told the jury to consider questions like: "What, if anything, did the person do or say? What result, if any, followed the person's conduct, and was that result the natural, necessary, and probable consequence of that conduct?" And he explained that fraud "can extend beyond economic concerns."

This is where Trump's contacts with David Pecker, the former publisher of the *National Enquirer*, and Hope Hicks, his longtime communications aide, will come in—to buttress Cohen on these questions.

Merchan then turned to Section 17-152 of New York State election law. It bars "conspiracy to promote or prevent an election by unlawful means"—a conspiracy the prosecution says began at the now infamous Trump Tower meeting in August 2015.

This state statute is obscure but should not be considered rickety. In fact, invoking it lends democratic grandeur to this case.

"Democracy gives people the right to elect their leaders, but that rests on the premise that the voters have access to accurate information about the candidates," Steinglass said in his closing argument. "[Trump] sought to deny that access, to manipulate and defraud the voters, to pull the wool over their eyes in a coordinated fashion."

But here's where the case gets legally intricate—like a Russian "nesting doll," as Cyrus Vance Jr., Alvin Bragg's predecessor as Manhattan DA, puts it. That intent to violate the New York election interference law must be connected to "unlawful means."

Vance, Bragg, and others from that office have compared it to New York's law on burglary, where intent to commit "other crimes" once inside the house (e.g., assault with a deadly weapon, vandalism) does not have to be spelled out. This is much tougher to explain in a business records case.

To meet the "other crimes" and "unlawful means" standards in the business records and election interference statutes, the prosecution offered three possibilities, any one of which would suffice: violation of the Federal Election Campaign Act (FECA), falsification of other business records, and violation of tax laws.

The core of the prosecutors' argument is that Trump caused Cohen to do all three. On FECA, Merchan instructed the jury that campaign contributions include "anything of value" given to the campaign by any person. He explained that in 2015–16, the legal limit on individual campaign contributions was $2,700.

Jurors didn't have to be mathematicians to figure that was a helluva lot less than Cohen's $130,000 in-kind contribution to Stormy Daniels, which got him in trouble with the Federal Election Commission.

Merchan's much-anticipated instruction on federal election laws was this: "Under federal law, a third party's payment of a candidate's expenses is deemed to be a contribution to the candidate unless the payment would have been made irrespective of the candidacy."

In other words, Cohen's $130,000 payment to Stormy Daniels was an undisclosed contribution to the Trump for President campaign unless he would have done it anyway—outside of a campaign—to, say, protect Melania. That's why all the testimony about suppressing those tawdry stories before the election was so important.

When I heard Merchan's instruction on FECA, I felt the odds move heavily in favor of conviction. The facts of the case had already badly wounded Trump—and now the law did, too.

Because Merchan was a state judge interpreting a federal statute, Republican lawyers think this could be Trump's most fruitful avenue of appeal.

But those who were not in the courtroom or did not read the motions and transcripts don't understand that even if Bradley Smith testified and Merchan had been a right-wing MAGA judge, Trump still would have likely been convicted. That's because there were two "other crimes."

Merchan told the jury it could consider the bank documents associated with Cohen's dummy corporations, the wire transfer of hush money to Keith Davidson, the invoices to one of the dummy corporations, and Cohen's Trump Organization 1099. All of them could be "unlawful" business records.

Cohen's tax fraud—his misrepresentations on local, state, and federal tax forms—could also be construed as unlawful "even if [they] do not result in underpayment of taxes."

At the end of the day, the prosecution didn't even need campaign finance violations.

Finally, Merchan focused on the thirty-four criminal counts. Thank God he didn't do so one at a time.

"The only difference is that each count pertains to a different business record and possibly a different date," he said.

After ending his complex instructions, the judge asked for volunteers among the jurors to handle the laptop they would use in the jury room to examine exhibits. Tech-savvy jurors #4 and #6 volunteered, and lawyers for both sides explained to them how to use it.

Speaking of tech, I'm wondering if anyone here will try to get a surreptitious shot of Trump when the verdict is announced. A few weeks ago, the comedian Robert Smigel suggested that I go to the SpyStore online and buy glasses that surreptitiously shoot video. That way I could get a shot of Trump, like the photographer who in 1928 tied a camera to his ankle and snapped a famous photo of the murderer Ruth Snyder in the electric chair inside Sing Sing. Alas, those glasses have a small red light on them that would alert the hovering court police guards and get me booted or worse.

ONE LAST HOPE

With the jury now deliberating, the judge reported a request to have the laptop disconnected from the internet.

I saw an energized Trump whispering to Todd Blanche and Emil Bove. My guess is that he wanted to know if the exhibits could be corrupted by forces outside the building, which would be an excellent argument for a mistrial.

But a few minutes later, the judge reported that the laptop of exhibits had never been connected to the internet in the first place. I have no idea if this had all been a rumor planted by the defense, though I have my suspicions.

With my superior seat, I got a good look at Trump as he turned to leave. He did a quick, lip-pursed intake of breath, which suggested some nervousness, then put on his game face as he went to the press pool pen and told the world, as usual, that the trial was "rigged."

"Mother Teresa could not beat those charges," he said, encouraging comparisons and lowering expectations.

After a couple of hours of deliberating, the jury rang the buzzy bell that indicated a verdict or a note to be delivered to the court. This was the latter. The jury wanted to hear four pieces of testimony read back:

- David Pecker being called out of a meeting with investors in New Jersey to take a call from Trump;
- Pecker's testimony on his decision not to finalize and fund the hush money for Karen McDougal;
- Both Pecker's and Cohen's testimonies about the 2015 Trump Tower meeting where the conspiracy to interfere in the election started.

Soon, the jury sent a second note saying it wanted the judge to reread the instructions. Some reporters groaned, but I understood. The law they were charged with applying wasn't simple.

The lawyers scuffled on a few points but mostly agreed on the relevant pages of the transcript that playacting court officials would read the next day.

I figured that since the jury would need time to hear all of that, I could come in later than usual on Thursday morning.

Big mistake.

5/30/24
CLOSE SHAVE

For six weeks, I've arrived at the courthouse at 7:30 AM, where I check in as #31, representing the *Washington Monthly*, on the Golden List of Al Baker, the unflappable and highly competent head of press at the courthouse. But today I figured I'd be fine if I arrived at 8:30 AM—a full hour before the trial resumed.

After deliberations began, things felt a little looser, and some rules were relaxed. Reporters began gathering in a large room for jury pools that was much easier to access and where we were free to eat and schmooze. And there was no chance of a verdict first thing in the morning because jurors had not yet heard the testimony they requested read back to them.

Coming in later would also give me a chance to finally get a good night's sleep. Emily's been abroad, so I've been sleeping for a couple of nights at my sister Jamie's in the Village.

I woke up early thinking of Steve Schwarzman, the billionaire whose name is plastered on the New York Public Library and the student center at Yale. I don't know Schwarzman but I busted him in *Newsweek* in 2010 when I found out that he privately told a charity group that Obama's tax increases on the super rich were "like Hitler invading Poland in 1939." Obama was furious about it and with good reason. I trust the *Times* to put that high in his obit.

Over a leisurely breakfast, I tell Jamie I'm disgusted by Schwarzman's recent endorsement of Trump. She pointed out that Republican politicians and business leaders are equally culpable in backing Trump—in putting self-interest over their country. My feeling is that the CEOs who claimed at Davos this year that there's little difference between Biden and Trump are just as unpatriotic as Mitch McConnell and Lindsey Graham.

I took my time heading downtown, and when I arrived at the courthouse, all the other reporters were inside. Al Baker said he had been looking for me. He told me he gave my pass away when I hadn't shown up. He said he could get me into the overflow room but not the courtroom.

Shit! I suddenly realized that I could miss the verdict because of my anger at Steve Schwarzman.

But Al took pity on me. He went inside and upstairs to see what he could do. I paced nervously for forty-five minutes outside the courthouse—fending off a woman who was weeping because she had waited seventeen hours in the line for spectator seats and still hadn't gotten in, even to the overflow room.

Finally, Al and a senior court police officer who knew my face came out and gave me the precious white paper pass with the date stamp on it. I was in again.

Not surprisingly, I had a bad seat on a bench at the very back of the courtroom in the morning, but—crucially—did fine in the afternoon, with a good sight line to the jury box.

When court resumed, we knew the jury wanted to be reminded of what David Pecker had told them five weeks ago. Did he corroborate Cohen's testimony? After all they had learned, they were now in a better position to know.

As two female court officials played the roles of Pecker, Cohen, and the lawyers, it was hard to read the tea leaves to determine which side this rereading of testimony favored. Same for the rereading of portions of the judge's instructions.

I was beginning to believe the jury would compromise by convicting Trump on nine out of thirty-four counts—the ones where his fingerprints were on the checks. I thought that if the jury bought the prosecution's theory of the case, it should convict on all thirty-four. But these kinds of jury room deals are not uncommon.

I was increasingly confident we wouldn't have a verdict today, and this was confirmed a little before 4 PM when Merchan came into the courtroom and told us he would summon the jury and excuse it until Friday.

This was good news for the defense table, where Trump and his lawyers were smiling and chuckling. They figured the longer the deliberations, the better the odds of a hung jury.

We heard nothing for more than half an hour—certainly not the buzzy bell we expected if the jury had a note to send the judge or a verdict.

Where was Merchan? He had left the bench to tell jurors he was excusing them and hadn't returned.

In the meantime, I began whispering with Andrew Giuliani, who, as a child, was immortalized in a hilarious Chris Farley skit on *SNL* before becoming Trump's golfing partner. He was spouting the usual MAGA talking points but we found common ground when I told him I liked his mother, Donna Hanover.*

Around 4:20 PM, Merchan mounted the bench and announced that he had received a note from the jury. Like other reporters, I first thought that it was

* In 2007, Hanover's ex-husband, Rudy Giuliani, who told the press about their separation before he informed her, was leading in the polls for the 2008 Republican nomination. Donna called me at *Newsweek* and asked to meet in an East Side coffee shop. She refused to say why on the phone. When we sat down, she told me directly: "You and your colleagues in the press must stop Rudy. He is a troubled man and isn't fit to be president."

another request for more evidence to be read back. This was a conscientious jury that had deliberated since midday on Wednesday—at this point, for more than nine hours.

Then came a shock: The note from the foreperson said, "We, the jury, have reached a verdict. We would like an extra 30 minutes to fill out the forms. Would that be possible?"

You could hear a collective gasp in the courtroom.

VERDICT

At 5:03 PM, the jury entered, led by the foreperson, Juror #1, a former waiter clad in a blue pullover.

I had been watching Juror #1 for weeks. From his looks, he might be MAGA—but only if he had been second- or third-generation Irish American. After all, most of the Irish American cops in this building are probably for Trump. But the foreperson is an *Irish-born* Irish American, a naturalized immigrant who spoke with a brogue during jury selection. This made me worry much less about him.

Today, he wouldn't be saying enough for the brogue to come through.

I savored the archaic language:

The clerk: "Will the foreperson please rise. Have the members of the jury agreed upon a verdict?"

Juror #1: "Yes, we have."

The clerk: "How say you to the first count of the indictment, charging Donald J. Trump with the crime of falsifying business records in the first degree, guilty or not guilty?"

"Guilty."

The clerk: "How say you to count two?"

"Guilty."

The clerk: "How say you to count three?"

"Guilty."

Juror #1 used the word thirty-four times in all:

"Guilty." "Guilty."

This was the most dramatic public moment I have ever witnessed.

The judge asked if either side wanted the jury polled, and of course Todd Blanche said yes. When the clerk asked, "Is that your verdict?" each of the other eleven jurors—their poker faces intact—calmly answered "Yes" or "Yes, it is."

Trump had become a felon.

Merchan thanked the jurors for their service in a "very stressful and difficult task" and told them they "are free to discuss the case, but you are also free not to. The choice is yours."

Blanche moved for a "judgment of acquittal" because there's "no way this jury could have reached a verdict without accepting the testimony of Michael Cohen."

The jury foreperson reveals the verdict (REUTERS/Jane Rosenberg)

Merchan thought he heard Blanche say that even the *judge* knew Cohen had perjured himself on the stand. The judge was not amused. Blanche backtracked, and the motion was denied with dispatch.

At the request of Blanche, who has other Trump legal proceedings to deal with in June, Merchan set sentencing for July 11.*

No sentence will be served until all appeals are exhausted, but the judge has great power over the felon now and could jail him for contempt at any time.

For the first time in his life, Trump had been held accountable for his conduct.

Merchan asked for the current bail status. In what may have been my favorite line of the day after "Guilty," Josh Steinglass said, "No bail, Judge."

In another trial, that might mean the felon had been denied bail. Here, it was a simple recognition of the stark reality that a jury had just convicted a former president of the United States, who would not be confined to a holding cell.

Trump's face had been impassive when the verdict was read. Now, he stood to begin his walk up the center aisle. He swung his right hand out to shake hands with Eric, but he did so with an exaggerated faux-bro wide-arc shake without looking directly at his son, much less hugging him.

As he walked up the center aisle, he seemed more hunched than usual, with pain on his face. He reminded me of a boxer who had just taken a shot to the solar plexus and was trying not to show it.

On exiting, Trump put on his game face for the cameras, but a photographer who has been shooting him for years told me in the elevator: "I have never seen him looking so tired."

I went outside, where a couple hundred protesters from both sides had gathered earlier to hear texted reports of the verdict. A police officer told me they had been evenly divided, but now, most of the pro-Trump activists have melted away.

---

* With the Supreme Court's immunity decision, the judge postponed sentencing until September 18 and suggested it could go longer.

I fell into a conversation with two cops—one Black, one white. The Black cop smiled when I described the verdict; the white cop repeated MAGA propaganda.

I wish I could tell you what happens next in this country. I can't. But the verdict was cathartic, and tonight, anyway, I plan to celebrate it.

PART THREE

"THEY ALWAYS GET IT RIGHT"

Not long ago, Charlotte reminded me of something I had forgotten. When she was nine years old, she asked me what would happen if a bad person was elected President of the United States. I told her that was impossible, and that impossibility was one of the things that made America a good place, despite its faults. Democracy allows average Americans to pick the president, I said, and while voters don't always choose the best candidates, they have a nose for the bad ones.

I was thinking of politicians like Alabama Governor George Wallace, a charismatic racist. (Many of his now-elderly supporters and their children love Trump.) Wallace ran three times for president and garnered a lot of support, even in the North, but he never came close. Even if he hadn't been shot in 1972, he would not have won that year's Democratic nomination.

So I was confident in my assurances and the timing of them was not coincidental, as another story from that same year suggests:

It was September 21, 1998—the surreal day that the videotape of President Clinton's sexually explicit and dodgy grand jury testimony in the Monica Lewinsky case ("I have said what it did not include. It did not include sexual intercourse") played endlessly on TV. Until Donald Trump was elected, this was arguably the most embarrassing day in the history of the American presidency.

I had spent the morning analyzing Clinton on NBC News. In the afternoon, I went downtown to NYU, where Clinton and British prime minister Tony Blair were speaking as part of a forum connected to the annual opening of the UN General Assembly. I napped through part of it.

Sidney Blumenthal, a journalist turned senior White House aide to Clinton, was headed for a small private reception afterwards. He invited me to come along. This was pre-9/11, and because I was chatting with Sidney on the way in, the Secret Service didn't notice that I had no pass.

Suddenly I was in a room with the president and first lady and maybe twenty-five other people, mostly senior diplomats. No other reporters or columnists were present.

In the Oval Office with Clinton, 1996

Neither Bill nor Hillary had spoken to the press in the eight months since the scandal began, and the unsmiling first lady was unhappy to see me. I approached her to chat informally about some global issue I've forgotten. She was polite but terse.

The president, on the other hand, greeted me with a big effusive smile and leaned in to talk. The first thing he said to me was that a Latin American head of state had approached him earlier that day at the United Nations and whispered, referring to the Republican calls for Clinton to be removed from office: "You're lucky. In our country, when they stage a coup d'etat, they use real bullets."

Clinton's approval rating was above 60 percent but he didn't know yet that—in reaction to all the tut-tutting about a liar and adulterer in the White House—the Democrats would defy historical trends and pick up seats in the 1998 midterm elections. Afterwards, hypocritical House Republicans impeached him, even as Speaker Newt Gingrich and his successor, Bob Livingston, both resigned amid sex scandals.

But even in September, Clinton already sensed that the American people would be his salvation, and he talked of them the way a man would speak of the woman he loved. He trusted them "totally," "completely," and said, "If they have the time and information to sort things out, they always get it right."

Even then, I took issue with the word "always." But I embraced the idea that voters are *usually* endowed with good judgment, and this meant that they *almost always* get it right.

Yes, voters elected Richard Nixon over Hubert Humphrey in 1968, Ronald Reagan over Jimmy Carter in 1980, and George W. Bush over Al Gore in 2000, with negative consequences after each wrong choice. But there were extenuating circumstances in those elections, and the innate wisdom of the American people remained intact.

Now, a quarter century after that chat with Clinton, my faith in this democratic wisdom—and in this country—is on trial. I'm no longer sure that if voters have the time, they will "sort it out" and "get it right."

Distracted by cultural effluvia and besieged by disorienting misinformation, we're not just divided but in danger of losing what—for all of our many faults—has made us so successful: a native common sense about who is fit for leadership and who is not.

TRIAL AFTERMATH

The jury in the Trump felony trial showed great common sense, but a lot of other folks out there were awful.

Between April and June, NYPD logged nearly five hundred threatening phone calls and emails, including fifty-six "actionable threats" against Alvin Bragg. The home address of one of the prosecutors was posted on one site, and another social media post included "sniper sights" on "people involved in this case or a family member of such a person." No wonder no jurors have surfaced to give interviews or write books. Doing so could get them killed.

After the verdict, Steve Bannon said Alvin Bragg "should be—and will be—jailed" if Trump returns to the White House. That's the America that MAGA wants.

Less crazed critics accuse Bragg of "selective prosecution." But public integrity cases are, by definition, selective because they require a decision to devote significant resources to trials that make examples of politicians who commit crimes, thereby deterring corruption. That Bragg prosecuted a less egregious offense than masterminding a coup attempt, or hoarding classified documents, hardly discredits his efforts. In fact, it ennobles him. As new evidence emerged, he followed the facts. With calm fortitude, he did his duty.

In the aftermath of the trial, I got a sense of what happened behind-the-scenes on both sides. Trump was a demanding client, of course, but he was asleep so often in court that beyond occasionally recommending that his attorneys offer more objections and foolishly insisting that Robert Costello testify, he usually left his attorneys alone. And he privately blamed the judge and jury more than his lawyers when he lost. "Clarence Darrow couldn't have won this case," a lawyer in Trump's Mar- a-Lago inner circle told me, apparently reflecting the views of his boss.

Prosecutors were nonetheless surprised by what they considered the incompetence of the other side. Why did Trump's lawyers put all their chips on discrediting Michael Cohen rather than offering a multi-pronged defense? Why did they put on a half-assed case with only one witness (Costello) instead of, say, calling Trump Organization witnesses to testify that Trump was so busy as president he couldn't possibly know trivial details like paying lawyers? Where were witnesses to impeach Stormy Daniels and Cohen, and to testify to what the Trump side presumably believed was the legitimate legal work Cohen did for Trump in 2017?

Some of the defense's tactics left prosecutors scratching their heads.) In pre-trial filings, Todd Blanche said the 194,000 documents held by federal prosecutors in the Southern District of New York included "voluminous exculpatory evidence," but he didn't introduce a single exhibit from them.

Defense attorneys had the right to introduce documents into evidence on cross examination, but they rarely did so beyond Stormy merch that they somehow imagined might discredit her. And even though Judge Merchan sustained about fifty percent of their objections, Trump's lawyers offered amazingly few. Prosecutors could not believe their luck when, for instance, Josh Steinglass asked David Pecker 342 questions on the second day of his direct testimony and Emil Bove objected only twelve times.

Outside the courtroom, the defense of Trump was even weaker. One of the striking things about the Republican screeching was that almost none of it was actually about the case. It was all about the "corrupt" Juan Merchan, the "crooked" Alvin Bragg, and the "biased" New York jury. No one has contested the mountain of evidence on the thirty-four counts. Even as rightwing legal analysts rejected the "other crimes" that made this a felony without having actually seen any exhibits—without knowing anything about the details of the case—they were essentially conceding that Trump broke the law on business records. These bootlickers didn't claim he didn't break the law; they said that it doesn't matter that he broke the law. Because he's Trump.

My smart lawyer friends from the courtroom tell me the odds are against Trump winning on appeal. His best shot is to get the case to the Supreme Court, not on an immunity claim but under a 2022 ruling that the Constitution requires unanimous jury verdicts. Might that be extended to every element of a verdict? Unlikely, though of course you can't rule out anything with this Trump high court.

On most other grounds for appeal, Merchan prepared well. He drew on ample precedent when he allowed the misdemeanor to be bumped up to a felony; protected himself from reversal on the grounds of Stormy Daniels's testimony being prejudicial by issuing his own objections and chastising the defense for not objecting more; did not rely solely on the federal campaign finance statute for the "other crimes"; and properly interpreted the underlying state law on interfering with elections.

All in all, Merchan was exactly the kind of meticulous judge needed in these circumstances.

HOBSON'S CHOICE

In late June, Bill Maher summarized the dilemma involved in prosecuting Trump, who has used the fallout from the trial to raise a boatload of money.

"It's a Hobson's choice always with him because he's always guilty," Maher said. "But the repercussions [of prosecuting Trump] might be worse." Maher argued that it would have been easier to prosecute in the court of public opinion if the case was about corruption instead of just sex. His view that the case is, at bottom, political is shared by Andrew Sullivan, Andrew Cuomo, and several others who are also not Trumpsters.

My answer to that is that every prosecution of a politician risks looking political. If you prosecute a politician from the other party, you're partisan; from the same party, you're just trying to get bipartisan brownie points when you run for higher office.

The question is not how something looks politically, or how one reads the tea leaves on "repercussions," or how sex cases are perceived differently than corruption cases.

The question is whether we're comfortable doing nothing when we have evidence that a former president of the United States broke the law.

FOR THE RECORD

Trump's felony conviction is the first time he got caught. But we shouldn't forget that it's hardly his first offense.

Let's recap: He illegally discriminated against Black renters; colluded with mobbed-up unions; engineered a massive tax fraud scheme to save his family hundreds of millions; colluded with the KGB's illegal efforts to elect him in 2016; boasted on audio about sexually abusing women; was accused by two dozen women of sexual improprieties; gave a Cabinet seat to a Florida prosecutor who covered up for Jeffrey Epstein.

Shall I continue? Trump's "foundation," his "university," and his business—the Trump Organization—have all been shut down as frauds, and in a civil case he has been found liable by a jury for sexual assault. For all the delays, he may yet face criminal charges in Georgia for racketeering, in Florida for hoarding nuclear secrets, and in Washington for trying to stage a coup d'etat. The federal cases will go away if Trump is reelected, but even with control of the department of justice, he cannot snap his fingers and make the Georgia case and the New York criminal conviction disappear.

TURNING PRESIDENTS INTO KINGS

Long after Trump rides off into the sunset in his golf cart, we'll be stuck with the poisonous majority opinions of his Supreme Court, two of which were issued in the tumultuous summer of '24. The Supreme Court's reversal of the Chevron case means that judges—not experts inside federal agencies—will determine how thousands of regulations work. This decision—*Loper Bright Enterprises v. Raimondo*—was an astonishing judicial power grab. It will likely have the most far-reaching consequences of any decision besides *Dobbs* this decade. Over time, this decision will unravel the administrative state—an essential bulwark of health and safety regulation against corporate power—that was born in the 1930s under FDR.

Then came the disastrous Supreme Court decision in the Trump immunity case. Chief Justice John Roberts issued a sweeping opinion that delayed and complicated Jack Smith's coup trial. But it also affected the hush money case. Judge Merchan felt obliged to postpone sentencing Trump, pending a hearing that sorts out how the Supreme Court decision might affect the case. Trump's attorneys will argue that anything Trump said as president to Hope Hicks, a senior White House staffer, was part of his official duties and thus cannot be used in the case against him. Hicks's testimony was important, but Manhattan prosecutors had plenty of evidence without it, which will likely give them the edge in long legal wrangling.

Justice Sonia Sotomayor summarized the larger threat posed by the SCOTUS immunity decision: If the president "Orders the Navy's Seal Team 6 to assassinate a political rival? Immune. Organizes a military coup to hold onto power? Immune. Takes a bribe in exchange for a pardon? Immune. Immune, immune, immune." She ended her fierce opinion with an instant classic: "With fear for our democracy, I dissent."

All six of the judges in the majority claim to be "originalists," but they have apparently never read *The Federalist Papers*, especially Federalist No. 69 where Alexander Hamilton said that after leaving office presidents would "be liable to prosecution and punishment in the ordinary course of law."

After the high court used a crowbar on the Constitution, my brother-in-law, Rob Warden, reminded me of a famous scene from Robert Bolt's *A Man for All Seasons*.

When William Roper says he would cut down every law in England to get at the Devil, Sir Thomas More responds, "Oh? And when the last law was down, and the Devil turned 'round on you, where would you hide, Roper, the laws all being flat?"

Rob asked: What if, with his newfound immunity, Biden ordered the FBI to seize without warrants the six justices in the majority and hold them incommunicado at some secret gulag in the wilds of northern Alaska?

Where would the justices turn, the laws that would have protected them now being flat?

Of course Biden would never do that, and that is my only consolation. We've had forty-five men serve as president (Grover Cleveland is counted twice, which is why Biden, technically, is the forty-sixth president). Many have lied, governed poorly, and started disastrous wars. But only two of them—Nixon and Trump—have been crooks.

If Trump wins, he will be emboldened and empowered to run roughshod over everyone. If he doesn't, we have some hope of reverting to the norm—a country where presidents don't need immunity because they don't break the law.

PROJECT 2025

The press has done a decent job explaining that Trump would use the presidency to retaliate against his enemies, but Trump has fuzzed it up with his usual response: I'm-rubber-you're-glue-what-you-say-bounces-off-of-me-and-sticks-to-you.

So he's pounding away at the Biden-Harris Administration for "weaponizing" law enforcement against him and turning the US into a banana republic—exactly what he did when he was in office.

Of course it's Trump who plans to wreck the FBI so he can revive it as his personal fiefdom; Trump who plans to smash the "deep state" so he can replace career civil servants with his political stooges; Trump who plans to sabotage

NATO and let Putin conquer Ukraine and try to reassemble the rest of the old Soviet Union.

And it's Trump who plans to use the National Guard to deport 15–20 million immigrants, ripping people away from their families who have been here for decades (including Dreamers), in an operation that essentially militarizes American society. They may not pull it off, but they sure as hell are going to try. It's one of the only issues Trump truly cares about.

Until late on the last night of the Republican National Convention, it seemed as if Trump would actually be able to do all of this. A giddiness infected the delegates, many of whom were wearing square white ear bandages to honor their chief. Trump began his acceptance speech by recounting his near-assassination and reading from the prompter the words of unity that had been prepared for him.

But then he veered off into an endless rant of moldy oldies that put some delegates to sleep and did nothing to win white women swing voters in the suburbs, who might not be vegetarians but aren't fans of rancid red meat.

With dizzying speed, Trump lost his convention bounce and J. D. Vance got clobbered for old quotes, with "childless cat ladies" and "I hate cops" especially harmful.

But the even more serious problem for the Trump-Vance ticket is that Vance wrote the introduction to the Heritage Foundation report, Project 2025, which Harris immediately wrung around Trump's neck.

Despite his attempts to run away from it, Project 2025 is Trump's blueprint for a second term. The best way to understand the authoritarian society he envisions is to recall what Trump told civics students at the White House in 2019: "I have an Article II [of the Constitution], where I have the right to do whatever I want as president."

The manager of this revolution would not be Trump himself. He has almost no interest in how the government works. It would be his vice president, J. D. Vance, and a guy almost no one's heard of: Russell Vought, a former budget director in the Trump White House. Vought is a self-described Christian nationalist and head of the Center for Renewing America, which is driving the Trump agenda. He is much smarter and more dangerous than Trump himself.

Vought believes the left has betrayed America and so we need what he calls "radical constitutionalism." In Trump, Vance, and Vought's government, all power would be centered in the Oval Office and the person of the president.

ASSASSINATION ATTEMPT

Just hours after Trump was nearly assassinated in Pennsylvania, J. D. Vance was already blaming liberals who say democracy is at stake in the 2024 election. He made it seem as if the twenty-year-old assassin—a registered Republican—was acting on orders from Democrats, an assertion based on zero evidence. The truth is that it is Trump and his MAGA acolytes who have stoked violence.

It's important to record this: Trump sanctioned violence against protesters, reporters, immigrants, and Hillary Clinton (with the help of "Second Amendment people"); made light of the attacks on Paul Pelosi and Gretchen Whitmer; used rhetoric that the shooters in El Paso and Pittsburgh's Tree of Life synagogue said inspired them; called the violent January 6 insurrectionists "hostages" and "martyrs"; predicted riots if he lost in 2024 and a "bloodbath for the country"; suggested that General Mark Milley be executed; and posted images of himself taking a baseball bat to Alvin Bragg.

At the same time, too many on the left went online to say that they regretted Trump's luck in avoiding assassination. These people are not only wrong and morally obtuse, they know little history.

Violence can be useful for autocrats but it has never been a solution to political problems in democratic societies. There's a reason Shakespeare gave Caesar's friend Marc Anthony the big part in his play, *Julius Caesar*. The assassination of Caesar in 44 BCE marked the end of the Roman republic and the beginning of autocratic emperors and all the kings and Caesar wannabes to come. We have to rid ourselves of Trump the old-fashioned Athenian way—through democracy.

WHAT I MISS

Sooner or later, Trump will be out of our lives, but in the meantime, a lot else has atrophied in American public life.

I miss the sovereignty of facts—the time in this country when facts mattered, words mattered, arguments mattered, journalism mattered.

I miss the vibrant (if often superficial) local press, the lungs of democracy. If you laid a map of "news deserts"—places with no local newspaper or digital news source—on top of a map of Trump counties, they would be almost perfectly congruent.

There are hundreds of good reporters out there still doing important work. Charlotte is one of them. A *TIME* cover story she wrote in advance of the 2022 midterms helped prevent the victory of election-denier candidates for secretary of state in four battleground states.

But the fragmentation of media has been consequential. It's harder to get traction with a story when so many people get their news from TikTok.

Maybe the old system gave too much power to people like me. Maybe it was wrong that a small group of reporters in Iowa and New Hampshire could force Gary Hart out in 1987 for monkey business aboard a yacht called *Monkey Business* (a story fueled by a photo in the *National Enquirer* of Donna Rice on Hart's lap); or push Biden out of the same race for (maybe) plagiarizing a story about coal miners from Neil Kinnock, a British politician; or turn front-runners into also-rans for a variety of other shortcomings.

But at least there was *some* vetting process in place after the Blackstone Hotel's smoke-filled rooms aired out. By 2016, there were no antibodies left to defend one of our major political parties. A draft-dodging fraudster named Trump could trash the 2008 Republican nominee (John McCain) for getting shot down and being held captive for five years and still be able to hijack the GOP.

Now, those batshit crazy letters on many subjects that I sometimes received in the 1980s at *Newsweek*, written with random exclamation points on the red typewriter ribbon (a dead giveaway), are not only more common online; they have infected the entire political debate.

I'm beginning to feel a little like Sy Feltz, the character in the *Fargo* television series who says: "The world is wrong. It looks like my world, but everything's different."

Then I realize that it's not my world anymore, so who am I to say it's wrong? And the things that are different—new media platforms, new ways of connecting, new AI applications—can be hugely exciting. The power of Kamala Harris's "We're not going back" message is that it frees us to, in Lincoln's words, "think anew and act anew" far beyond the bounds of politics.

NO SUGARCOATING

As we feel our way to the future, it's important not to sugarcoat the past. We didn't even have anything resembling democracy in the South until the passage of the 1965 Voting Rights Act. Before that, only 7 percent of Black Mississippians were registered to vote. "Whites-only" primaries had been declared unconstitutional in 1944 but remained the norm in the South, and racial discrimination was rampant in the North, too.

I'm old enough to remember 1968, when the tensions were even higher than they are today. That year ended badly—with Nixon's election—but we survived.

And we would survive Trump's election, too, one way or another. The difference is that Trump's disregard for the norms that even Nixon respected is so far-reaching—and his plans for governing as an authoritarian are so plain—that we have no precedent for what might happen.

Still, it's not accurate to say that we're in uncharted waters. The waters have been chartered in Hungary, the country that MAGA is looking to as a model. There, strongman Viktor Orban has destroyed a fine university, corrupted the judiciary, and turned elections into mere formalities. I'm less worried about sugarcoating the past than I am about sugarcoating this kind of future.

HITLER AND TRUMP

I've always been a little suspicious of Hitler-Trump comparisons. Watching Trump strut a stage or balcony, I'm more taken with the Mussolini analogy, though Mussolini was much smarter and more competent than Trump. To me, the best comparisons are to Trump's modern-day role models: not just Orban but Xi Jinping, Vladimir Putin, Nicolas Maduro, Jair Bolsinaro, and other strongmen who love money and power and use their authority to get more of both. Trump makes no secret of his respect for these thugs with blood on their hands.

Until recently, Hitler analogies were verboten in American journalism. Using them was a sign of simplistic historical analogizing of the kind that Richard Neustadt would reject. So why do we hear so much about Hitler? Because Trump himself keeps injecting Nazis into the conversation.

This isn't a new habit. In 1990, Marie Brenner wrote an article in *Vanity Fair* about Trump's divorce from Ivana, who told her lawyer that from time to time her then-husband would read a collection of Hitler's speeches, *My New Order,* that he kept in a cabinet by his bed.

Trump almost certainly didn't read it; his aides have said for years that he doesn't read anything except his press clips—not even intelligence briefings. But an interest in Nazis is clearly lodged in his brain, and it has been growing since he left the presidency.*

Trump actually plagiarizes Hitler, only with immigrants subbing for Jews. He dehumanizes immigrants by calling them "vermin" who are "poisoning the blood of our country"—Hitler's exact words for the Jews. He echoes Hitler's depiction of "the enemy within," and he constantly talks about the nonexistent threat of "Marxists," a favorite Hitler target.

In the White House, Trump complained that his military commanders were not "totally loyal" to him and he wondered aloud to his White House chief of staff, retired Marine Corps general John Kelly: "Why can't you be like

---

* In 2016, J. D. Vance, Trump's future running mate, wrote to a friend that Trump could become "America's Hitler."

the German generals?" (Kelly had to remind him that some of those generals tried to kill Hitler.) Trump, whose grandparents were German (a fact he tried to cover up), told cabinet members that "Hitler did some good things" and was pleased when German chancellor Angela Merkel compared the size of his crowds to Hitler's.

In 2022, Trump hosted Holocaust deniers and Jew haters Nick Fuentes and Kanye West at Mar-a-Lago, which didn't seem to hurt him much. Nor did a campaign video, posted on his Truth Social account, promising that if reelected, his industrial recovery would be "driven by the creation of a unified Reich." Trump pulled down the video but didn't bother with his normal "just kidding" excuse.

Why does Trump do this? The answer is that—like Hitler, who also started as a clownish figure—he must constantly up the ante to keep his fanatic followers engaged and his critics shocked and appalled. It's also because the only sincere part of Trump is his entirely honest thirst for total power. If he gets it, he will use it to crush his enemies, not all at once but over time.

In 1940, George Orwell wrote a book review of *Mein Kampf*. He said Hitler was "appealing" because "he is the martyr, the victim, Prometheus chained to the rock, the self-sacrificing hero who fights single-handed against impossible odds." This sounds a lot like Trump, who, as Hitler did, uses "drums, flags and loyalty-parades" to cement his support.

Everything Hitler did, he promised in *Mein Kampf*. Everything Trump would do, he is promising now, from bringing "retribution" to his enemies to "suspending the Constitution." One of the starkest lessons of history is that when a strongman tells you that he wants to hurt you, believe him. It's the only thing he's telling the truth about.

THE DICTATOR

I signed my contract for a book on Franklin Roosevelt's famous first one hundred days on Monday, September 10, 2001.

In the weeks that followed, as I went repeatedly to Ground Zero and tried to wrestle with a changed America, I thought my FDR book was irrelevant and dead.

A week after 9/11, President George W. Bush visited a mosque in Washington, where he urged Americans not to take vengeance on innocent Arabs and Muslims, a move that Trump would never make. His short war to remove the Taliban was successful and his speeches were strong.

Then, in 2002, Bush began marshaling support for an attack on Iraq and politicizing what he called "homeland security."

I woke up in the middle of the night and thought: *Our challenges now involve presidential leadership.* I began working again on FDR, who saved democracy twice—first in 1933, when pulled the country out of the fetal position after millions of Americans had given up on democracy and favored a dictatorship, and again in early 1941, when his much-maligned Lend-Lease program saved our allies from being conquered by Nazi Germany. Arguably, he did so a third time in 1944 with D-Day.

I remember being struck by how many Americans admired Mussolini in the 1920s and early 1930s. My Grandpa Harry merely sold him a radio; Lowell Thomas, the most famous broadcaster of the era, extravagantly praised him on it. I was surprised to learn that the revered columnist Walter Lippmann, whom Mom hoped I would emulate, recommended to FDR that he assume some dictatorial powers, and even Eleanor Roosevelt, more liberal than her husband, told him that he might need to be "a benevolent dictator." Studebaker had a car called the Dictator that sold well.

Nowadays, with so many Republicans enabling Trump's plans to be a "dictator for a day" (as if he'd stop after that), the public's weakness for strength in the early 1930s is more comprehensible. They yearned for a strong leader to set things right.

Roosevelt was tempted. In one of my favorite research discoveries, I found in the files of his library at Hyde Park a speech he never gave. On the second day of his presidency, he was set to deliver a radio address to the American Legion in which he was prepared to tell decommissioned veterans in their thirties that he might draft them into a Mussolini-style private army: "I reserve to myself the right to command you in any phase of the situation which now confronts us." This was dictator talk, but FDR decided not to give that speech. He rejected going extraconstitutional (even his 1937 court-packing scheme was a failed bill to reform a horrible Supreme Court, not a power grab), and he worked with a Congress that was not as pliant as many historians assume.

Roosevelt's isolationist Republican opponents, like today's MAGA movement, were scarier than even the dopiest progressives. In 1939, the German American Bund, a pro-Nazi organization, held what it called a "pro-American" rally at Madison Square Garden. More than 20,000 people attended, many with regalia featuring swastikas. The US Congress contained several pro-Nazi lawmakers. Arthur Schlesinger wrote that the fight between isolationists and interventionists—known as "those angry days"—brought the deepest divisions in American society of his lifetime.

The country came together only after Pearl Harbor. If Harris loses, it might take some other shock to the system to change our current political trajectory and restore my faith in our common sense.

TEMPERAMENT

When assessing presidential leadership, Richard Neustadt wrote that "temperament is the great separator," an observation connected to a famous story. During the first week of his presidency, FDR visited retired Supreme Court Justice Oliver Wendell Holmes to celebrate his ninety-second birthday with a little bootleg champagne (akin to Biden smoking a little weed with Stephen Breyer). When Roosevelt left, Holmes remarked: "Second-class intellect; first class temperament."

The same could be said of Biden, who, like FDR, was never much of a student but knew how to get things done. Jimmy Carter possessed the reverse—a first-class intellect and a second-class temperament. He was close to the top of the heap in terms of raw intelligence but had a prickly personality that undermined his powers of persuasion. Yet his decency, good judgment, and, yes, much-maligned attention to detail constituted its own kind of productive temperament in the presidency.

Clinton and Obama both had first-class intellects *and* first-class temperaments, but the latter took distinct forms. Clinton's temperament was shaped by a superior political intelligence, though one that was hampered by his personal flaws; Obama was missing the schmooze gene but he compensated for it with immense coolest-kid-in-school magnetism.*

Bush Sr. was at the upper end of second-class in both categories, and his son on the lower side. Trump, exclusively transactional and self-interested, breaks Holmes's formulation entirely. He can be clever and his political instincts, especially about the juncture of television and politics, are superior. But he has little interest in policy and—in the words of more than forty of his former senior appointees—is temperamentally unfit to be president.

Temperament is a product of motivation, and vice versa. What is the motive for a president's struggle to win and wield power? Trump's fight is entirely about himself—his battle to stay out of jail, bolster his ego and political position by mobilizing resentments against "the other." Kamala Harris's fight is for her campaign, of course, but also for an agenda to help Americans get ahead and to put MAGA in the rear view mirror.

Even in normal times, I've always thought that presidential leadership counts more than people realize. Imagine how much worse the situation in the Middle East would be today if Israel and Egypt were mortal enemies, as they were until Jimmy Carter engineered the Camp David Accords. Imagine a world where if someone in your family fell seriously ill, you had to sell your home or declare personal bankruptcy. That was the case for millions of American families until Obamacare. Imagine we had more of Trump's useless "Infrastructure Weeks" instead of Biden's trillions of dollars of investment in infrastructure, chips, and clean energy.

---

* We think of Obama as an inspiring orator, but because he spoke in beautiful paragraphs, not pithy sentences, few of his lines have stood the test of time.

After the Tower of Babble collapses under its own weight, it's policy that remains—programs and ideas with the potential to be harmful or transformational.

BUSH-WHACKED

Trump's only domestic achievement as president—if you can call it that—was his gargantuan tax cut for the rich. But George W. Bush, whose father raised taxes in 1990 to put the government on a path to a balanced budget, is the one who first succumbed to the GOP's mania for tax cuts. Trump was just picking up where Bush left off.

In 2000, my *Newsweek* colleague, the late Howard Fineman, and I interviewed Bush during a long van ride in New Hampshire. Dubya, as the press called him, showed no concern about last-minute prepping for a GOP debate that night, an insouciance (or arrogance) that would hurt him in the presidency.

I asked Bush why he wanted to end the inheritance tax, noting that his fellow Republican, Theodore Roosevelt, was a strong believer in it. TR thought unearned wealth was "bad for young men" and that great fortunes should be returned upon death to the commonweal. Bush scoffed. He said today's heirs would buy fancy cars and other expensive stuff, and that would recirculate the money—the Maserati dealer theory of wealth creation.

It's far down the list of sins, but one of the bad things about Trump is that he makes George W. look OK by comparison. Junior wasn't any good in the job—and he serves as a rebuke to the dynastic impulses of the American electorate.

At the same time, Bush's tie with Al Gore in 2000 and very narrow win over John Kerry in 2004 are clearly within the normal parameters of American politics, hanging chads and all. And as bad as the Iraq War turned out to me, no one worried that Bush would trash democratic institutions.

The 2000 election was the first in 112 years in which the popular vote winner was not elected. I didn't expect to see another such undemocratic outcome in my lifetime and it never occurred to me that the loser of both the popular vote and the election itself in 2020 would lie incessantly about how he really won—"and by a lot." Another shock to our system—and to my own.

EYEBALL TO EYEBALL

Carter, Clinton, and Obama all explained to me at various times that the job of president is mostly about reacting to events. Trump was lucky he faced no major foreign policy crisis between 2017 and 2021; he is unlikely to be so fortunate again. His illusions about his relationships with Putin, Xi, and Kim Jong Un are dangerous. According to John Bolton, Trump's former national security adviser, "They think he's a laughing fool, and they're fully prepared to take advantage of him." Trump and his vice president, J. D. Vance, who said "I don't really care about Ukraine," would be fine with that.

With Putin now prepared to ship the technology to Kim that would allow North Korean missiles to hit the United States, this could get very ugly very fast.

I'm reminded of why I always list John F. Kennedy in the first tier of American presidents. In 1962, JFK was a forty-five-year-old president who on foreign policy often deferred to the older and wiser men of the Senate, Richard Russell and William Fulbright. As the thirteen-day Cuban Missile Crisis unfolded, there were two options on the table for dealing with the presence of Soviet missiles a mere ninety miles from the United States: an air strike to take out the missile bases or a naval blockade directed against Soviet ships carrying more missiles to Cuba.

The Joint Chiefs of Staff favored an air strike. So did Russell and Fulbright. But Kennedy chose a naval blockade, and after the US and the Soviet Union went "eyeball-to-eyeball," as Secretary of State Dean Rusk put it, the Soviet ships turned back and the crisis was over.

At a 1992 conference, Fidel Castro said that if the US had invaded, "I would have agreed to the use of tactical nuclear weapons," launched without the permission of Soviet authorities and with the knowledge that it would possibly mean the destruction of Cuba. We can't know for sure if that would have happened, but had Kennedy done nothing else in office (and his legislative record, beyond funding NASA for the moon shot, was middling), his willingness to stand up to the hawks at this moment by itself qualifies him for greatness.

JFK's secretary of defense was Robert S. McNamara, whom I interviewed several times. I'll never forget McNamara putting his thumb and forefinger a fraction of an inch apart and saying on camera, "We came this close to nuclear war."

I doubt Trump could have been elected during the Cold War, when Americans took the threat of nuclear war seriously and cared who had his finger on the button. Voters were more aware that with the wrong leadership, there are lots of ways to stumble into Armageddon.

LOSERS AND SUCKERS

For most of my childhood, Dad didn't talk about the war. He wasn't traumatized, just wary—like McCain—of coming off as some kind of hero when so many others of his generation served, too. But over time, he appreciated that he had seen combat in the largest military conflict in human history, and he wrote a fine short book about it.

Like navy veteran Jimmy Carter, Dad's priority was always peace. The biggest political disagreement we ever had was over the Iraq War. I believed Colin Powell, whom I had traveled with and respected, when he said there were weapons of mass destruction in Iraq. So I described it as "right war, wrong commander-in-chief." Dad thought it was a double wrong, and he was right.

Dad disliked "chicken hawks"—people like George W. Bush, Dick Cheney, and Pat Buchanan who had taken steps to avoid combat when they were young but were later perfectly willing to send young men off to die for their illusions. Biden's college deferments wouldn't have bothered him because they weren't hawks, but Trump's five deferments, supposedly because of "bone spurs" we never heard about again, would have irked him, as it did McCain. Trump told Howard Stern in 1998 that with STDs, dating was like combat. "It's Vietnam," Trump said. "It is very dangerous. So I'm very, very careful."

In 2018, Trump canceled a visit to a military cemetery outside of Paris because he feared the rain would hurt his hair, but he also had no interest in seeing the "losers" buried there. He's denied saying it, but does anyone believe that? General Kelly, his chief of staff, who lost a son in Iraq, heard the "losers" line and other slurs directly and later described Trump as: "A person that thinks those who defend their country in uniform, or are shot down or seriously wounded in combat, or spend years being tortured as POWs are all 'suckers' because 'there is nothing in it for them.' A person that did not want to be seen in the presence of amputees because 'it doesn't look good for me.' A person who demonstrated open contempt for a Gold Star family—for all Gold Star families—on TV during the 2016 campaign, and rants that our most precious heroes who gave their lives in America's defense are 'losers' and he wouldn't visit their graves in France."

There's a lot that I don't understand in this strange world, and one of them is how anyone connected to the military can vote for this man.

BLACK SWAN SUMMER

In 2007, Nassim Nicholas Taleb wrote an influential book called *The Black Swan: The Impact of the Highly Improbable.* Taleb argued that Black Swan events (e.g., 9/11 or the development of Google) share three criteria: they are extremely rare, extremely impactful, and—in spite of being outliers—explainable and even predictable after the fact.

Both Donald Trump's felony conviction and Joe Biden's late withdrawal in favor of a dynamic Kamala Harris will be seen as Black Swans if Harris goes on to win the election. These events weren't just improbable and impactful; they were also, in retrospect, predictable. Why shouldn't a criminal president be held to account and a frail president be forced to stand down? On the other hand, if Trump wins, the trial and the passing of the torch to Harris will fade as Black Swan events, while his near-assassination will qualify as one.

If Trump loses the 2024 election, the pivotal moment will have been his decision on May 15 to agree to Biden's request that they debate in June. Biden's team hoped to reset the campaign with an unprecedented mid-year debate. That miscalculation doomed his candidacy. Trump might have doomed his own by not waiting until the fall to debate, at which point it would have been too late for the Democrats to replace Biden.

I got a heads-up on what might happen. On Father's Day, eleven days *before* the historic June 27 CNN debate, I spoke to a senior Democratic senator who told me that if Biden did poorly in the debate, Democrats would have to find another presidential nominee. Surprised by this, I immediately broke (again) my New Year's resolution not to scheme against Biden.

The debate was a fiasco from the moment the cadaverous president walked on stage. The idea that, if somehow reelected, he would still be president in 2028 at age eighty-six was alarming for many of his supporters. For half an hour, Trump steamrolled him. Biden was so weak that everyone ignored not just Trump's dozens of lies but his viciousness, which we apparently now take for granted. He even had the nerve to go after Nancy Pelosi for not protecting the Capitol on January 6, as he incited his mob to kill her and his vice president and watched TV for 187 minutes without ordering help. Biden has said privately that Trump is "a sick fuck" for repeatedly joking about the home invasion that almost killed Paul Pelosi. Why couldn't the president have managed to say some less profane version of that in the debate? Why was he so bad?

The answer was obvious. Age had robbed Biden of what Richard Neustadt taught me forty-five years ago is the only real power any president has: the power to persuade. He had lost his connection to the American people at least eighteen months earlier. Now it was clear that he couldn't be Harry Truman, coming from behind to beat Tom Dewey in 1948. He wasn't up to it.

My family couldn't bear to watch the debate to the end. I did, and I stayed up until 2 AM writing the first of three *New York Times Opinion* pieces advocating an open audition process for a new nominee. That afternoon, the *Times* published an historic editorial that called for Biden to withdraw, describing his nomination as a "risky gamble." Ezra Klein, Crooked Media, James Carville, David Remnick, Michelle Goldberg, and Tom Friedman were among the early big voices insisting that the president must immediately stand down, with David Axelrod's view that Biden's chances were "very slim" also highly influential.

While the idea of an open nomination process was always a bit of a pipe dream, it proved to be an effective fantasy. Democrats began to see the debate fiasco as a blessing in disguise, offering them the chance to nominate a fresh young candidate who had not been dented in fractious Democratic primaries. By making the idea of a "blitz primary" seem real, the *Times* gave Democrats uncomfortable with Kamala Harris permission to speculate about other possible nominees. If big donors had thought their only choices were Biden and Harris, they might have continued to fund Biden, assuring his nomination.

The effort to sideline the president was brutal and it briefly divided the party. But given the stakes, it wasn't enough just to murmur, "It's up to him." Biden had to be gently cajoled in private and pushed harder in public, so that he would finally realize there was "no path," as political strategists say.

It wasn't easy. Bess Truman in 1952 and Lady Bird Johnson in 1968 both thought it sensible for their husbands to stand down and said so early in the election season. (When an exhausted LBJ announced he wasn't running, he was fifty-nine, the same age as Kamala Harris.) By contrast, Jill Biden was all-in on Joe seeking reelection. Hunter Biden, too.

For two weeks, the president seemed to be in denial. He appreciated all of the comparisons to George Washington giving up power but still preferred to be in the company of successful two-term presidents Eisenhower, Reagan, Clinton, and Obama, rather than one-termers Carter, H.W. Bush, and Trump, whom he continued to think—against all odds—that he could beat again. On July 5, George Stephanopoulos asked him what he would do if a delegation of congressional leaders came to the White House and asked him to step aside. He confidently predicted that wouldn't happen, but did not close the door.

The key figure in getting Biden to change his mind was Pelosi, who drew on their forty-year friendship. At first, she thought Biden could survive what he described as his "bad night." But Pelosi is an institutionalist; she loves the House, and her nightmare of not regaining control of that chamber (when Democrats were so close to winning it back) seemed to be coming true. With Republican control of the presidency, both houses of Congress and the Supreme Court, who would check Trump's authoritarian impulses? After Biden under-performed with Stephanopoulos, Pelosi expected that Bill Clinton, Barack Obama, and the Democratic leadership on Capitol Hill would stage an intervention. "But the men were MIA," one insider told me. "She wasn't happy that the only bloody fingerprints on the knife were hers."

The week of July 8, Pelosi went to the White House amid great secrecy and opened a channel to the president with an I'm-here-for-you tone, followed by several phone chats. When the poll numbers of endangered House Democrats worsened, her concerns deepened. A fly on the wall would have seen a master class in subtle politics, as the former speaker—a velvet-gloved boss for our times—maneuvered with great sensitivity to ease the president of the United States out of power. "She'll cut your head off and you'll never even know," one of her friends told me.*

To put pressure on Biden, Pelosi matched her inside game with a subtle public effort. On July 10, she told Joe Scarborough and Mika Brzezinski on MSNBC's *Morning Joe* that Biden has been a "great president" before saying, "It's up to the president to decide if he's going to run." Of course Biden had already decided to run, which made Pelosi's comments an easy-to-decode message for others to resume pushing him to stand down once the NATO summit in Washington ended. This set the stage for George Clooney in public and scores of big donors in private to turn off the money tap.

By the end of the week, the men got more involved, as Hakeem Jeffries and Chuck Schumer made sure Biden saw devastating polls that his top campaign aides had been hiding from him or interpreting with confirmation bias. On July 18, Biden tested positive for Covid-19. During his time recuperating at home in Delaware—which overlapped with the coronation of the nearly martyred Trump at his convention in Milwaukee—he saw polls showing him in danger of losing long-blue New Mexico, Virginia, and Minnesota.

Biden's intimates viewed Covid as the last straw. It took him off the road and seemed to underline the gloom of the moment, with the tide of Democratic opinion that favored a new nominee showing no signs of receding. If the president hadn't tested positive, he might well have run out the clock, lashing

* This was not the first time Nancy Pelosi showed her LBJ-level political skills. In 2010, she stiffened Obama's spine and shepherded the Affordable Care Act to passage against great odds. And in 2021, she helped shape Biden's multitrillion-dollar legislative program before modeling a transition to younger leaders by not seeking reelection as speaker.

himself to a party that increasingly viewed him as a selfish loser. The White House, the campaign, and the Democratic National Committee were fully on board with this lambs-to-the-slaughter approach and they needed to hold the line for only two more weeks before delegates would nominate Biden by virtual roll call. But with Covid, the endgame began. After denial (on display in interviews) and bargaining (over which polls to believe), Biden's grief for the death of his presidency finally moved toward acceptance.

As he weighed this momentous political decision, he cut himself off for more than four days from almost everyone outside his family. The wounds of what he called "Obama's deal with the Clintons" in 2016 were still surprisingly fresh, and he consulted none of them in this period—an extraordinary decision in itself. He would make this excruciating call without the wisdom of the fellow presidents he had once considered good friends.

In the nine years since Beau's death, Biden had become much less joyful. The solemnity had its compensations: he was a steady, well-grounded, and philosophical president. Like his friend John McCain, he had seen worse, and the enduring pain helped keep him calm. It was no coincidence that on Friday, about forty-eight hours before he withdrew, he told Cindy McCain—hardly a close friend—that he would likely step aside. Even his chief of staff, Jeff Zients, hadn't heard that yet.

After finalizing his decision with aides Mike Donilon and Steve Ricchetti on Saturday, Biden got up Sunday, July 21, and began telling people, including Harris. Senior staff heard the news only moments before the world did. Pelosi found out when she was performing community service with Jon Bon Jovi in New Jersey; Obama was playing golf. Just one hour before withdrawing, Biden was on the phone with the president of Slovenia putting the finishing touches on the largest prisoner swap since the Cold War, more proof that he was still a global leader of great skill and compassion.

When he finally bowed to reality, Biden went out with class. Less than half an hour after he issued a statement withdrawing from the race, he passed the torch to Harris, who moved with impressive speed to unite the Democratic Party behind her. Two days later, Biden's eloquent Oval Office address included a deft insertion of great presidents into today's struggle for democracy and decency. He conjured "Thomas Jefferson, who wrote the immortal words that guide this nation. George Washington, who showed us presidents are not kings. Abraham Lincoln, who implored us to reject malice. Franklin Roosevelt, who inspired us to reject fear." The president never mentioned his former opponent, but it was hard to miss the message: Trump defiled the temple that his transcendent predecessors had built.

The speech reminded me of an ailing FDR—in much worse health than Biden— addressing Congress after returning from the Yalta Conference in 1945, only six weeks before he died. The postwar international order that Roosevelt designed is the one that Biden has done so much to reenergize. It's the world that Eleanor Roosevelt conveyed to Mom and that she and Dad and my great teachers conveyed to me—a world of alliances, not autocrats; cooperation, not chaos.

As I reviewed why Biden had to stand down, I had a flashback that at first seemed disconnected from the extraordinary story of a political party trying to replace a successful president on the ticket. I thought about how the common experience of so many Americans having gay friends and relatives helped speed support for marriage equality in the early years of the twenty-first century—an issue on which Biden was ahead of Obama. In the same vein, the common experience of gently taking the car keys away from elderly parents helped lead two thirds of Democrats to the conclusion that Biden was too old to run again.

In retrospect, I'm glad I was passionately committed to Biden's withdrawal, in print and in private conversations. Like my father in a single airplane, I played a very small role but it made me feel that I was doing everything I could to help protect democracy.

REBIRTH

When politicians reach a certain level, they take on the capacity to be born anew. Kamala Harris, who went from maligned vice president to thrilling presidential candidate overnight, is only the latest to experience this phenomenon.

Governor Franklin D. Roosevelt was widely derided as a lightweight when he first ran for president in 1932. Even after he was barely nominated on the fourth ballot at the Chicago convention, pundits said it was "a kangaroo ticket—stronger in the hindquarters," a reference to FDR's Texan running mate, John Nance Garner. It wasn't until his galvanizing acceptance speech that the Democratic Party united behind Roosevelt and his "new deal."

In 1960, Senator John F. Kennedy was seen as a risky candidate. He was Catholic, and the only previous Catholic nominee—Governor Al Smith of New York—had lost badly to Herbert Hoover in 1928. Besides, Kennedy talked funny and was seen as a callow senator. Once the campaign began in earnest, the Democratic Party united behind him and he eked out a victory over Richard Nixon.

In 1980, former Governor Ronald Reagan was initially seen as a gaffe-prone ("Air pollution is caused by trees") and trigger-happy cowboy who was too extreme to survive a general election.

The point is, fortune favors candidates who can paint a compelling picture of the future, where presidential campaigns are always won or lost.

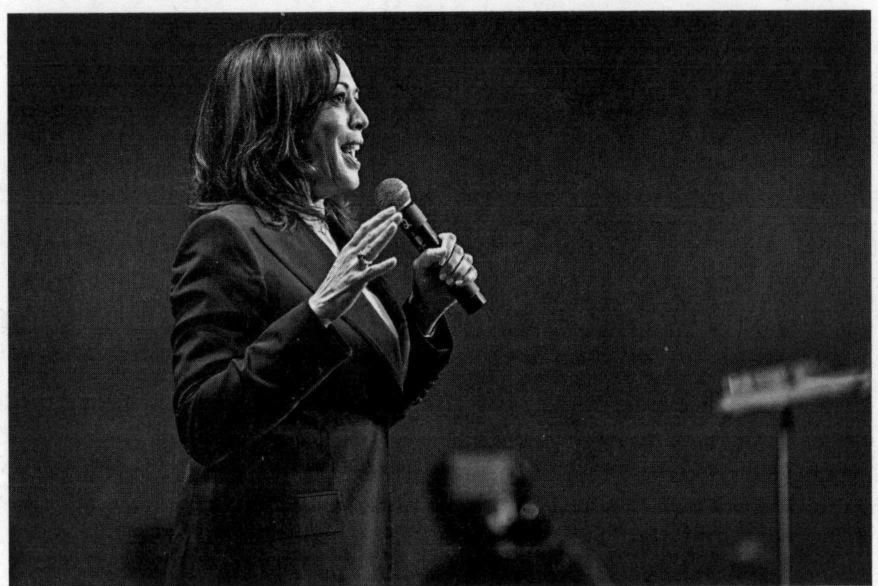

Kamala Harris bringing it.

From the moment Biden stood down, Kamala Harris electrified the Democratic Party and gave herself—and the country—a chance to be reborn.

I wish Mom was here to see Harris, the embodiment of everything she dreamed of from that day Eleanor Roosevelt sat on her bed at Mount Holyoke.

ALWAYS THE RACE CARD

Donald Trump began polluting national politics in 2011 by peddling the racist lie that Barack Obama had not been born in the United States.

We often forget how brazen this was, more than forty years after politicians gave up explicit racial politics in favor of "school busing," "welfare cheats," and other code words and dog whistles.

After Obama produced his long-form birth certificate, Trump doubled down, offering to give $5 million to a charity of Obama's choice if he released his college applications and transcripts. The man George Will called a "bloviating ignoramus" claimed Obama—a former editor of the *Harvard Law Review*—had been too stupid to be admitted to college except as an affirmative action case.

A dozen years and hundreds of insults later, a bullying Trump went on stage at the National Association of Black Journalists convention and slimed Kamala Harris as an Indian woman who "happened to turn Black, and now she wants to be known as Black," comments that would get any CEO in America fired. This was a lie (Harris graduated from Howard University) and a slur intended to stir fear of "the other." Inserting this poison into the heart of his campaign, he followed up with more racist and misogynist rants. Trump is determined to get reelected playing the same race card he brought to the table in the first place. On top of a verdict on the future of NATO, reproductive rights, and democracy itself, American voters will have to decide what they think about this kind of politics. Will it be sloughed off as a forgivable reaction to "woke excesses"—or repudiated as the foul residue of a country we no longer want to be?

WE DO OUR PART

I'm hearing people muse about leaving the country if Trump is elected. I'm not sure they're serious but it reminds me that this is exactly what rightwingers have wanted ever since those "America—Love It or Leave It" bumper stickers in the 1960s.

I also didn't like the liberal bumper sticker from those years: "America—Fix It or Forget It." I don't want to leave America or fuhgeddaboudit either, as Jimmy Breslin or John Gotti might say.

Why hand over the country to these weirdos?

If Trump wins, we'll fight him in the courts, in Congress, and, peacefully, in the streets. We'll need to protect immigrants—many of whom have been here for decades—from being rounded up and deported. We'll need to serve democracy in a hundred other ways that are hard to predict.

The main difference between our current challenges and what we've faced in the past is that all of the haters and demagogues and con men in our history have operated at a level below that of the president of the United States.

In that sense, Trump presents unique threats that, of necessity, involve far more of us than were needed to confront, say, Huey Long or Joe McCarthy, or the broader "paranoid style" that has always been present on the fringes of American politics.

After the Jack Smith case was delayed, it became a truism in the commentariat that no trial could stop Trump. Only the voters could do that.

Truisms are often true, but this one is incomplete. Democracy is a set of muscles and they work best when exercised throughout the body politic. Trials, turnout, journalism—it's all important. Politics is a game of inches, so anything might make the difference.

All citizens need to think of what we can do to meet the moment, as my father and George H. W. Bush and so many other brave men and women have done before us. Electing Kamala Harris would protect democracy but mark only the beginning of the revival of democratic values. With MAGA having metastasized, the battle against authoritarians at home and abroad will be, as JFK described the Cold War, a "long twilight struggle."

In the meantime, what we know for sure about Donald Trump is that he will challenge the election returns if he loses and continue to inflict himself on us. Every time we think he has finally touched bottom, he crashes through the floor.

In the early years of the New Deal, at the depths of a Depression much more painful and disruptive than anything we have experienced since, Franklin Roosevelt launched the National Recovery Administration. Shopkeepers and homeowners attached a decal to their windows featuring a blue eagle—the symbol of recovery—and a legend below that read: WE DO OUR PART.

Will we do ours?

LINCOLN

The history of American democracy is a story of unruly struggle and of common sense, a handy tool passed down like a practical family heirloom.

Abraham Lincoln was a natural storyteller but also a listener, and he craved hearing the horse sense possessed by the people—the voters that FDR, Clinton, and other politicians so trust. Lincoln enjoyed hosting big public events at the White House, which he viewed as "my public opinion baths"—essential for any success. "Public sentiment is everything," he said. "With it, nothing can fail; without it, nothing can succeed." He applied this even to children, whose voices he wanted to hear.

One day after court, I wandered four blocks south of the courthouse to what in the nineteenth century was the notorious Five Points, as readers and viewers of *Gangs of New York* may recall. Lincoln went there, too, in 1860, not long after he bought a new suit at Brooks Brothers and a stovepipe hat and had his photograph taken by Mathew Brady.

At Five Points, Lincoln visited the House of Industry, a grim workhouse for desperately poor children. The children's faces, a witness reported, "would brighten into sunshine as he spoke cheerful words of promise." When told he had inspired the children, Lincoln responded, "No, they inspired me."

Lincoln's speech about slavery that week at the Cooper Union would help catapult him to the presidency. He wrote the ending in all capital letters so he would know to stress it in his reedy tenor:

LET US HAVE FAITH THAT RIGHT MAKES MIGHT, AND IN THAT FAITH LET US, TO THE END, DARE TO DO OUR DUTY AS WE UNDERSTAND IT.

Trump, inverting Lincoln, echoes strongmen like Putin who believe might makes right, and that "doing our duty" is for suckers. He celebrates Jan. 6 insurrectionists who flew a Confederate flag inside the Capitol that Lincoln helped build.

The 2024 election is the most crucial in American history with the possible exception of 1864, when President Lincoln faced dashing General George B. McClellan, who opposed the abolition of slavery.

In 1865, less than six weeks before he was assassinated, Lincoln delivered his brilliant second inaugural address beneath the partially completed Capitol dome.

He said:

"The mystic chords of memory, stretching from every battlefield and patriot grave to every living heart and hearthstone all over this land, will yet swell the chorus of the Union, when again touched, as surely they will be, by the better angels of our nature."

I'm not a natural optimist, but I have always been hopeful. I'm convinced that our angels are better than so many now assume, and that those mystic chords of memory will, over time, swell our chorus and carry us home.

ACKNOWLEDGMENTS

After four books on American presidents in which I avoided attitude and the first person, this one is a major departure for me. It wouldn't have been written in the first place without David Kuhn, co-CEO of Aevitas Creative Management, who along with Helen Hicks and Nate Muscato figured out in a matter of days how to turn my courtroom reporting into a book, then sell it. David was the one who said it had to be personal, and he was right. The autobiographical sections helped me access episodes of my life I hadn't thought about in years, which was fun.

My publisher, BenBella Books, is a great example of how independent book publishers are revolutionizing the industry. They produced this book in an astonishing three months, which no corporate publisher could do. Thanks to BenBella's public-spirited CEO, Glenn Yeffeth, who told me early on that if the book convinced even a handful of voters of the true stakes in the election, it was worth publishing; Leah Wilson, my talented editor; and Monica Lowry, Aaron Edmiston, Jennifer Canzoneri, Adrienne Lang, Sarah Avinger, Susan Welte, Alicia Kania, and Madeline Grigg.

I was rescued by friends and relatives who read the very rushed manuscript, including Jill Abramson, Liz Fine, Dale Russakoff, Cliff Sloan, Jeff Toobin, Keith Ulrich, and Michael Waldman. In my family, Jennifer Alter Warden,

Jamie Alter Lynton (who should be a book editor!), Harrison Alter, Rob Warden, and Lee Greenhouse all read various drafts, as did our kids, Charlotte Alter, Tommy Alter (thanks for Black Swan analogy!), and Molly Alter, plus our son-in-law Mark Chiusano. Everyone had great suggestions.

I'm grateful to my good friends Paul Glastris and Matt Cooper of the *Washington Monthly*, who helped me get my credential for the trial and published my dispatches from the courtroom, and to Katie Kingsbury, Patrick Healy, and David Firestone, editor extraordinaire, of *New York Times Opinion*, who gave me a contract and a chance to write blog posts for "The Point" twice a day. Meredith Stark, the producer of my Substack newsletter, did her usual great work on *Old Goats*.

At the Manhattan Criminal Courthouse, I am indebted to Al Baker, the communications chief, who got me the seat and was unfailingly helpful. Special thanks to my courthouse buddies Harry Litman, Norm Eisen, George Grasso, Adam Klasfeld, and Lawrence O'Donnell. I also got good insights from Lisa Rubin, Valerie Jarrett, Andrew Rice, and George Conway, among others. Outside the courtroom, Michael Lynton, Michael Ryan, Chris Cerf, Stephen Colbert, Garry Trudeau, Bud Trillin, Andy Clayman, and Julian Zelizer had good thoughts. Thanks to Garry, Jane Rosenberg, and Barry Blitt for sketches.

And finally, a big hug for my lovely wife, Emily, who once again saved me from myself. Maybe.

INDEX

NAMES

Page references in *italic* refer to images.

SECTIONS

ABOUT THE AUTHOR

Jonathan Alter is the bestselling author of four books on American presidents, most recently *His Very Best: Jimmy Carter, a Life*. He is a political analyst for *NBC News* and MSNBC and also covered the Trump felony trial for *New York Times Opinion*, the *Washington Monthly*, and his Substack newsletter *Old Goats*.